Appropriating the Dao

Also Available from Bloomsbury:

Weird Confucius, Zhao Lu

Dynamism and the Ageing of a Japanese 'New' Religion, Erica Baffelli and Ian Reader

Philosophical Enactment and Bodily Cultivation in Early Daoism, Thomas Michael

Appropriating the Dao

The Euro-American Esoteric Reception of China

Edited by
Lukas K. Pokorny and Franz Winter

BLOOMSBURY ACADEMIC
LONDON • NEW YORK • OXFORD • NEW DELHI • SYDNEY

BLOOMSBURY ACADEMIC

Bloomsbury Publishing Plc, 50 Bedford Square, London, WC1B 3DP, UK
Bloomsbury Publishing Inc, 1359 Broadway, New York, NY 10018, USA
Bloomsbury Publishing Ireland, 29 Earlsfort Terrace, Dublin 2, D02 AY28, Ireland

BLOOMSBURY, BLOOMSBURY ACADEMIC and the Diana logo are trademarks
of Bloomsbury Publishing Plc

First published in Great Britain 2024
Paperback edition published 2026

Copyright © Lukas K. Pokorny, Franz Winter and contributors, 2024

Lukas K. Pokorny and Franz Winter have asserted their rights under the Copyright,
Designs and Patents Act, 1988, to be identified as Editors of this work.

Cover image: Éliphas Lévi, *Dogme et Rituel de la Haute Magie*, 1861

All rights reserved. No part of this publication may be: i) reproduced or transmitted in any form, electronic or mechanical, including photocopying, recording or by means of any information storage or retrieval system without prior permission in writing from the publishers; or ii) used or reproduced in any way for the training, development or operation of artificial intelligence (AI) technologies, including generative AI technologies. The rights holders expressly reserve this publication from the text and data mining exception as per Article 4(3) of the Digital Single Market Directive (EU) 2019/790.

Bloomsbury Publishing Plc does not have any control over, or responsibility for, any third-party websites referred to or in this book. All internet addresses given in this book were correct at the time of going to press. The author and publisher regret any inconvenience caused if addresses have changed or sites have ceased to exist, but can accept no responsibility for any such changes.

A catalogue record for this book is available from the British Library.

A catalog record for this book is available from the Library of Congress.

ISBN: HB: 978-1-3502-8956-7
PB: 978-1-3502-8960-4
ePDF: 978-1-3502-8957-4
eBook: 978-1-3502-8958-1

Typeset by Deanta Global Publishing Services, Chennai, India

For product safety related questions contact productsafety@bloomsbury.com.

To find out more about our authors and books visit www.bloomsbury.com
and sign up for our newsletters

Contents

List of contributors ... vi

China in the Euro-American esoteric imagination: Contouring a lacuna
   Lukas K. Pokorny and Franz Winter ... 1

1. Daoism and Kung Fu as occult sciences: Historical comparisons between Chinese practices and mesmerism *Julian Strube* ... 15
2. Looking out for magic in Ancient China: The *Yijing*, its trigrams and the Figurist tradition in Éliphas Lévi *Franz Winter* ... 35
3. The Theosophical *Daodejing*: The beginnings *Lukas K. Pokorny* ... 61
4. The Daoist who wasn't: Albert de Pouvourville, Matgioi, Nguyễn Văn Cang and the problem of Indochinese masters in *fin de siècle* occultism *Davide Marino* ... 83
5. Turning further East: C. H. A. Bjerregaard and the esoteric enthusiasm for Daoism *Johan Nilsson* ... 109
6. Do what dao wilt: The integration of East Asian concepts and practices into Aleister Crowley's Thelema *Gordan Djurdjevic* ... 125
7. An exoticism of rationality and social order? Examining the East–West binary in late nineteenth- and early twentieth-century esoteric representations of China *Johan Nilsson* ... 145
8. The archetypal Dao: A look at C. G. Jung's reception of Chinese thought *Karl Baier* ... 163
9. Be water my friend: Esotericism, martial arts and entangled histories *Tao Thykier Makeeff* ... 201

Index ... 223

Contributors

Karl Baier is a professorial research fellow in Religious Studies at the University of Vienna, Austria. His research focuses on mesmerism, the history of modern yoga and meditation and alternative religions and cultures of self-cultivation during the nineteenth and twentieth centuries including the intersections between psychotherapeutical schools and the religious field. He is the author of *Yoga auf dem Weg nach Westen. Studien zur Rezeptionsgeschichte* (1998) and *Meditation und Moderne. Zur Genese eines Kernbereichs moderner Spiritualität in der Wechselwirkung zwischen Westeuropa, Nordamerika und Asien* (2009).

Gordan Djurdjevic, independent scholar, is author of *India and the Occult: The Influence of South Asian Spirituality on Modern Western Occultism* (2014) and co-author of *Sayings of Gorakhnāth: Annotated Translation of the* Gorakh Bānī (2019). He co-edited, with Henrik Bogdan, a collection of essays on *Occultism in a Global Perspective* (2013), and contributed to the anthologies *Aleister Crowley and Western Esotericism: An Anthology of Critical Studies* (eds. Henrik Bogdan and Martin P. Starr; 2012) and *Handbook of Religion and Secrecy* (eds. Hugh B. Urban and Paul C. Johnson; 2022). He currently works on two related volumes that concern the new religious movement of Thelema approached from a hermeneutical and comparative perspective.

Tao Thykier Makeeff received his Ph.D. in the History of Religions from Lund University, Sweden, with the award winning dissertation *Do Satyrs Wear Sneakers? Hellenic Polytheism and the Reception of Antiquity in Contemporary Greece, a Study in Serious Play*. He is an affiliated researcher at Lund University and the University of Stavanger, Norway, where he was also recently employed as a postdoctoral fellow (2020–22). His research focuses on Contemporary Paganism, ritual innovation, historical reception and nationalisms. He has published and lectured extensively on contemporary receptions of Greek Antiquity, the Viking Age and East Asian martial arts and religion. His first monograph on Hellenic Polytheism in contemporary Greece is in preparation for publication.

Davide Marino is a research fellow at the University of Vienna. He holds a Ph.D. in Religious Studies from The Chinese University of Hong Kong. His current research focuses on esoteric receptions of Chinese religions, with particular attention to the history of French Traditionalism. He is particularly interested in the ideological implications of essentialist understandings of Asian religion. His latest publication is a paper entitled 'Mircea Eliade and René Guénon: Patterns of Initiation and the "Myth of Affinity"' published in *Aries: Journal for the Study of Western Esotericism*.

Johan Nilsson is a postdoctoral researcher in the History of Religions at the Centre for Theology and Religious Studies at Lund University, Sweden, where he also received his Ph.D. with a thesis entitled *As a Fire Beneath the Ashes: The Quest for Chinese Wisdom within Occultism, 1850–1949*. His research focuses on esotericism and new religions movements during the nineteenth and twentieth centuries. He is currently working on a research project about the reception of Buddhism in Swedish Theosophy.

Lukas K. Pokorny is Professor and Chair of Religious Studies at the University of Vienna, Austria. Large parts of his current research focus on millenarianism and esotericism (specifically the reception history of East Asia) as well as new, alternative and Asian diasporic religions in Austria. Recent publications include, among others, the *Handbook of East Asian New Religious Movements* (co-edited with Franz Winter; 2018), *The Occult Nineteenth Century: Roots, Developments, and Impact on the Modern World* (co-edited with Franz Winter; 2021), and *Religion in Austria*, so far published in eight volumes (2012–23). He is also the editor-in-chief of the *Vienna Journal of East Asian Studies*.

Julian Strube is Assistant Professor in Religious Studies at the University of Vienna, Austria. He works from a global historical perspective on the relationship between religion and politics since the eighteenth century, focusing on exchanges between India, Europe, and North America. He has published widely on global religious history, religious comparativism, colonialism, esotericism, socialism and far-right extremism. Recent publications include *Global Tantra: Religion, Science, and Nationalism in Colonial Modernity* (2022); *New Approaches to the Study of Esotericism* (co-edited with Egil Asprem; 2021), and a special issue on 'Global Religious History' for *Method & Theory in the Study of Religion*, co-edited with Giovanni Maltese.

Franz Winter is Professor and Chair of Religious Studies at the University of Graz, Austria. His research interests cover the history of religious and cultural contacts between Asia and Europe from antiquity to modernity. Recent publications include the *Handbook of East Asian New Religious Movements* (co-edited with Lukas Pokorny; 2018), *The Occult Nineteenth Century: Roots, Developments, and Impact on the Modern World* (co-edited with Lukas Pokorny; 2021), and *Religious Diversity, State, and Law: National, Transnational and International Challenges* (co-edited with Joseph Marko et al.; 2023), as well as various contributions in academic journals, including *Numen*, *Religion* and *Zeitschrift für Religionswissenschaft*.

China in the Euro-American esoteric imagination

Contouring a lacuna

Lukas K. Pokorny and Franz Winter

European images of China and the esoteric lacuna

Due to various recent political and economic developments, the question of how to deal with modern China from a Western perspective is becoming an object of growing public and intellectual interest from various perspectives and across diverse academic disciplines.[1] Part of such a discourse is also intrinsically related to the general perception about China and its millennia-old cultural tradition. The way non-Western cultural contexts – particularly Asia – are perceived is naturally closely aligned to various developments and constellations that are constantly changing. Presently, the idea that China sooner or later might prevail over Europe and the 'West' is a persistent subject in public and intellectual debates. From a broader historical perspective, this is only one of many other notions that developed in the course of the ongoing contact with and the growing knowledge about China.

There are many studies examining the European encounter with China, which has a long history of its own, going back to antiquity as the Roman Empire maintained commercial and even diplomatic relationships with China (for an overview, see McLaughlin 2010: 120–40; also Raschke 1978). These were continued during the medieval times (Reichert 1992), but it was mainly during early modernity in Europe that substantial contacts were established. Prior to the sixteenth century, only a few Europeans managed to overcome the geographical distance, thereby most of the knowledge about China was rooted in legends and myths. Several factors formed the conditions for the subsequent interest in China and the Chinese religious traditions in the early modern period. The sixteenth century was the starting phase of a large-scale expansionist, colonialist agenda in Europe, which included missionary endeavours all over the (then known) world, but also had a strong commercial aspect that aimed at increasing the financial and economic power of the countries involved. New intellectual concepts triggered by a fresh reading of ancient sources during the Renaissance as well as the recent scientific discoveries at the time transformed the way the world and its history were seen. Such changes posed a challenge to traditional interpretations that were closely aligned to specific readings of the Christian Bible, but had seemingly no place for accommodating the surge of new insights and developments. David E. Mungello points to several specific junctions in this vast cultural transformation process in early modern Europe that became particularly important with respect to China. These relate to the search for a universal language coupled with new insights in the sciences and also includes the history of Hermeticism, which became an important intermediary in the reception of the religious culture of China (Mungello 1985: 23–43).

The transformative trajectory of Europe distinctively shaped the encounter with China. The Portuguese arrived in 1557, and it was due to their lasting presence in the country and under their patronage that the first Catholic missionaries embarked on their pioneering intellectual assessment (Latourette 2019: 78–101). In spite of their failure to create a sizeable Christian community, let alone evangelize the whole of China (Latourette 2019: 185–98), the reverberations of this encounter were immense. Particularly in its first phase and under the Jesuit banner, knowledge of Chinese cultural traditions and related religious and literary materials were for the first time made accessible to the Western public (Brockey 2007). Western reception commenced with reports and 'letters' sent to Europe by the missionaries, which contained primary materials and insights into this hitherto virtually unknown country (Mungello 2009: 81–112). Soon the first (partial) translations and appraisals of major textual sources – such as the *Yijing* 易經 (Classic of Changes) and the *Daodejing* 道德經 (Classic of the Way and Virtue) – were added, growing significantly in number in the following centuries (see, e.g., the detailed study by von Collani 2007). A number of Jesuit theologians also started their own attempts to integrate elements of the Chinese tradition into a seemingly coherent system of interpretation, whose main features developed into a current known as Figurism (Wei 2020; von Collani 2010). All the new information made it obvious that China possessed an immense cultural, literary and religious tradition and concomitantly raised the need for thorough contextualization and assessment.

The Jesuit missionary encounter was indeed the starting point for a deeper understanding of the country. Evidently, the portrayal of China in the Western imagination was extremely diverse. Whereas some Enlightenment philosophers, such as Gottfried Wilhelm Leibniz (1646–1716) and Voltaire (1694–1778), who based their approach mainly on the Jesuit accounts, introduced China as a veritable utopia and a rational and ordered society centred on meritocracy (Perkins 2004), others like Pierre Bayle (1647–1706) and Montesqieu (1689–1755) were critical and pointed to China's strictly hierarchical and despotic emperor system or its society being prone to polytheism and other sociocultural atavisms.[2] Hence, there were two extremes – namely, Sinophilia and Sinophobia – that became dominant in the subsequent perception of China (Mungello 2009: 125–30). An important element for the further reception of China was the emergence of the academic discipline of sinology, which was pioneered at the beginning of the nineteenth century by Jean-Pierre Abel-Rémusat (1788–1832) who held the first chair for the study of Chinese at the famous Collège de France in Paris from 1814 (Cheng 2019; Will 2015). The establishment of sinology led to a much more nuanced view of China, gradually professionalizing the interaction with and reception of the country's history and culture.

The contributions of this volume are concerned with one specific area in the reception history of China that has hitherto hardly been of any scholarly concern – that is, the Euro-American esoteric encounter.[3] The main focus of the contributors is the nineteenth and early twentieth centuries, when a network of esoteric movements and individuals emerged sharing a common interest in extra-European sociocultural traditions and, specifically, their spiritual contribution.[4] Interest in China and East Asia[5] was intrinsically connected to fundamental presuppositions marshalled by these actors, such as the idea of a universal truth comprising the core of the world's religions. Involving 'foreign' traditions was particularly important as it was meant to serve as validating evidence for such claims. Asia had particular significance as it comprised cultures that extended over millennia and developed a rich and distinct cultural productivity, more specifically by having generated an extensive corpus of religious literature that started to become broadly accessible at the time.

Predictably, the esoteric interest in Asia had two favourites: China and India. Both underwent individual stages of reception and interpretation, shaped by varying perspectives and shifting historical contexts across the centuries. Knowledge of the respective languages was one key factor why India received both early and more attention,[6] for (most of) the relevant Indian languages make up part of the Indo-European linguistic repository and were previously accessible to the intellectual public (see Halbfass 1990: 36–83; as for the early history, see Windisch 1917: 26–73). Especially facilitated by the Romantic tradition (Halbfass 1990: 69–83), this led to an immensely positive reception of India more often than not resulting in an idealized depiction as a stronghold of religion and (as it would be later called) 'spirituality' – a general perception that is prevalent to this day (King 2013).

Another crucial aspect why India became more important – especially in (but not limited to) the esoteric reception history – is related to the influence of the Theosophical Society which enthusiastically engaged with Indian traditions under the aegis of its foundress Helena P. Blavatsky (1831–91) and especially by her immediate successors (Rudbøg and Reenberg Sand 2020). The Theosophical Society's Indophilia had Blavatsky even relocate its headquarters to India.

Therefore, most of the scholarship dealing with the relationship between esoteric movements and Asia is expectedly focused on India (e.g. Djurdjevic 2014; de Michelis 2004). Related research also includes studies on the influence of Indian religious traditions (Hanegraaff 2020; Strube 2022; Urban 2003) or the concrete networks developing between Europe and India in this particular religious area (Čapková 2020b; Cox and Turner 2020; Myers 2020).

The interest in China and East Asia has its own specific history within the wider context of Euro-American esotericism. The most eminent early intermediary was the famous German Jesuit polymath and prolific writer Athanasius Kircher (1602–80), who had access to a copious treasure trove of materials, both due to his standing as one of the chief intellectuals of his time and because he was located at the Jesuit Collegium Romanum. His approach was mainly informed by a unique fusion of Christian and Hermetic ideas (for an overview, see Trompf 2011). Consequently, Kircher focused his attention on Egypt and its tradition. But alongside, China – where he reportedly wanted to go as a missionary (Fletcher 2011: 20–1) – became his object of interest owing to the pioneering accounts that arrived from early missionaries at the time (Mungello 1985: 135–73). All this culminated in the publication of the seminal *China illustrata* (1667). Although therein he reduced China to the status of a stale imitation of the great Egyptian culture (e.g. he thought of Chinese characters as being pale copies of the hieroglyphs), the portrayal of China as an eminent cultural tradition remained important in the course of its further reception (Stolzenberg 2013: 50–1). Kircher was a crucial precursor of the later esoteric interest despite the peculiar information in *China illustrata* which was criticized already at the time of publication (on early critics, see Fletcher 2011: 179–80). As already pointed out by Mungello (1985: 29–31), the connection with Hermeticism was an important catalyst for the incipient esoteric interest. In the (esoteric) search for a universal language, Chinese always had a special place

(Mungello 1985: 34–5; Kern 1996: 68–101). In addition, elements of Kircher's approach became relevant for the early Figurists within their integrative approach towards China. In her concise characterization of Figurism, Claudia von Collani (2010: 668–9) isolated three traits: (1) a typological exegesis, which is bound to reveal alleged hidden meanings in the Old Testament; (2) a *prisca theologia* frame, which presupposes the idea of some type of 'divine revelation' by non-Christian figures (with Melchizedek, Pythagoras, Plato, Orpheus and Zoroaster being some of the 'usual suspects', a list that can be readily extended); and (3) a reference to the Christian Kabbala as an overarching concept or interpretative tool. The latter two characteristics became also important in the early esoteric perception as they were easily integrated into a wider framework beyond the confines of the biblical context.

The far smaller appreciation of esotericists vis-à-vis China is also related to a major shift in the overall perception. The said ambiguity, viz. Sinophilia versus Sinophobia, was to be resolved by clearly shifting towards the latter during the late eighteenth and nineteenth centuries (Mungello 2009: 81–145; Dijkstra 2022: 266; Osterhammel 2018: 372). One major factor for this development was the emergence of racial theories: whereas India remained part of the presupposed Aryan sphere, the Chinese were racially inferiorized.[7]

Contouring the Euro-American esoteric reception of China and East Asia

In the last two decades, a growing number of scholars have embarked on exploring both the impact-cum-reception (e.g. Akai 2009; Yoshinaga 2009; Wu 2018) and transplantation (e.g. Čapková 2020a; Chuang 2020; Jammes 2020) of Euro-American esotericism as well as the formation and expression of the esoteric current in East Asia (e.g. Gaitanidis and Stein 2019; Yoshinaga 2021; Junqueira 2021). So far, the study of 'occult East Asia' has engaged specifically with the case of Japan since the late nineteenth century (and less so with China, Korea and Vietnam). Yet, whereas there is an increase in studies that examine Japan et al.'s reception of esoteric themes coming (back) from the Euro-American context, the 'other end' of this entangled phenomenon, that is, the Euro-American esoteric reception of East Asia, remains a desideratum.

One of the guiding principles of the present volume is to contextualize the approach towards East Asia with a focus on China within a broader cultural and historical framework. This is closely aligned with the idea that esoteric and occult traditions constitute part of basic cultural, religious as well as social developments. Indeed, the history of esoteric currents is undoubtedly a vital aspect of the religious history of Europe and beyond – therefore, they must not be regarded as instances of isolated curiosities or some sort of negligible peculiarity. On the contrary, the immense cultural influence of esotericism has been highlighted by many scholars. One of the seminal features of the esoteric current is the appreciation, integration and promotion of extra-European cultures and traditions. In fact, from early on, esotericists have been important advocates for and facilitators of a particular interest in non-European religious and cultural traditions. Often this was accompanied by a pronounced idealization of 'the other', which was presented as a superior alternative. The reception of India and its image as the supposed 'home of ideal religion and spirituality' in the twentieth century owes therefore much to its overall positive early reception within the esoteric milieu.

Another subject to which the volume contributes refers to the question found at the core of an ongoing debate within the academic study of esotericism, namely, how (if at all) to apply the designation 'Western' in the umbrella term 'Western Esotericism'. In the founding days of the discipline the use of this compound was deemed imperative as it was understood to clearly spell out crucial boundaries defining the very scholarly field, thereby keeping at bay the emic discourse. As the contributions in the volume demonstrate, the 'East–West' logic cannot be upheld with a view to the formation and identity of the global esoteric current, which is indeed not monolithic but intrinsically entangled (Asprem and Strube 2021).

The chapters of this volume highlight the vibrant, multifaceted and intricate esoteric reception of China and Chinese thought, a process still reverberating to this day. Moreover, this collection contours – admittedly not exhaustively – major discursive trajectories and influential figures in this particular thread of reception history pertaining to China and East Asia. Today's popular imagination about China and East Asia would not have been the same without these individuals – including many others as well, whom future scholarship will need to properly introduce. The esoteric contribution, especially to the formation of the popular appreciation of the Chinese and overall East Asian religious thought and philosophy, can hardly be overstated.

Julian Strube illustrates an early network of relations that are centred on the interpretation of the European tradition of mesmerism in comparison with Chinese concepts such as the *yin-yang* 陰陽 dyad. Strube's major focus is a most fascinating exchange between Beijing and Paris in the eighteenth century, namely, between the French Jesuit Joseph-Marie Amiot (1718–93) and (his friend) the Chinese prince Hongwu 弘旿 (1743–1811) but also including the famous Huguenot masonic author Antoine Court de Gébelin (1725–84) and a French lieutenant general-cum-Mesmerist. This transcultural contact exemplifies the close entanglement of individual actors, thereby dissolving the classical 'East–West' binary.

Franz Winter deals with one of the most eminent figures in the history of esotericism whose influence is conspicuous even today. Alphonse-Louis Constant (1810–75), better known by his later pen name Éliphas Lévi, virtually fathered the modern notion of 'magic' through his seminal writings. References to China, particularly to the *Yijing*, neatly fit into his design of 'magic' as an all-encompassing, transcultural current whose traces could be explored ubiquitously. Winter interrogates these references within a wider cultural and historical context while considering Lévi's biography, which includes a training at a Catholic seminary and intense involvement in early socialist movements in France. Notably, Lévi approaches China, among others, through a Figurist lens.

Lukas K. Pokorny investigates the early translation history of the *Daodejing* with a focus on the Theosophical reception and contribution towards the end of the nineteenth century. In particular, he traces which translations and verses were employed by Theosophical writers at the time and what status they assigned to this Daoist classic. He pays special attention to the first two full renditions crafted by the well-known Theosophists Walter Richard Old (1864–1929) and Franz Hartmann (1838–1912) – both being in circulation to this day. Pokorny notes that their Theosophically minded translations were essentially an exercise in creative (Old) or blunt copying (Hartmann).

Davide Marino explores another key figure of the early esoteric reception of East Asian religious concepts in Europe, whose publications were formative for the French esoteric imagination of East Asia: the Martinist Eugène-Albert Puyou de Pouvourville (1861–1939) who spent several years in French Indochina (modern-day Vietnam) and began to publish works on East Asian religions or the 'Far-Eastern metaphysics' under the nom de plume Matgioi. Marino engages with the question of authenticity regarding de Pouvourville's Vietnamese informant but also interprets his work in relation to major patterns of European colonialism.

Johan Nilsson introduces another chief protagonist of the early esoteric interpretation of Chinese religious thought: the Danish-American Carl Henrik Andreas Bjerregaard (1845–1922), a Theosophical connoisseur of Daoism. Nilsson places Bjerregaard's writings in the context of the early twentieth-century esoteric fascination with China, which was also formed and transformed by his writings.

Gordan Djurdjevic turns to the landmark figure of occultism Aleister Crowley (1875–1947), who immersed himself in (what he understood as) Chinese wisdom at least in his self-perception. Crowley went so far as to publish his own 'translations' of important Chinese classics, including the *Daodejing*. In addition, he was deeply intrigued by the idea that there was a correlation between the eight trigrams of the *Yijing* and the occult model of the so-called Tree of Life. Djurdjevic intimately follows the biographical genesis of Crowley's views on China and its alleged wisdom, underlining the importance of this largely uncharted area of the history of esotericism.

In his second contribution, *Johan Nilsson* deals more generally with the question of the 'spiritual East–materialistic West' binary in esoteric depictions of Chinese culture in the late nineteenth and early twentieth centuries. He argues that, contrary to the wider public image of China, the esoteric perception indeed employed this binary to some degree but did not do so vigorously. The esoteric reception of Chinese wisdom was many-layered, involving educational, social and political issues alongside the spiritual dimension.

Karl Baier meticulously studies a pivotal figure for the twentieth- and twenty-first-century esoteric reception of Chinese thought – the Swiss psychologist Carl Gustav Jung (1875–1961). Jung's encounter with Daoism and the *Yijing* (but also Zen Buddhism) proved enormously influential for the area of alternative religiosities from the 1960s Counter Culture to the present-day holistic milieu. Baier sheds light on the fruitful relationship between Jung and his chief sinological informant, Richard Wilhelm (1873–1920), and scrutinizes Jung's orientalist understanding and integration of Daoism and the *Yijing*.

Finally, *Tao Thykier Makeeff* navigates into more recent times in his discussion of the esoteric entanglement with Chinese martial arts. More particularly, he draws on the martial artist legend Bruce Lee (1940–73) and various Hermetic Taijiquan 太极拳 masters. Makeeff stresses that these agents' identities and self-conceptions are the complex result of globally enmeshed reception processes which clearly defy the 'East–West' binary stereotype. He rightly alerts that one runs the risk of reductionism or outright misattribution when trying to capture the formative elements of these figures and traditions.

As stated at the beginning, this volume is a first attempt to explore in a more focused manner a thus far highly understudied subject. Admittedly, this can only be a humble attempt, opening the field for much-needed further elaborations and more detailed studies. As mentioned, whereas the Euro-

American esoteric prism of the reception cast upon India has received relatively wide attention in recent years, China and East Asia remain a veritable *terra incognita* in this respect. Being the first of its kind, this collection attempts to remedy this scholarly lacuna by sketching chief contours of the Euro-American esoteric reception project. However, many topics of interest remain to be explored, such as, for example, Japan and Japanese religions, which are only mentioned in passing. Likewise, with the exception of one chapter, emphasis is clearly put upon the long nineteenth century (and slightly before and beyond). The subsequent period, especially from the 1960s onwards, led to a surging esoteric interest in things East Asian. Austrian-born Fritjof Capra's (b. 1939) influential *The Tao of Physics* (1975) is such an example, spearheading an entirely new book genre in which modern-day science and East Asian religious thought were esoterically appropriated (Clarke 2000: 75–6). For this collection, we designated a regional and temporal focus, for China represented the uncontested centre of the Euro-American esoteric interest involving East Asia for the longer part of its reception history. Follow-up research will need to fill the remaining gaps and thoroughly expand on the directions set by the contributions of this volume.

Notes

1. 'Euro-American' is a qualifier that is intended to *geographically* delimit the globally entangled esoteric discourse. That is, the contributions in this volume predominantly refer to sources that were crafted (however globally intertwined the production processes may have been) by individuals who lived or (originally) resided in precisely this geographical context (i.e. Europe and North America). Moreover, the writings of these individuals were primarily addressed to and/or received by a likewise European/North American audience. Of course, many of these sources circulated globally and found interested audiences around the world. The use of the term 'Western' in this volume has to be understood in the same vein as an admittedly vague geographical limitation and not as a (cultural) essentialist category.
2. On Bayle and Montesquieu, see Kow 2017: 41–78, 135–99; see also the concise overview of French Enlightenment philosophers and their take on China in Pinot 1932.
3. Rare exceptions include Irwin 2004; Sacco 2008; Nilsson 2013, 2020; Paolillo 2013; Statman 2019; Faxneld 2021; and Redmond 2021. Moreover, the subject is touched upon by Cohen 2022. A follow-up to this collection is the special issue on 'Euro-American Esoteric Readings of East Asia' (Pokorny and Winter 2024a; for the

individual contributions, see Marino 2024; Nilsson 2024; Pokorny 2024; Strube 2024; and Winter 2024).

4 In this volume, and in line with our definition given in Pokorny and Winter 2024b: 3, '"esotericism" is understood as an umbrella notion comprising largely non-hegemonic teachings and currents with shared structural features, foremostly centring on the idea that higher or special (practical) knowledge distilled from a discourse deemed secretive can be (incrementally) utilized by its practitioners to salvific or otherwise self-cultivational ends, thereby uncovering ulterior dynamics of life, nature, and/or the cosmos at large'.

5 Drawing on our definition (Pokorny and Winter 2018: 4–6), we understand 'East Asia' to comprise today's nation-states of China (excepting Tibet) and Taiwan, Japan, South and North Korea and Vietnam.

6 Adding to this, of course, is the fact that the European encounter with India preceded that with China (also due to the lesser travel distance), rendering the former 'more familiar'. China's sheer vastness and the general impression of a more closed and alien society likewise favoured India's reception.

7 On the transformation process that eventually also led to the idea of the Chinese as 'yellow' race, see Demel 1992.

References

Akai, T. (2009), 'Theosophical Accounts in Japanese Buddhist Publications of the Late Nineteenth Century: An Introduction and Select Bibliography', *Japanese Religions*, 34 (2): 187–208.

Asprem, E. and J. Strube, eds (2021), *New Approaches to the Study of Esotericism*, Leiden: Brill.

Brockey, L. M. (2007), *Journey to the East: The Jesuit Mission to China, 1579–1724*, Cambridge, MA: Belknap Press of Harvard University Press.

Čapková, H. (2020a), 'A Brief History of the Theosophical Society in Japan in the Interwar Period', *The Journal of CESNUR*, 4 (5): 3–26.

Čapková, H. (2020b), 'Theosophy as a Transnational Network: The Commission of the Golconde Dormitory in Puducherry (1935–ca. 1948)', in J. Strube and H. M. Krämer (eds), *Theosophy Across Boundaries: Transcultural and Interdisciplinary Perspectives on a Modern Esoteric Movement*, 373–400, Albany: State University of New York Press.

Cheng, A. (2019), 'Abel-Rémusat e Hegel: Sinologia e filosofia nell'Europa del XIX secolo', *Rivista di estetica*, 72: 139–51.

Chuang, C. (2020), 'Theosophical Movements in Modern China: The Education Provided by Theosophists at the Shanghai International Settlement', in J. Strube and H. M. Krämer (eds), *Theosophy Across Boundaries: Transcultural and*

Interdisciplinary Perspectives on a Modern Esoteric Movement, 149–78, Albany: State University of New York Press.

Clarke, J. J. (2000), *The Tao of the West: Western Transformations of Taoist Thought*, London: Routledge.

Cohen, E. (2022), *The Psychologisation of Eastern Spiritual Traditions: Colonisation, Translation and Commodification*, London: Routledge.

Cox, L. and A. Turner (2020), 'International Religious Organizations in a Colonial World. The Maha-Bodhi Society in Arakan', in J. Strube and H. M. Krämer (eds), *Theosophy Across Boundaries: Transcultural and Interdisciplinary Perspectives on a Modern Esoteric Movement*, 281–316, Albany: State University of New York Press.

de Michelis, E. (2004), *A History of Modern Yoga: Patañjali and Western Esotericism*, London: Continuum.

Demel, W. (1992), 'Wie die Chinesen gelb wurden: Ein Beitrag zur Frühgeschichte der Rassentheorien', *Historische Zeitschrift*, 255: 625–66.

Dijkstra, T. (2022), *Printing and Publishing Chinese Religion and Philosophy in the Dutch Republic, 1595–1700: The Chinese Imprint*, Leiden: Brill.

Djurdjevic, G. (2014), *India and the Occult: The Influence of South Asian Spirituality on Modern Western Occultism*, New York: Palgrave Macmillan.

Faxneld, P. (2021), 'Martial Arts Spirituality in Sweden: The Occult Connection', in L. Pokorny and F. Winter (eds), *The Occult Nineteenth Century: Roots, Developments, and Impact on the Modern World*, 221–43, Cham: Palgrave Macmillan.

Fletcher, J. E. (2011), *A Study of the Life and Works of Athanasius Kircher, "Germanus incredibilis". With a Selection of his Unpublished Correspondence and an Annotated Translation of his Autobiography*, edited for publication by E. Fletcher, Leiden: Brill.

Gaitanidis, I. and J. Stein (2019), 'Japanese Religions and the Global Occult: An Introduction and Literature Review', *Japanese Religions*, 44 (1–2): 1–32.

Halbfass, W. (1990), *India and Europe: An Essay in Philosophical Understanding*, Delhi: Motilal Banarsidass.

Hanegraaff, W. J. (2020), 'Western Esotericism and the Orient in the First Theosophical Society', in J. Strube and H. M. Krämer (eds), *Theosophy Across Boundaries: Transcultural and Interdisciplinary Perspectives on a Modern Esoteric Movement*, 29–64, Albany: State University of New York Press.

Irwin, L. (2004), 'Daoist Alchemy in the West: The Esoteric Paradigms', *Esoterica*, 6: 31–51.

Jammes, J. (2020), 'Theosophying the Vietnamese Religious Landscape: A Circulatory History of a Western Esoteric Movement in Southern Vietnam', in J. Strube and H. M. Krämer (eds), *Theosophy Across Boundaries: Transcultural and Interdisciplinary Perspectives on a Modern Esoteric Movement*, 109–48, Albany: State University of New York Press.

Junqueira, L. F. B. (2021), 'Revealing Secrets: Talismans, Healthcare and the Market of the Occult in Early Twentieth-century China', *Social History of Medicine*, 34 (4): 1069–93.

Kern, R. (1996), *Orientalism, Modernism, and the American Poem*, Cambridge: Cambridge University Press.

King, R. (2013), *Orientalism and Religion: Post-Colonial Theory, India and The Mystic East*, London: Routledge.

Kow, S. (2017), *China in Early Enlightenment Political Thought*, New York: Routledge.

Latourette, K. S. (2019), *A History of Christian Missions in China*, Piscataway: Gorgias Press.

Marino, D. (2024), 'Albert de Pouvourville's Occultisme Colonial', *NVMEN. International Review for the History of Religions*, 71 (1): 71–93.

McLaughlin, R. (2010), *Rome and the Distant East: Trade Routes to the Ancient Lands of Arabia, India and China*, London: Bloomsbury.

Mungello, D. E. (1985), *Curious Land: Jesuit Accommodation and the Origins of Sinology*, Stuttgart: Steiner Verlag Wiesbaden.

Mungello, D. E. (2009), *The Great Encounter of China and the West, 1500–1800*, Lanham: Rowman and Littlefield.

Myers, P. (2020), 'Affinity and Estrangement: Transnational Theosophy in Germany and India during the Colonial Era (1878–1933)', in J. Strube and H. M. Krämer (eds), *Theosophy Across Boundaries: Transcultural and Interdisciplinary Perspectives on a Modern Esoteric Movement*, 217–52, Albany: State University of New York Press.

Nilsson, J. (2013), 'Defending Paper Gods: Aleister Crowley and the Reception of Daoism in Early Twentieth Century Esotericism', *Correspondences*, 1 (1): 103–27.

Nilsson, J. (2020), 'As a Fire Beneath the Ashes: The Quest for Chinese Wisdom within Occultism, 1850–1949', PhD diss., Centre for Theology and Religious Studies, Lund University, Lund.

Nilsson, J. (2024) '"If the Kingdom be Ruled according to the Tao": Politics as "Eastern Wisdom" in Aleister Crowley's Reception of the *Daodejing*', *NVMEN. International Review for the History of Religions*, 71 (1): 94–109.

Osterhammel, J. (2018), *Unfabling the East: The Enlightenment's Encounter with Asia*, Princeton: Princeton University Press.

Paolillo, M. (2013), 'Il simbolismo del Centro e dell'Asse Verticale nelle pratiche di realizzazione secondo le più antiche fonti taoiste', *Perennia Verba. Il deposito sacro della tradizione*, 13: 145–88.

Perkins, F. (2004), *Leibniz and China: A Commerce of Light*, Cambridge: Cambridge University Press.

Pinot, V. (1932), *La Chine et la formation de l'esprit philosophique en France (1640–1740)*, Paris: Paul Geuthner.

Pokorny, L. K. (2024), 'The Ascended Confucius: Images of the Chinese Master in the Euro-American Esoteric Discourse', *NVMEN. International Review for the History of Religions*, 71 (1): 29–47.

Pokorny, L. K. and F. Winter (2018), 'East Asian New Religious Movements: Introductory Remarks', in L. K. Pokorny and F. Winter (eds), *Handbook of East Asian New Religious Movements*, 3–13, Leiden: Brill.

Pokorny, L. K. and F. Winter (2024a), 'Euro-American Esoteric Readings of East Asia', *NVMEN. International Review for the History of Religions*, 71 (1).

Pokorny, L. K. and F. Winter (2024b), 'Euro-American Esoteric Readings of East Asia: Introductory Remarks', *NVMEN. International Review for the History of Religions*, 71 (1): 1–8.

Raschke, M. (1978), 'New Studies in Roman Commerce with the East', in H. Temporini (ed.), *Aufstieg und Niedergang der römischen Welt: Geschichte und Kultur Roms in der neuen Forschung. II Principat*, Vol. 9, 604–1361, Berlin: De Gruyter.

Redmond, G. (2021), 'The *Yijing* in Early Postwar Counterculture in the West', in B. W. Ng (ed.), *The Making of the Global Yijing in the Modern World: Cross-cultural Interpretations and Interactions*, 197–221, Singapore: Springer.

Reichert, F. (1992), *Begegnungen mit China: Die Entdeckung Ostasiens im Mittelalter*, Sigmaringen: Thorbecke.

Rudbøg, T. and E. Reenberg Sand (2020), 'H. P. Blavatsky's Early Reception of Hindu Philosophy', in T. Rudbøg and E. Reenberg Sand (eds), *Imagining the East: The Early Theosophical Society*, 107–32, New York: Oxford University Press.

Sacco, L. (2008), 'La tradizione taoista nel pensiero di René Guénon', *Aries*, 8 (1): 63–89.

Statman, A. (2019), 'The Tarot of Yu the Great: The Search for Civilization's Origins between France and China in the Age of Enlightenment', in P. Findlen (ed.), *Empires of Knowledge: Scientific Networks in the Early Modern World*, 246–68, London: Routledge.

Stolzenberg, D. (2013), *Egyptian Oedipus: Athanasius Kircher and the Secrets of Antiquity*, Chicago: The University of Chicago Press.

Strube, J. (2022), *Global Tantra: Religion, Science, and Nationalism in Colonial Modernity*, New York: Oxford University Press.

Strube, J. (2024), 'Esotericism between Europe and East Asia: How the "Esoteric Distinction" Became a Structure in Cross-Cultural Interpretation', *NVMEN. International Review for the History of Religions*, 71 (1): 9–28.

Trompf, G. (2011), 'Introduction: Athanasius Kircher as Esoteric Thinker and the State of Kircher Scholarship', in J. E. Fletcher (ed.), *A Study of the Life and Works of Athanasius Kircher, "Germanus incredibilis": With a Selection of His Unpublished Correspondence and an Annotated Translation of His Autobiography*, xxi–xxxiv, Leiden: Brill.

Urban, H. B. (2003), *Tantra: Sex, Secrecy, Politics, and Power in the Study of Religion*, Berkeley: University of California Press.

von Collani, C. (2007), 'The First Encounter of the West with the Yijing', *Monumenta Serica*, 55 (1): 227–387.

von Collani, C. (2010), 'Figurism', in N. Standaert (ed.), *Handbook of Christianity in China: 635–1800*, Vol. 1, 668–79, Leiden: Brill.

Wei, S. L. (2020), *Chinese Theology and Translation: The Christianity of the Jesuit Figurists and their Christianized Yijing*, London: Routledge.

Will, P.-E. (2015), 'Jean-Pierre Abel-Rémusat (1788–1832) et ses successeurs', *La lettre du Collège de France*, 40: 26–8.

Windisch, E. (1917), *Geschichte der Sanskrit-Philologie und indischen Altertumskunde*, Teil 1, Berlin Erscheinungsort nicht ermittelbar: De Gruyter Mouton; Karl I. Trübner Verlag.

Winter, F. (2024), 'Introducing "the Heavenly Empire of China" (le Céleste Empire de la Chine): China versus India in the Quest for an Ancient Model Society in Joseph Alexandre Saint-Yves d'Alveydre', *NVMEN. International Review for the History of Religions*, 71 (1): 48–70.

Wu, Y. (2018), 'Techniques for Nothingness: Debate over the Comparability of Hypnosis and Zen in Early-Twentieth-century Japan', *History of Science*, 56 (4): 470–96.

Yoshinaga, S. (2009), 'Theosophy and Buddhist Reformers in the Middle of the Meiji Period: An Introduction', *Japanese Religions*, 34 (2): 119–31.

Yoshinaga, S. (2021), 'Spiritualism and Occultism', in E. Baffelli, F. Rambelli, and A. Castiglioni (eds), *The Bloomsbury Handbook of Japanese Religions*, 229–39, London: Bloomsbury.

1

Daoism and Kung Fu as occult sciences

Historical comparisons between Chinese practices and mesmerism

Julian Strube

Comparison and cultural exchange

Eighteenth-century authors widely discussed Asian subjects in terms of supposedly 'occult' and 'esoteric' practices and traditions. As I have demonstrated elsewhere, this language was employed since the seventeenth century and then exponentially proliferated during the eighteenth, mostly within theological and orientalist writings (Strube 2023). Until the nineteenth century, the notions of 'occult' and 'esoteric' were firmly established within orientalist scholarship and comparative religion, primarily focused on Indian, Persian and Arabic contexts. Similarly, references to China and wider Asia have been widespread (Strube 2024). This raises some important questions that concern the emergence of religious comparative categories during the professionalization and institutionalization of orientalist and philological studies, which pertain to the present-day applicability of categories such as 'religion' or 'esotericism' beyond 'the West'. In previous studies, I have argued that our categories do warrant theoretical reflection and critical interrogation, yet without assuming that they should be merely regarded as unilateral Western projections or impositions. Rather, current debates about religious comparativism would greatly benefit from a consistent historicization of our categories, which implies approaching and exploring them as the constantly contested and re-negotiated outcomes of often ambiguous processes of global exchanges (Strube 2022: 1–33, 242–51). In this chapter, I will propose some insights into historical acts of comparison in which Daoism and Kung Fu were identified as 'occult sciences', interpreted through the lens of contemporary mesmerism and situated within the historiography of a Eurasian 'primitive culture'. By doing so, I will dive into a remarkable cross-cultural exchange that illustrates the historical complexities of comparison.¹

This exchange unfolded between Jesuits in Beijing, their local interlocutors and French intellectuals invested in scientific experiments, historical speculations about the origin of civilization, mesmerism, the 'esoteric' masonic current of Martinism (also referred to as illuminism) and the so-called occult sciences encompassing astrology, alchemy and magic. On the Chinese side, I will concentrate on the French Jesuit Joseph-Marie Amiot (1718–93) and his friend, the prince Hongwu 弘旿 (1743–1811). Among the learned French who corresponded with Amiot, I will focus on the Huguenot masonic author Antoine Court de Gébelin (1725–84), famous for his nine-volume *Monde primitif analysé et comparé avec le monde moderne* (1773–82), and Louis-Raphaël-Lucrèce de Fayolle, Comte de Mellet (1727–1804), a lieutenant general, regional governor and follower of mesmerism who prominently contributed an essay on the Tarot to one of Gébelin's volumes.

These authors corresponded about the identification of Chinese practices with mesmerism, supposedly derived from a shared primordial science. Their writings are particularly interesting because they can hardly be understood as products of the imaginations of Westerners, that is, from the viewpoints of either the spatially distant France or those of the local Jesuit mission in Beijing. Rather, we are dealing with an intricate tangle in which the highly abstract and historically erroneous speculations of Gébelin and Mellet met with the local experience of Amiot, shaped by Qing 清 intellectuals such as Hongwu, and, as we shall see, Amiot's observation of everyday Chinese practices. All of this unfolded within globally entangled debates about the origin of religion and its relationship to science. For a considerable time, Amiot was a major source for European scholars interested in China, well until the beginning of the nineteenth century, when the first academic sinologist Jean-Pierre Abel-Rémusat (1788–1832) and philosophers such as Hegel (1770–1831) took inspiration from his writings. As Alexander Statman points out in his seminal article on the friendship between Amiot and Hongwu, it was through the latter's 'help and encouragement' that the Jesuit was able to communicate this knowledge about China (Statman 2017: 117). In fact, Amiot's 'harsh early criticism of most practices beyond Catholicism and Confucian orthodoxy' was radically transformed through his interactions, and 'he began to approach other knowledge traditions of China with an open-mindedness almost unmatched in the history of the Jesuit mission to China'. He especially praised Daoism for its physical, metaphysical and spiritual truths. By the early 1790s, 'Amiot had come to believe that "the principles of all the sciences" of Europe and China, particularly in physics, were mutually complementary'. Mesmer's theory of animal magnetism was a case in point, as it had been anticipated by the principles of *yin* 陰 and *yang* 陽, rooted in an ancient pan-Eurasian tradition (Statman 2017: 111).

It bears emphasizing that Amiot's identification of Chinese practices with magnetism and occult sciences was the outcome of his embeddedness in local Chinese culture. Amiot formulated his ideas about mesmerism while closely collaborating with Hongwu, within a context marked by dialogue between missionaries and Chinese intellectuals (Statman 2017: 92). During that time, European scholars were confronted with an exploding wealth of information about Asia, which stimulated the emergence of orientalist studies and the development of various theories about the origin of language, 'races' and religion in particular. Gébelin's *Monde primitif* featured prominently among the numerous works that were published at that time, next to those by scholars such as Jean Sylvain Bailly (1736–93), to whom I will return; Charles François Dupuis (1742–1809), author of *Origine de tous les cultes, ou la religion [sic] universelle* (1794); and Constantin François Volney (1757–1820), whose studies of the supposed links between Europe and Asia were highly influential (App 2010: 440–79). These European theories of human history became intertwined with the ideas of scholars such as Hongwu, leading to, in the words of Statman, 'a truly cross-cultural conversation that drew on European and Chinese learning to formulate an alternative narrative of historical progress' (Statman 2019: 248).

Apart from being fascinating in their own right, these historical developments allow for instructive insights into more theoretical issues revolving around the issue of comparison. After discussing the source material related, first, to magnetism and occult sciences in China, and second, to the underlying historiography that informed it, I will then offer some reflections on why and how historical actors engaged in these acts of comparison and the identification of certain ideas and practices.

Science and magic at the Beijing North Church

Having requested to be sent to China as a missionary during his training as a priest, Amiot eventually arrived in Macao in 1750. About a year later, he entered the Jesuit mission in Beijing, where he stayed until his death (for more on his biography, see Hermans 2019). During the 1750s and 1760s, the Jesuits received support from the Qianlong 乾隆 emperor (1711–99; r. 1735–99), who was interested in Western science, debated astronomical theories with the missionaries and had them perform electrical experiments. However, this constellation changed drastically in the 1770s, when the Society of Jesus, which for about two centuries had transmitted almost all knowledge about China, was suppressed in Europe in 1773. On the Chinese side, the emperor reacted to the Wang Lun 王倫 uprising of 1774 by identifying sectarianism as the major threat to Qing stability. As a result, exchange between learned Chinese and the now 'secular priests' was heavily restricted. The latter were now supported by the French state rather than the Church or the Qing authorities (Statman 2017: 90). As Statman points out, these unfavourable circumstances reduced interactions between the missionaries and the Chinese, but they did not put an end to them. Hongwu's activities are an impressive illustration of this. The prince had an extraordinarily inquisitive and unconventional spirit, interested in matters artistic and scientific (for more on his life, see Statman 2017: 92–6). After his political ambitions did not materialize, he turned away from Confucianism and immersed himself into Daoism and Buddhism, possibly even engaging with Christianity. Hongwu had been in contact with the Jesuits since his upbringing at the Qing court and began to frequent their North Church in Beijing from around 1780 (Statman 2017: 98–9).

After the suppression of the Society of Jesus, the missionaries had to withdraw to their private quarters at the North Church, which possessed one of the most extensive European libraries in Asia (Statman 2017: 105). By 1784, Hongwu had become a regular and a close friend of Amiot, conducting experiments together and exchanging ideas. This is not least significant because these interactions directly manifested in the fifteen-volume *Mémoires concernant les Chinois*, which were published between 1776 and 1791. They contain many letters, treatises and translations done by the 'ex-Jesuits', among whom Amiot was the leading figure. All this was possible due to the patronage of the French minister Henri-Léonard Bertin (1720–92), who funded the mission, sent them yearly packages up until the French Revolution and maintained full control over the correspondence (Statman 2017: 100).

The friendship between Hongwu and Amiot was not least the result of their shared enthusiasm for scientific experiments. From 1751 onwards, Amiot had worked on astronomy and physics, carrying out numerous experiments on magnetism (Parr 2019: 242). According to Amiot, Hongwu had 'inherited from his august grandfather the love of the sciences and of French people' (Statmann 2017: 104). Amiot was the ideal partner to pursue these interests, and together they conducted experiments at the North Church – using some of the most sophisticated equipment worldwide – and built a new laboratory at Hongwu's mansion. Aware of the difficult circumstances and fearing for the negative reception of their activities, they kept their investigations secret and never made their results public. Yet, as Amiot put it, Hongwu did become 'initiated in all the mysteries of physics' (Statmann 2017: 106).

This interesting expression of scientific experiments in the language of 'initiation' might appear superficial, a mere form of speech, but it does point to a highly fascinating and instructive tension between the cutting-edge scientific activities at the North Church and the Chinese traditions that the collaborators increasingly related to them. In 1784, Hongwu reportedly pondered the knowledge and skill of ancient Chinese alchemists, and it is 'likely not coincidental that at about this time, Amiot began to take Daoism and Chinese alchemy in particular more seriously than almost any European had before' (Statmann 2017: 101–2). Indeed, like most scholars of the late imperial period, Hongwu was apparently convinced that Western scholarship was only rediscovering what the ancient Chinese had already known – an argument that was frequently employed by missionaries (Zhang 2015: 5–12; Statman 2017: 107). Yet, Hongwu and Amiot were careful. On the one hand, they intensified their research: an electric machine that had been delivered to the North Church in 1764, but was never assembled, was now set up in 1785, causing great fascination and an interest in therapeutical applications. On the other hand, Hongwu advised to hide the machine, especially from the emperor. The missionaries agreed, as they feared that they might be taken for magicians (Statman 2017: 108–9). Nonetheless, Bertin pushed for the continuation of the performances, sending more state-of-the-art equipment. As he wrote to Amiot, explaining the physical principles behind the electrical device would be the best 'cure of all credulity in magic'. The machine was eventually used only for 'purely physical experiments', not for medical use, and public demonstrations were discontinued (Statman 2017: 110).

These concerns about the perceptions of electric experiments as magic, especially when conducted with medical applications in mind, are but one manifestation of the tensions between 'science' and 'magic' that – for different but yet interrelated reasons – can be observed both in Europe and China. As will become obvious later, whereas Hongwu was primarily worried about local political and social conditions, Amiot's caution becomes tangible in the remarkable contrast between his published writings in both the *Mémoires* and his private correspondence. The worlds of Hongwu and Amiot were not separate, however, which is evident taking into consideration that the latter's approach to electricity and magnetism was decisively shaped by his interaction with Chinese learning. For instance, Amiot had brief contact with the Imperial Academy of Sciences in St. Petersburg in 1755, where he sent the results of his experiments with magnetism and electricity. He never received a response, although his findings did indeed circulate among European scholars (Parr 2019: 245–6). In a letter from 1784, which was reprinted in a volume of the *Mémoires*, he recalled this unanswered attempt at establishing contact, describing how, decades earlier, he had been theorizing about the existence of a 'universal agent' behind the phenomena of electricity and magnetism. In fact, he believed that these were 'derived from one principle and formed like two main branches of the same trunk' (Amiot 1786: 570).

As I will discuss below, at the time of his writing, Amiot had already equated these two branches of the same principle with both the concept of yin and yang and mesmerism. Yet, neither of them is mentioned anywhere in the letters published in the *Mémoires*. This stands in stark contrast to Amiot's private correspondence, where he discussed them extensively. This suggests that, in parallel to his public activities and writings, which he deemed more acceptable, Amiot increasingly engaged with Chinese practices and traditions which he positively related to mesmerism and the occult sciences. This happened in close exchange with Hongwu and, most likely, other learned Chinese. As will become clear in what follows, the Jesuit seems to have been most intrigued by the mesmerist and Chinese perspectives.

Mesmerism and Chinese occult sciences

It was through *both* Amiot's engagement with mesmerism and his friendship with Hongwu that his view on Chinese practices would be radically transformed in the early 1780s. Several years prior to the onset of the North Church collaboration, an essay by Amiot about what he termed the 'Kung Fu of the Bonzes of Tao-sée' was published in the *Mémoires*. In the language common among missionaries at the time, Amiot explained that the *Tao-sée* were those who followed the teachings of *Lao-tsée*, especially monks ('Bonzes'). These 'monks' practiced the postures of *Cong-fou*, about which we read (Amiot 1779: 441):

> The thick clouds of superstition and the dreadful shadows of idolatry have concealed the true theory of *Cong-fou* from the masses so much that they are led to believe, according to the accounts of the Bonzes, that it is a true exercise

of religion which, by curing the body of its infirmities, frees the soul from the servitude of the senses, prepares it to enter into commerce with the Spirits, and opens to it the door of some immortality to which one arrives without passing through the grave.

Clearly, Amiot was anything but sympathetic towards the Daoists. He held that they had deluded even emperors and were generally smiled upon by Confucian scholars, who yet continued to lend credibility to the Bonzes' 'chimeras'. At the same time, Amiot was curious about the 'true theory' of Kung Fu, which revealed 'ideas common with our Alchemists of the Great Work'. He was convinced that behind the mist of superstition lay 'an ancient practice of Medicine based on principles and completely independent of the absurd doctrine of the Tao-tsée', which deserved examination for the sake of 'the Physicists and Doctors of Europe' (Amiot 1779: 442). Amiot explained that Kung Fu consisted of bodily postures and the way of breathing, describing the respective techniques in some detail and providing illustrations (Figure 1.1) (Amiot 1779: 443–7).

Some years later, Amiot's condescending curiosity would give way to appreciation and outright admiration. This was the direct result of a correspondence with Mellet in the early 1780s, at exactly the same time when his friendship with Hongwu solidified. Mellet's mother, Charlotte, was Bertin's sister, an illustration of how closely knit the network of mesmerism enthusiasts was that became connected to Beijing (Parr 2019: 268–9; Statman 2017: 111). In his letter from 1 October 1783, Amiot confessed that he had first thought Kung Fu to be buffoonery, but that his view had completely changed: 'What you tell me about the prodigies that Mesmer performs in your country [*chez vous*] opens my eyes, and I can already see, as if through a cloud, that it could well be that the same applies to both Chinese Kung Fu and the medicine of Mesmer' (Huard, Solonet, and Wong 1960: 62–3). Amiot declared that, already nearly six thousand years ago (Huard, Solonet, and Wong 1960: 63–4):

> [...] there was here a method of curing illnesses more or less similar to that of Mesmer, there is no doubt that we can still find some vestiges of it. I have no doubt that some remnants of it can still be found. I have no doubt, given the esteem, respect, and veneration that people have for the ancients, that there are still doctors who practice it, patients who submit to their procedures, and secret admirers who attest to its marvelous effects. If there are only two or three of them in the vast city of Peking, I will dig them up and give you an account of their operations, their way of working and the principles on which they base themselves.

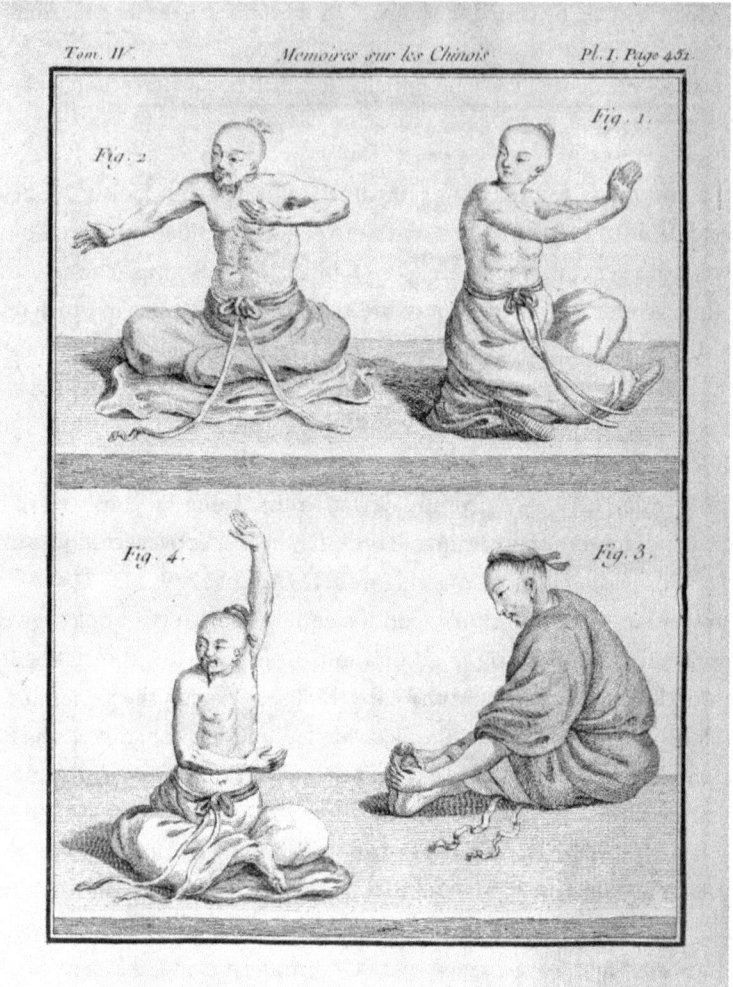

Figure 1.1 Kung Fu postures, from Amiot, *Mémoires concernant l'histoire, les sciences, les arts, les moeurs, les usages, &c. des Chinois*, volume 4 (1779).

In the meantime, I believe I can explain what Monsieur Mesmer explains by animal magnetism by the physical principles that the Chinese admit in nature, and I can, it seems to me, explain it in a clearer and more satisfactory way than the German doctor ....

Amiot was convinced that the phenomena of electricity, magnetism and attraction could be much better elucidated by the Chinese doctrine 'the *Tai Chi* is this universal agent, essentially constituted by yin and yang, with which it makes a whole, which is in all and by all' (Huard, Solonet, and Wong 1960: 64).

Discussing Mesmer's approach to healing patients, Amiot argued (Huard, Solonet, and Wong 1960: 66–7):

> Since illness can only be caused by an excess or a deficiency of activity in the *Ki*, the vital principle, it is obvious that by subtracting what is in excess, or by making up for what is lacking, the balance is re-established, and this is precisely what Music and baths contribute to.

The shift from Amiot's previous assessment could hardly be more striking than in his following statement: 'what may seem to you to be unintelligible jargon, is to me a language as luminous as that of your Newtonian Philosophers and others' (Huard, Solonet, and Wong 1960: 67–9). Amiot emphasized: 'These three monosyllables (*ki, yn* and *yang*) are used to explain all the other sciences, and this without any other help than that of the Quaternary [*Quaternaire*], much more sacred, without comparison, than the one whose invention is attributed to Pythagoras, and infinitely more fertile in property' (Huard, Solonet, and Wong 1960: 68). It is astonishing that the Jesuit would put the Chinese doctrine above both Newton and Pythagoras – the contemporary reference points for the pinnacle of science and philosophy. It suggests that he was convinced by the legitimacy and utmost importance of mesmerism, while he believed it to be inferior to Chinese tradition. This was highly significant, as he unambiguously juxtaposed the "Western" imagination of a lineage leading from Pythagoras via Newton to Mesmer – an omnipresent narrative among mesmerists and their sympathizers – to ancient Chinese wisdom. His preference for the latter was not due to the influence of his French interlocutors but his collaboration with Hongwu and other Chinese.

In another letter to Mellet from 18 October 1784, Amiot further elaborated his ideas after thanking his correspondent for sending him several brochures through the channel of Bertin. Confirming 'the existence of a universal agent', he described the Chinese system in some more detail, highlighting that animal magnetism offered only partial insight into the complex interplay between yin and yang (Huard, Solonet, and Wong 1960: 73–5). In fact, he stressed that '[e]verything Monsieur Mesmer has said about Animal Magnetism has been said by the Chinese about Yin-yang for nearly four thousand years' (Huard, Solonet, and Wong 1960: 81–2). It appears that Amiot did follow through with his aforementioned plan to trace the remnants of these ancient practices to the present. In another letter from 24 February 1790, he provided some amazingly detailed descriptions of his observations of Chinese 'magnetizers' (Huard, Solonet, and Wong 1960: 86):

> When I speak of a *Magnetizer*, do not imagine a Marquis, a Count, a Knight, or even a Doctor. Those who magnetize here are simply ordinary men who are counted by the thousands in the various districts of the city, and who are called *ty-teou*, as we would say in French, *raseur de tête*, if the word *raseur* were French. In your country [*chez vous*], they are called *Barbier*, because unlike in China, they shave beards more often than heads. After all, it does not matter by what name they are called: they shave and they magnetize when they are required to do so; that is all I wanted to say; but I must add that the way in which they magnetize differs in many respects from the way in which you do it. They do not put so many preparations into it. They have no rooms, no tubs, no ropes to form the Chain, no iron rods for conductors; everything is simple as nature, everything breathes confidence and decent freedom.[2]

The subsequent detailed descriptions, which would merit further study in their own right, show that Amiot made great effort to observe these practices in both the city and countryside; he emphasized that most of them took place in villages. He pointed out that 'it is rare that on my way I do not meet some Magnetizer currently in practice', but that it was 'only since I have been initiated into the science of Magnetism that I have seen things as one should see them' (Huard, Solonet, and Wong 1960: 87–8). Mesmerism provided him with a lens to explain the Chinese practices, which, in turn, led him to understand better what animal magnetism failed to fully penetrate.

These sympathetic accounts that breathe an air of fascination and amazement underline Amiot's rapidly growing appreciation, fascination and even admiration for these Chinese practices. Again, these reports stand in stark contrast to what we encounter in the *Mémoires*, which reproduced a letter written in quite a different tone to an unidentified recipient on 16 October 1787. This indicates that, depending on his correspondent, Amiot chose carefully how to express his ideas about Chinese practices. It should also be kept in mind that the *Mémoires* were a heavily curated, redacted collection that excluded subjects deemed too abstruse (Statman 2019: 250). At the outset of his well-known letter 'About the Sect of the Tao-sée', Amiot highlighted their rivalry to the Confucian scholars and the fact that they had fallen into disrepute: 'it originated in the country itself, and was the first to corrupt the ancient national doctrine, by joining to the noble simplicity of the primitive dogmas, the most absurd principles of the crudest errors' (Amiot 1791: 208). While his treatment of the *Tao-sée* was highly critical, he did go into some detail about their teachings, which were taught according to the disciple's progress through instructions by masters (Amiot 1791: 210):

It was only after they had made the most of the lessons of these strong teachers and masters, that some adepts finally obtained the right to penetrate to the sanctuary of nature, in order to read there all that is within the purview of the occult sciences, such as magic, the cabala, judicial astrology, etc. They admit as principle that everything that exists or can exist is matter, with the exception of the Supreme Being, whom they designate by the names of *Tien*, *Chang-tien*, *Chang-ti*, and other similar names .... This matter, they say, emanated from the omnipotence of this Being, & enclosed in the *Tay-ki*, under the envelope of *yin-yang* of which this *Tay-ki* is composed receives perpetually different modifications by the generation, the destruction, and the regeneration of beings.

Amiot here explicitly identified the practices of the *Tao-sée* as occult sciences and he did not fail 'to point out that the cabal, magic, and the others that we understand under the general name of the *occult sciences* have always been known to the Chinese, but they were considered as harmful sciences that brought misfortune to those who practiced them' (Amiot 1791: 227-8). We also learn about the triumph of the Confucian scholars of the Hanlin 翰林 Academy over 'the absurdities of the occult sciences' (Amiot 1791: 256), which is another allusion to the opposition between Confucianism and Daoism. This account differs remarkably from the more nuanced discussion in Amiot's letter to Mellet (Huard, Solonet, and Wong 1960: 78). This difference becomes even more obvious in his discussion of the workings of yin and yang, which is much more distanced than his outright enthusiastic portrayals in the unpublished letters. In order to comprehend this enthusiasm, it is crucial to turn to the historiography that largely informed the correspondence between Beijing and Paris (Figure 1.2).

Atlantean origins

Amiot's insistence that Daoism had 'originated in the country itself' and corrupted the pure 'primitive dogmas' is highly significant. In the eighteenth century, practically all scholars in Europe agreed on the extreme antiquity of Chinese culture, but opinions were divided over its origins (Statman 2019: 248-51; cf. Amiot 1777). Most Jesuits believed that the Chinese were direct descendants of Noah (Amiot 1780: 53). Others, following the orientalist Joseph de Guignes (1721-1800) and the earlier conjectures of the Jesuit antiquarian Athanasius Kircher (1602-80), regarded China as an ancient Egyptian colony (App 2010: 207-231; Hartman 1998). This theory was extensively and frequently discussed in the *Mémoires*, the first volume of which included an

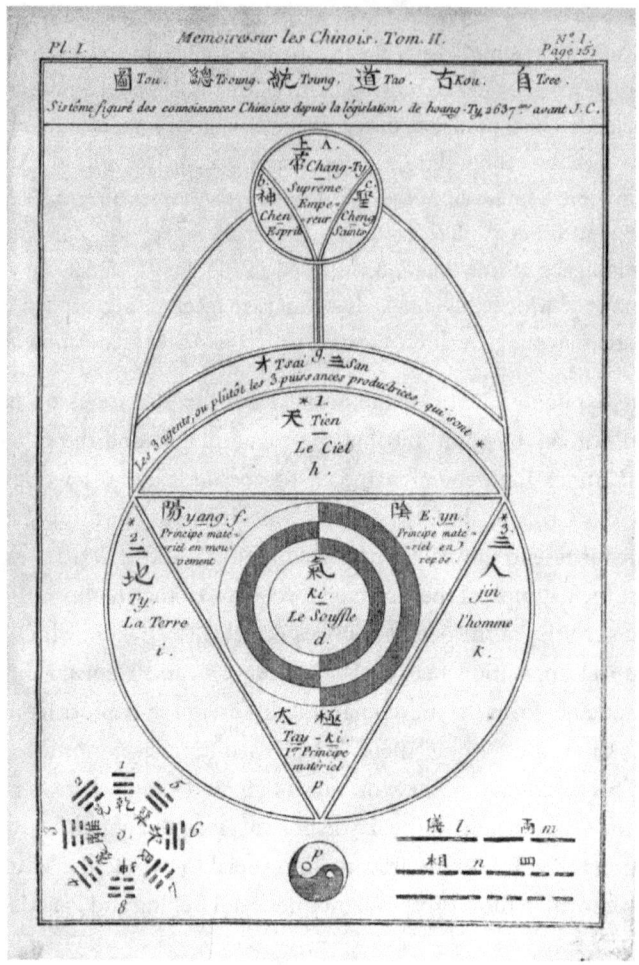

Figure 1.2 The Workings of the Universal Principle, from Amiot, *Mémoires concernant l'histoire, les sciences, les arts, les moeurs, les usages, &c. des Chinois*, volume 2 (1777).

essay on the parallels between Chinese and Egyptian scripts (Amiot 1776; cf. Parr 2019: 204–5, 246–50). Another theory, proposed by the Dutch historian Cornelius de Pauw (1739–99), claimed that the Chinese were an offshoot of the 'Tartars' or 'Scyths' from Central Asia (Parr 2019: 256–7). Notably, none of these theories placed the origins of Chinese culture in China. Amiot's argument for the emergence of Daoism in China, then, must indeed be understood as referring to the later, local corruption of a pristine doctrine that had originated elsewhere.

It did not take long before Amiot became convinced by a new solution to the question of the provenance of Chinese culture, spearheaded by Bailly and

Gébelin, which argued for its antediluvian origins in Atlantis. This theory was not least attractive because it made plausible the idea of a primitive Eurasian culture at the root of its Chinese, Indian, Persian, Egyptian and eventually European branches. It also thrusts in the middle of a far-reaching conflict between conceptions of history as either progressive or retrograde: whereas some authors viewed history, with Condorcet (1743–94), in terms of the progressing perfectibility of humanity, others looked back to a distant golden age, whose ancient wisdom now awaited its rediscovery after a long period of decay. Hence, the extreme antiquity of Chinese culture, which allegedly had remained in a state of stasis over millennia, could be perceived as either retrograde or as an authoritative source of *prisca scientia* (ancient wisdom) for the very same reasons (Statman 2019: 246). Amiot discussed these ideas in Beijing with his Chinese friends and scholars, who confirmed them on the basis of Chinese historiography. At the same time, he became a self-described 'disciple' of Bailly and Gébelin, actively reaching out to offer evidence for their theories (Statman 2019: 247). As in the case of mesmerism, Amiot's ideas were formed by both European and Chinese scholarship. His admiration of the *prisca scientia* supposedly conserved in Chinese learning, critically channelled through the prism of French historiography, becomes tangible in his letter to Mellet from 1784 (Huard, Solonet, and Wong 1960: 77):

> Let us admit, Monsieur, that our presumptuous scholars, who consider the Chinese to be such bad physicists, would be very surprised if they were to adopt the same system of these same Chinese, as being, if not the true one, at least the most satisfactory and the closest to the truth: And as this system is so very old among them that they do not name its author and that they have it by tradition since the first time of the Monarchy, it would be necessary to conclude with Mr. Bailly that they received it from an earlier people, from a lost people, in a word, from the Antediluvian people, who were probably more advanced in the sciences than we can be today.

These speculations emerged within a feedback loop between Paris and Beijing. In 1787, Mellet wrote to the Marquis de Puységur (1751–1825), one of the leading and most influential proponents of animal magnetism that Mesmer had rediscovered an antediluvian medicine that was linked to both magnetism and electricity (Castenet de Puységur 1807: 383–4):

> I had seen a medicine of attitudes in Chinese memoirs, which gave me pause for thought; I therefore made a small collection of works on Mesmerism, and I sent it to Peking, to Father Amiot, a missionary of great learning, whose truly

apostolic complacency for the progress of science and the happiness of humanity I knew, and I asked him to tell me if the Cong-fou would not relate to all this.

This is just a glimpse into the theories that diffused through the connections between Paris and Beijing, directly flowing into major contemporary debates about the origin of civilization and the relationship between science and religion. For Amiot, the crucial starting point had been the work of Gébelin, which he mentioned in his correspondence with Mellet (Huard, Solonet, and Wong 1960: 80). As early as 1777, Amiot had read Gébelin's *Monde primitif* and was so amazed by it that he compiled a collection on ancient China for Bertin to forward to Gébelin. In the fascinating correspondence that ensued, Gébelin attempted to relate his famous theory about the card game of Tarot to material that Amiot had sent to him, particularly an ink rubbing of the supposedly ancient 'Stele of Yu' (Statman 2019: 251–6). Gébelin had claimed that the Tarot was actually a symbolistic representation of ancient Egyptian teachings (Court de Gébelin 1781: 365–94), a theory that was further elaborated by an essay by Mellet on the 'Book of Thot', contained in *Monde primitif*, in which Mellet also linked the Tarot to the Kabbalah (Mellet 1781; cf. Decker, Depaulis, and Dummett 1996). Gébelin argued that the Stele of Yu displayed the same system conserved in the Tarot, linking China to Egypt.

Amiot was intrigued but sceptical. It is quite possible that he discussed the stele with Hongwu, who might have referred him to Wang Chang 王昶 (1724–1806), a leading Chinese expert on such monuments and with whom the matter was possibly discussed directly (Statman 2019: 253). Amiot's exchange with Gébelin made it into the chapter in *Monde primitif*, from whence it found its way into the works of later esotericists such as Éliphas Lévi (i.e. Alphonse-Louis Constant, 1810–75), who cemented the association of the Tarot with both Egypt and China (Strube 2016).[3] Amiot, however, was eventually not convinced by Gébelin's rather fantastic argument, but this did not diminish his respect for him. As Statman put it, this was due to their agreement that 'valuable truths were known to the ancients, and it was the task of modern scholars to dig them up them – to exhume their debris and to reconstruct their monuments' (Statman 2019: 256).

The Atlantean origin of the Chinese was also proposed by Bailly, who was a friend of Bertin's and of Louis-George de Bréquigny (1715–95), the latter being the publisher of the *Mémoires*. Bailly was a famed scholar of the highest rank, belonging to all three French academies and later becoming a prominent figure of the French Revolution. He certainly was a *philosophe* in the most proper Enlightenment sense, yet at the same time he was deeply immersed into the world of 'esoteric' masonry and referred to (in both negative and positive senses) as an *illuminé* (Statman 2019: 256–9). Bailly held that the Chinese, Egyptians, Indians and Chaldeans descended from the same ancient Eurasian civilization rooted in hyperborean homelands, sharing ideas of a golden age, a universal flood and central doctrines. This had direct ramifications for the present: 'it is the spirit of Asia that animates Europe' (Bailly 1779: 258). Bailly took inspiration from Gébelin's oeuvre to work towards the revival of the perfect science of this advanced ancient civilization. The study of Chinese culture was crucial for this endeavour by virtue of its supposed conservatism that had preserved the ancient doctrine. This is probably why Bailly entered the network between Paris and Beijing by the 1780s. Bertin forwarded Bailly's work to Amiot, and indeed he found it most convincing (Statman 2019: 260–2). This was not least due to the fact that Chinese scholars seemed to agree with it, considering their aforementioned conviction that modern Western science was only recovering ancient Chinese wisdom – a circumstance that Bailly seems to had become aware of, as he invoked the authority of contemporary Chinese scientists in his writings (Statman 2019: 261).

In turn, Amiot appears to have grown quite sympathetic to the form of masonry widely termed illuminism, in which Bailly, Mellet and Gébelin were all involved in different yet interconnected ways. This can be illustrated by a remarkable reference to Louis Claude de Saint-Martin (1743–1803), a leading figure of Martinism, who flourished at the time among the *illuminés* and *théosophes* (Mehltretter 2009; McCalla 1998). In his correspondence with Mellet, Amiot wrote (Huard, Solonet, and Wong 1960: 68):

> You are, Monsieur, too gallant a man for me to refuse to initiate you; I am therefore going to put you among the Adepts; but it will be on condition that you guard against the curiosity of the prophane. These gentlemen, who usually blaspheme what they do not know, would not fail to call me a visionary if, unfortunately, they did not first see in your kind of Mystagogy something to learn in their own way, or at least something to amuse themselves.

> Take the trouble to cast your eyes on the figure that I dare to draw for you here, contemplate it at leisure, and do not lose a word of the short explanation that I must necessarily accompany it to facilitate your understanding. You can boldly call it the Universal Cipher [*le Chiffre universel*], I will call it by that name myself.

On the basis of a drawing contained in the letter, Amiot went on to explain the workings of *taiji* 太極, which the 'Newtonians and all the attractionists, both ancient and modern, could without trouble adopt' as the unknown principle of their different attractions (Huard, Solonet, and Wong 1960: 69).

Amiot stressed that the philosophers of Europe would benefit greatly from this Chinese wisdom, whose diffusion would, in fact, 'be sufficient, it seems to me, to institute a new order, in the style of those already established to honour the different kinds of merit, such as nobility, value, services rendered to the State and the like' (Huard, Solonet, and Wong 1960: 70). This order could be called 'the Order of the Universal Cipher', the organization and details of which Amiot described in bewildering detail, including ranks, functions, rituals and a medallion depicting the Universal Cipher. The order would certainly attract 'Mr B', possibly Bailly. Mellet, he suggested, could become its grand master, paving the path for someone even better, 'the unknown Philosopher', who had given the public his work *Des erreurs et de la verité, ou les hommes rappellés à au principe universel de la science* (Huard, Solonet, and Wong 1960: 72). This was a reference to none other than Saint-Martin, who featured prominently in the milieu frequented by Bailly, Mellet and Gébelin.

Indeed, Amiot appears to have derived the notion of the Universal Cipher from Saint-Martin's *Erreurs* (1775). Therein we encounter this concept developed against the background of Saint-Martin's reception of Pythagoreanism (Mehltretter 2009: 129–36). More specifically, Saint-Martin had conceived of numbers as the representations of Being, the 'images' in which the 'laws' of the Creator were constituted, thus forming the eternal 'principles' of Truth. Saint-Martin especially venerated what he termed the *quaternaire*, a manifestation of the divine emanation showing itself in creation. The human individual is 'positioned' within these Laws, which form 'the four columns of the edifice' of creation (Saint-Martin 1775: 535):

> In a word, it is necessary to admit that the one who will be able to possess the key of this universal cipher, will not find anything hidden for him in all that exists, since this cipher is that of the Being who produces all, who operates all, and who embraces all.

We are now able to comprehend the passage cited earlier from Amiot's letter to Mellet in 1783, in which he put the Chinese doctrine above Pythagoras's 'Quaternary'. During the correspondence with his Parisian interlocutors, Amiot found that the work of Saint-Martin confirmed what he had learnt in China, but – similar to his engagement with mesmerism – concluded that the Chinese had been closer to truth for thousands of years. This was possible not least because of his conviction that Chinese culture had preserved the pristine antediluvian doctrine in a purer and more complex way, despite its later corruptions.

Conclusion: A tangle of exchanges

Considering the Jesuit technique of *accomodatio* – that is, the adaption of doctrinal language to local circumstances for the sake of conversion – it might be tempting to surmise that Amiot adroitly adjusted his tone to his different correspondents, intentionally conversing with Mellet and Gébelin in the language of French illuminism and mesmerism. It seems, however, that he was as sincerely convinced by the value of mesmerism as he was by the value of the Chinese teachings and practices he had observed on the ground. His learned discussions and experiments with Hongwu and other Chinese scholars, as well as his study of 'peasant' practices in the countryside and in villages, shaped his view on the relationship between mesmerism and Daoism as much as his engagement with orientalist scholarship and the French magnetizers.

These developments beg the question whether Amiot had indeed identified Chinese forms of 'esotericism' or 'occultism' that had their counterparts in other places of the world. Today, the notion of esotericism is widely used by scholars to discuss Chinese traditions (e.g. Goble 2019), but it is not entirely clear how it emerged historically. Considering the vast challenges arising from religious comparativism (e.g. Freiberger 2019; Bergunder 2016), this is an important lacuna – not least because the term 'esoteric' is conspicuously absent from the sources linked to Amiot. We have seen how Amiot related Daoism to the occult sciences, whereas both Bailly and Gébelin only passingly addressed 'occult qualities' in a way that was common since medieval natural philosophy (e.g. Bailly 1785: 198; Court de Gébelin 1781: 400). We could also observe how self-evidently Amiot referred to Daoism as 'cabala', which mirrors contemporary orientalist scholarship, especially on yoga and Sufism (Strube 2023).

As I have pointed out at the outset of this chapter, the notions of 'esoteric' and 'occult' were commonplace in scholarship on other parts of Asia – and the perceptions of yoga, 'Sufi cabalists', or far-flung speculations about Eurasian civilizational origins do indeed parallel eighteenth-century sources focused on the area spanning from India to the Mediterranean. Yet, these references hardly pass as established scholarly categories, not least because of the striking difference in writings about Arabic, Persian and Indian topics. More research is necessary to comprehend how this orientalist vocabulary developed with regard to various subjects and how it relates to local practices, traditions and terminology.

If Daoism would later come to be conceived of as a form of 'Chinese esotericism', not least due to occultist writings since the second half of the nineteenth century, this terminology appears to have been absent a century earlier. However, Daoism had already been identified with alchemy, magic, astrology and other occult sciences, as it was with mesmerism and the supposed Pythagorean tradition manifesting the writings of French illuminism. Amiot's case is particularly instructive for this process because of the frank and vivid correspondence revealing how he developed these comparisons himself: having encountered the barber-magnetizers on the streets for a long time, it was only after his 'initiation into mesmerism' that he could make sense of their practices. Similarly, his previous dismissal of Daoism as superstitious buffoonery gave way to admiration in light of its supposed scientific values that had originated in an advanced antediluvian civilization. In other words, the concrete historical context *made* certain traditions and practices comparable in the first place. This was not merely the projection of a Western observer. Rather, it was the complex outcome of a tangle of exchanges between Paris and Beijing, which underlines the need for a decentred historiography of the comparative categories that we continue to debate so passionately in the present day.

Notes

1   I thank Karl Baier for initially providing me with the source material that stimulated the research for this article. I am also grateful to Alexander Statman for our friendly correspondence. The Amiot exchange is discussed in more depth and width in Statman (2023).
2   It is conspicuous that Amiot juxtaposes the French term *raseur de tête* with the German word *Barbier*, which might suggest that the recipient spoke German. However, the expression 'in your country' (*chez vous*) does not necessarily suggest a country other than France since Amiot at another point also refers to 'your Europe'. Statman has assured me that the recipient was indeed Mellet.
3   On Lévi, see the chapter by Franz Winter in this volume.

References

Amiot, J.-M. (1776), 'Lettre sur les caractères Chinois', in J.-M. Amiot, *Mémoires concernant l'histoire, les sciences, les arts, les moeurs, les usages, &c. des Chinois*, Vol. 1, 275–323, Paris: Nyon. [Although the author is not indicated in this volume, it is Amiot's text.]

Amiot, J.-M. (1777), 'Antiquité des Chinois, prouvée par les monuments', in J.-M. Amiot, *Mémoires concernant l'histoire, les sciences, les arts, les moeurs, les usages, &c. des Chinois*, Vol. 2, 5–364, Paris: Nyon.

Amiot, J.-M. (1779), 'Notice du Cong-Fou des Bonzes Tao-sée', in J.-M. Amiot, *Mémoires concernant l'histoire, les sciences, les arts, les moeurs, les usages, &c. des Chinois*, Vol. 4, 441–51, Paris: Nyon.

Amiot, J.-M. (1780), 'Idée générale de la Chine et de ses relations avec l'Europe sur le nom de Chine', in J.-M. Amiot, *Mémoires concernant l'histoire, les sciences, les arts, les moeurs, les usages, &c. des Chinois*, Vol. 5, 1–68, Paris: Nyon. [As in the first reference above, Amiot is not given as the author of this text.]

Amiot, J.-M. (1786), 'Extrait d'une autre lettre de M. Amiot, écrite de Pé-king le 15 Novembre 1784', in J.-M. Amiot, *Mémoires concernant l'histoire, les sciences, les arts, les moeurs, les usages, &c. des Chinois*, Vol. 11, 569–76, Paris: Nyon.

Amiot, J.-M. (1791), 'Extrait d'une lettre de M. Amiot, missionnaire, écrite de Péking, le 16 Octobre 1787, sur la secte des Tao-sée', in J.-M. Amiot, *Mémoires concernant l'histoire, les sciences, les arts, les moeurs, les usages, &c. des Chinois*, Vol. 15, 208–59, Paris: Nyon.

App, U. (2010), *The Birth of Orientalism*, Philadelphia: University of Pennsylvania Press.

Bailly, J. S. (1779), *Lettres sur l'Atlantide de Platon et sur l'ancienne histoire de l'Asie*, London and Paris: Elmesly and Debure.

Bailly, J. S. (1785), *Histoire de l'astronomie moderne depuis la fondation de l'école d'Alexandrie jusqu'à l'époque de 1730*, Vol. 1, 2nd edn, Paris: De Bure.

Bergunder, M. (2016), 'Comparison in the Maelstrom of Historicity: A Postcolonial Perspective on Comparative Religion', in P. Schmidt-Leukel and A. Nehring (eds), *Interreligious Comparisons in Religious Studies and Theology*, 34–52, London and New York: Bloomsbury Academic.

Chastenet de Puységur, A. M. J. d. (1807), *Du magnétisme animal: Considéré dans ses rapports avec diverses branches de la physique générale*, Paris: Desenne.

Court de Gébelin, A. (1781), *Monde primitif analysé et comparé avec le monde moderne*, Vol. 8, Paris: L'Auteur, Valleyre and Sorin.

Decker, R., T. Depaulis, and M. Dummett (1996), *A Wicked Pack of Cards: The Origins of the Occult Tarot*, London: Duckworth.

Freiberger, O. (2019), *Considering Comparison: A Method for Religious Studies*, New York: Oxford University Press.

Goble, G. C. (2019), *Chinese Esoteric Buddhism: Amoghavajra, the Ruling Elite, and the Emergence of a Tradition*, New York: Columbia University Press.

Hartman, J. (1998), 'Ideograms and Hieroglyphs: The Egypto-Chinese Origins Controversy in the Enlightenment', *Dalhousie French Studies*, 43: 101–18.

Hermans, M. (2019), 'Amiot's Life', in A. Parr (ed.), *The Mandate of Heaven: Strategy, Revolution, and the First European Translation of Sunzi's Art of War (1772)*, 224–74, Leiden and Boston: Brill.

Huard, P., J. Solonet, and M. Wong, eds (1960), *Mesmer en Chine: Trois lettres médicales du R.P. Amiot, rédigées à Pékin de 1783 à 1790*, Paris: A. Michel.

McCalla, A. (1998), 'Illuminism and French Romantic Philosophies of History', in A. Faivre and W. Hanegraaff (eds), *Western Esotericism and the Science of Religion*, 253–68, Louvain: Peeters.

Mehltretter, F. (2009), *Der Text unserer Natur. Studien zu Illuminismus und Aufklärung in Frankreich in der zweiten Hälfte des 18. Jahrhunderts*, Tübingen: Narr.

Mellet, L.-R.-L. d. F. Comte de (1781), 'Recherches sur les tarots, et sur la divination par les cartes des tarots', in A. Court de Gébelin (ed.), *Monde primitif*, Vol. 8, 395–410, Paris: L'Auteur, Valleyre, and Sorin.

Parr, A. (2019), *The Mandate of Heaven: Strategy, Revolution, and the First European Translation of Sunzi's Art of War (1772)*, Leiden and Boston: Brill.

Saint-Martin, L.-C. d. (1775), *Des erreurs et de la verité, ou les hommes rappellés à au principe universel de la science*, Edimbourg.

Statman, A. (2017), 'A Forgotten Friendship: How a French Missionary and a Manchu Prince Studied Electricity and Ballooning in Late Eighteenth Century Beijing', *East Asian Science, Technology, and Medicine*, 46 (1): 89–118.

Statman, A. (2019), 'The Tarot of Yu the Great: The Search for Civilization's Origins between France and China in the Age of Enlightenment', in P. Findlen (ed.), *Empires of Knowledge*, 246–68, London and New York: Routledge.

Statman, A. (2023), *A Global Enlightenment: Western Progress and Chinese Science*, Chicago: University of Chicago Press.

Strube, J. (2016), *Sozialismus, Katholizismus und Okkultismus im Frankreich des 19. Jahrhunderts. Die Genealogie der Schriften von Eliphas Lévi, Religionsgeschichtliche Versuche und Vorarbeiten*, Berlin and Boston: De Gruyter.

Strube, J. (2022), *Global Tantra: Religion, Science, and Nationalism in Colonial Modernity*, New York: Oxford University Press.

Strube, J. (2023), 'The Emergence of 'Esoteric' as a Comparative Category: Towards a Decentered Historiography', *Implicit Religion*, 23 (3–4): 353–83.

Strube, J. (2024), 'Esotericism between Europe and East Asia: How the "Esoteric Distinction" Became a Fundamental Structure in Asianist Scholarship', *NVMEN. International Review for the History of Religions*, 71 (1): 9–28.

Zhang, Q. (2015), *Making the New World Their Own: Chinese Encounters with Jesuit Science in the Age of Discovery*, Leiden and Boston: Brill.

2

Looking out for magic in Ancient China
The *Yijing*, its trigrams and the Figurist tradition in Éliphas Lévi

Franz Winter

Introductory remarks: 'Magic'

'Magic' is a dazzling and glamorous catchword that is and has been used in an immense variety through the centuries. A modern approach to this term abstains from any essentialist definition and refers to it as a signifier that is the object of various and ever-changing interpretations, closely connected to the interpretative frame that is relevant for them, including the various approaches to demarcate 'magic' from other generic classifications such as 'religion' or 'science' in the last centuries.[1] Consequently, a constant need for a contextualized view on the references and usages of the terms is at stake. Beyond doubt, one of the pivotal figures in a contemporary understanding of magic and closely connected to its current popularity in various (alternative) socioreligious contexts was the French author, political activist and occult writer Alphonse-Louis Constant (1810–75), better known with his *nom de plume* Éliphas Lévi. Some of his publications are a major source for the modern usage and framing of 'magic' because they became seminal within specific cultural and religious contexts. Lévi's cultural influence has been far-reaching and includes – in addition to and closely intertwined with his framing of the term 'magic' – such diverse arenas as the modern esoteric interpretation and popularity of the Tarot or the fashionable popular iconography with the (in)famous but persuasive emblematic depiction of the goat-headed Baphomet as its probably best-known example (for a full interpretation, see Strube 2017; on the iconography and its history, see also Fernandes, Rodriguez de Sá, and Gansohr 2013: 1131–3).

One major characteristic of Lévi's work is the all-encompassing interpretation of the history of humankind that includes both 'the West' and all the major cultural regions with their various philosophical and religious traditions. As will be shown, this take is guided by some major interpretative trajectories that are based on a couple of presuppositions such as the idea of the one 'true' tradition, which develops through the ages and cultures and whose traces are visible and detectable if one has the correct knowledge and the right tools to access it.

This chapter aims at taking a deeper look into Lévi's take on China and Chinese cultural, philosophical and religious traditions that make up part of a specific reception history within the European context. I will try to show the dependence of Lévi's take on Chinese materials on the then available information that heavily relied on the information coming from Jesuit missionaries in the so-called Figurist tradition. The latter was a very specific and intellectually influential – albeit not long-lived – approach to the traditions of China from a Catholic perspective with an integrative mode, that is, an attempt to interpret its lore within an incorporating trajectory. As will be shown, Lévi was indebted not only to the materials provided within this particular strand but also to the intellectual and epistemological framing of China that he transferred into his own cosmos of understanding the history of humankind. However, it is important to state from the outset that Lévi lacks any systematic approach towards both his sources and the information therein that he often referred to erratically. Yet, a sincere study of his interests provides the unique opportunity for contextualizing a major source of contemporary alternative religiosity in the broader framework of the religious history of his time.

Introducing the founder of modern magic: Éliphas Lévi

Alphonse-Louis Constant, alias Éliphas Lévi, is perceived as one of the most prolific writers of the nineteenth century whose major publication *Histoire de la magie* (History of Magic; 1860) is reprinted to date, being available in various forms and translations in the book market (and, nowadays, in digitized versions on the internet as well). It is precisely this book together with the two-volume *Dogme et rituel de la haute magie* (Doctrine and Ritual of High Magic;[2] 1854–6), as well as *La clef des grands mystères* (The Key to the Great Mysteries; 1861), *La Science des esprits* (The Science of Spirits; 1865) and the posthumously edited *Le Grand Arcane: ou l'occultisme dévoilé* (The Great Arcane, or Occultism Unveiled; 1898) that are often perceived as the founding texts of the modern perception of magic as a crucial aspect of occultism. Consequently, many scholarly works attribute to Lévi a pivotal influence on important developments, introducing him as a major cultural force within the nineteenth century with enormous reverberations in the subsequent ones (Strube 2016a; Otto 2015; McIntosh 2014; Davies 2012: 39–41; Otto 2011: 524–32; Hanegraaff 2010; Laurant 2006a). One important example of his influence is a direct line of transmission that connects Lévi's work to the publications of the co-founder of Theosophy, Helena Petrovna Blavatsky (1831–91), as she copiously used his publications in her own work (Strube 2016a: 592; Zander 2008: vol. 1, 85), which itself became a quarry for esoteric movements and alternative religiosity in the twentieth and twenty-first centuries.

Within religious studies, Lévi and his work was not the object of serious academic interest for a rather long time. This was mostly caused by the scarcity of information available about Lévi himself, as well as his convoluted and difficult to handle and interpret publications. It is only recently that important major studies have fully dealt with his work and clearly showed that his life and work are deeply intertwined with complex French cultural conflicts and particularly Catholic and socialist discourses of his time (see the important publications of Julian Strube [2016a, 2016b]).[3] Initially trained in a Catholic seminary, he had to abandon his clerical career shortly before the final consecration as a priest. Thereafter, he became one of the most radical French socialists of the 1840s and immersed himself into a pulsating and vibrant activists' scenery publishing books and pamphlets. The publications of this time include passionate manifestos, such as *La Bible de la liberté* (The Bible of Liberty; 1841a) that contained a mix of socialist, religious, Romantic and feminist topics, or the even more radical pamphlet *La Voix de la famine* (The Voice of Famine; 1846).[4] Both publications led to his imprisonment (in 1841 and 1847) and he was also deeply affected by the so-called June uprising of 1848 (commonly referred to in French as *les journées de Juin*), an anti-monarchist insurrection whose failure was a major blow for the socialist reformist groups that emerged in the first half of the nineteenth century (Beecher 2021: 1–10, for a summary 405–7; see also Beecher 2001).

To a certain extent, both socialism and Catholicism remained the main pillars of his self-understanding throughout the following period when he seemingly set sail into (hitherto) unknown waters. The period after 1848 was marked by an intense personal uncertainty and is connected with an obvious shift in his interest that eventually would bring forth the 'occult' writer Éliphas Lévi.[5] Taken from this mere biographical angle, the penchant for the occult seemingly started rather late, when Lévi was already in his forties. The long accepted common approach in the academic literature on Lévi to explain this shift pointed to a kind of conversion and initiation into the occult that has nothing to do with his Catholic and socialist upbringing and early socialization. This is part of a frequently cited biographical information indicating that this change was the direct result of Lévi's contact with the Polish emigré and polymath Joseph Maria Hoëné-Wronski (1776–1853).[6] Against this common interpretation, Strube was able to show that this is a later constructed view on his life to isolate the 'occult' Lévi from the aforementioned factors, and the result of a kind of emic, that is, later manufactured view by occultists on the movement's very own history. This widespread view interprets Lévi as the quasi-renovator of a seemingly lost and suppressed occult tradition before him and/or the founder of modern occultism.[7] On the contrary, Lévi's occult publications are deeply embedded in the aforementioned complex cultural constellations, and particularly the Catholic and socialist discourses of his time. To a certain extent and within the limits of a contribution such as this one, I follow this line of argumentation by focusing on the references to China and its prehistory.

China and its place in the history of 'magic' according to Éliphas Lévi

The major frame: How to interpret the history of humankind

In order to understand Lévi's take on China it is important to highlight his major conceptual approach towards the religious, philosophical and cultural history of humankind that is guided by the idea of vast lines of transmission of a presupposed tradition of absolute truth. This stream of wisdom is referred to as 'magic' (the most dominating catchword throughout these publications) and defined as 'exact and absolute science of nature and its laws' (*science exacte et absolue de la Nature et de ses lois*; Lévi 1860: 1), itself a kind of conciliation of religion and science, a 'universal science' (*science universelle*; see Strube 2016b: 374).[8] Hence, it is more often than not introduced as 'high science' (*haute science*)[9] or 'absolute science' (*science absolue*).[10] This special wisdom would have been revealed to humanity at the beginning of time, since it 'was, so to say, born with the world' (*née pour ainsi dire avec le monde*; Lévi 1860: 34) and then handed down – to cite one of the common trajectories indicated by Lévi – from the biblical Seth to Zoroaster and from the Chaldaean *magi* to

Abraham, subsequently taken by Joseph to and by Moses out of Egypt and was eventually incorporated in some major traditions, with the Jewish-Christian Kabbalah as the most important among them.[11] This scheme, which is flexible and by no means fixed, undergoes a couple of changes and emendations with the obvious aim to include other cultural regions and religious traditions as well. To broaden this approach and make it more flexible, Lévi made use of another explanatory tool, namely, the concept of differing and sometimes opposing streams of 'magic' that are identified as right and wrong ways (Otto 2015: 433–6). As will be shown, this idea goes back to early European approaches to the multifaceted arena of philosophies and religions of 'the East' and is often connected to important biblical figures who are interpreted as the originators of these opposing traditions. This interpretation often concurs with the presupposed transmission of 'sacred texts', that is, books that are said to be relics of an antediluvian age that were later discovered and identified as such.[12] This was important in the evaluation of Asian religious texts such as the Veda and also a major interpretative frame for the evaluation of the *Yijing* (for a summary, see App 2010: 363–439, particularly 435–9; for the general background, see also Winter 2018: 48–50).

In addition to this idea of a (hidden) stream of wisdom, another aspect is crucial to understand the following material. Lévi had great interest in the search for instruments or tools that are connected to the magic tradition. It is basically about charts and tables that might be used in the authentic occult and magical practice, and which are introduced and interpreted in his writings with rather convoluted and complex argumentations. These key instruments make up part of his presentation and most of them owe their origin to the vast repertoire of grimoires that were published abundantly in Europe in the eighteenth and nineteenth centuries in general (Davies 2012: 78–81) and in France in particular (Davies 2009: 93–109). One of the texts often referred to by Lévi is the so-called *Clavicula Salomonis* (The Key of Solomon). Its origin might be traced back to the fifteenth century (see Otto 2015: 532–6; Silva 2009, with a thorough study of the text and its translation history; see also Strube 2016a: 550–1; Otto 2015: 423–4) and made up part of the French *Grand Grimoire* that became extremely popular since the eighteenth century, being the 'first explicitly diabolic massmarket grimoire' (Davies 2009: 101). Together with other popular books, these charts are used by Lévi in various contexts (Strube 2016a: 551–2). As will be shown later, another most valuable source for his imagery is the Tarot deck, whose 'occult' interpretation began in the eighteenth century and was greatly triggered by Lévi (Piegeler 2020: 266).

The described scheme is relevant for the references to China and its lore, since Lévi identified the ancient divination manual *Yijing* 易經 (Classic of Changes) as one of those occult and magic tools. As will be shown, the high esteem for this important, but rather enigmatic and difficult to interpret ancient Chinese text has its roots in early Jesuit concepts, mostly pertaining to the Figurist school of interpreting Chinese cultural traditions where the *Yijing* received a very special place.

China

In the following, two of Lévi's crucial publications will be scrutinized, namely, the *Histoire de la Magie* and the *Dogme et Rituel de la Haute Magie*, both being the most important sources for his interest in things Chinese (see Nilsson 2020: 76–82). Although the *Histoire* was published after *Dogme et Rituel*, it will be dealt with first as it explains Lévi's take on China more thoroughly, whereas the latter refers to it on the basis of conceptual presuppositions that are not explained in the volumes themselves.

The *Histoire* is basically an attempt to root 'magic' in a solid historical frame that encompasses the whole history of humanity with literal biblical dimensions (Otto 2015: 421). The most important information on China and its lore is given at the beginning of the sixth book, which is noteworthy given that this section is dealing with the topic 'magic and revolution' (*la magie et la révolution*) and is mostly about the French eighteenth century. The header of the first chapter is not referring to China but to 'remarkable authors of the eighteenth century' (*auteurs remarquables du XVIIIe siècle*; Lévi 1860: 408), who are introduced right after the China-related preamble. Curiously, China does not make up part of one of the preceding sections which are devoted to the historical genesis and predecessors of the magic tradition in various cultural contexts; particularly the first book, with its musings on the prehistory of magic in, among others, the ancient oriental context with Zarathustra, ancient Greek mythology, the hermetic tradition, or India, would have been a natural place for that section to be included (Lévi 1860: 11–117). Taken from this angle, and at first glance, the information on China seems to be a mere addendum, a kind of later arrival that serves as a preface to the following expositions that are dealing with a completely different content. However, by starting with this reference to an ancient and esteemed tradition, the following references to modern authors seem to get a different standing, as a kind of century-long trajectory of the presupposed magic tradition connecting, so to say, eighteenth century France with ancient China is suggested.

In his exposition, Lévi introduces both the legendary mythic Fuxi 伏 羲 (referred to as *Fo-hi* in his texts) and Confucius as central figures in the presupposed true lineage of magic because they are related to the history of the *Yijing* (*I'y-Kim*), which is perceived to be a key-text of the presupposed magic truth tradition. Therein, Lévi fully focuses on Fuxi, who, in the Chinese tradition, is credited with some important inventions and reformations in early Chinese mythological historiography (including hunting, fishing, but also music), as well as being the originator of the basic eight *trigrams* (*bagua* 八卦) of the *Yijing*. In the traditional mythological presentation, the trigrams were revealed to Fuxi in the markings of a mythical animal that emerged from the river Luo 洛 when he was sitting at its banks.[13] The animal is most commonly described as a *longma* 龍馬, that is, a dragon-horse hybrid, which is also the version Lévi follows when describing it as 'sphinx', that is, an 'allegoric animal with the mixed form of a horse and a dragon' (*un animal allégorique ayant la forme mixte d'un cheval et d'un dragon*; Lévi 1860: 409).

Generally, information on Fuxi, his importance and the connection with the *Yijing* was widely accessible in the nineteenth century, as it was already included in some substantial publications on China and its history that emerged in the wake of the Jesuit missionary activities. One eminent example was the famous *Description geographique, historique, chronologique, politique et physique de l'empire de la Chine et de la Tartarie chinoise* by the Jesuit Jean-Baptiste du Halde (1674–1743), a four-volume compilation of important materials sent to Europe by early Jesuit missionaries. Fuxi makes up part of the presentation of history as he is introduced as China's first emperor (du Halde 1735: 271–3) and the aforementioned story is given therein, although in this version it has a demythologizing spin: Fuxi is said to have told the story with the dragon-horse to impress the people, 'to give more credit to his recently introduced laws' (*pour donner plus de credit à ses nouvelles Loix*). This demythologizing tendency was not untypical for some of the early Jesuit reports, whereas others clearly delved into the mythological material (for the eighteenth-century French authors and the differences in their take on mythology, see Standaert 2016: 94–5 and particularly 116–63). The latter layer would also be the frame that is more relevant to Lévi's presentation and, in this particular case, there is even the possibility to dig deeper into the sources, as in the *Histoire* Lévi mentions his alleged own reference in this very passage (which is not often the case): he refers to a 'Vay-Ky' by a 'Léon-Tao-Yuen' of the 'Soms' dynasty. It is highly probable that this refers to the historian Liu Shu 劉恕 (1032–78), whose courtesy name was Daoyuan 道原 (or 道源) and who composed a work entitled *Zizhi tongjian waiji* 資治通鑑外紀 (also called, in shorter form, *Tongjian waiji* 通鑑外紀).[14] This was written as a supplement to Sima Guang's 司馬光 (1019–86) influential historical work *Zizhi tongjian* 資治通鑑 (literally, Comprehensive Mirror to Aid in Government) that is one of the most important traditional histories of China, second only to Sima Qian's 司馬遷 (c. 145–86 BCE) *Shiji* 史記 (Records of the Historian). Liu Shu extended Sima Guang's history back into the earliest times (Standaert 2016: 26–7).

The *Zizhi tongjian* and the other works surrounding it were highly important historical works and available in European languages since the Jesuits' first attempts to present Chinese history to the West (Standaert 2016: 98–9; 107–8; 131–2). An important French intermediary of that material would be the translation of an abridged compilation of the *Zizhi tongjian* by the Confucian scholar Zhu Xi 朱熹 (1130–1200), the *Zizhi tongjian gangmu* 資治通鑑綱目 (Outline of the Comprehensive Mirror for Aid in Government). The Manchu version was translated into French by the Jesuit missionary Joseph-Anne-Marie de Moyriac de Mailla (1669–1748) and published posthumously by Jean-Baptiste Grosier (1743–1823) with the aid of Michel-Ange-André Le Roux Deshauterayes (1724–95), a professor of Arabic (with a knowledge of Chinese as well), in thirteen volumes entitled *Histoire générale de la Chine, ou Annales de cet Empire* (A General History of China, or the Annals of that Empire) in the period between 1777 and 1783. These books remained for some time the most complete history of China available in Europe and information on Fuxi and his relation to the origin of the 'Y-king' was available therein (see de Mailla 1777: 5–10, with a table showing the trigrams as well as a chart of the hexagrams as he maintains that they were also invented by Fuxi already). This text, however, is again a good example of a version that does not mention the mythic story of the detection with the help of the dragon-horse. However, the aforementioned version was also available early. It was included in a sample of compilations on Chinese history provided by the Jesuit missionary Joseph de Prémare (1660–1736), which was printed as the preface to the widely distributed translation of the ancient Chinese compilation *Shujing* 書經 (Classic of Documents, which is basically a heterogeneous collection of various documents that were probably compiled in the middle of the first millennium BCE) by Antoine Gaubil (published in 1770 and revised by the orientalist Joseph de Guignes [1721–1800]; see Camus 2007: 12–13). This is an important edition given that de Prémare, who belonged to the Figurist tradition (Mungello 2019; Lundbaek 1991), thoroughly informs about his Chinese sources (Standaert 2016: 128–32; see also von Collani 2007: 233) and explicitly includes the aforementioned Liu Shu, which would be 'Lieou-tao-yuen' and his work 'Tong-kien-vay-ki', that is, the *Tongjian waiji* (de Prémare 1770: liii n. 1). The full story of the eight trigrams on the back of the dragon-horse and its discovery is given in the account on Fuxi (de Prémare 1770: ci).

In Lévi's exposition, Fuxi introduced the 'high science' in China, but it was not fully understood, with the following periods marked by deterioration. After him, Confucius is introduced as the one who merely revealed or 'unveiled' 'this Kabbalah': '*Koug-fu-tzée*, or *Confucius*, was only the revealer or *unveiler* of this Kabbalah . . .' (Koug-fu-tzée ou Confucius, n'eût été que le révélateur ou révoilateur de cette *kabbale*; Lévi 1860: 410). According to Lévi, Confucius did not fully grasp the *Yijing*, which is why he compared him to the Jewish thinker Maimonides (1135–1204), who likewise had reportedly not been fully aware of the importance of a major tool of the presupposed Hebrew truth tradition, namely, the *Clavicula Salomonis*. As will be noted in more detail in the following, this portrayal of Confucius is a little bit off compared to other (more positive) references to him in Lévi's publications but seems necessary here to introduce the idea of a distorted line of transmission that is a typical model employed by Lévi. To push this even further, the next step in the downfall of the Chinese tradition of magic according to Lévi was the introduction of 'the worship of Fo' (*le culte de Fo*), that is, Buddhism, which would have been a major blow for the further positive unfolding of the truth and even 'paralyzed the progress of the sciences in China' causing a collapse 'into routine and dumbness' (*dans la routine de dans l'abrutissement*; Lévi 1860: 411). This agreed with a view of Buddhism that was also quite popular in the materials Lévi had at hand when writing his *Histoire* as will be shown later.

As indicated earlier, this short excursus on the Chinese tradition serves as an introduction to the main object of attention in this section of the *Histoire* (namely, some 'remarkable authors of the eighteenth century'). The linking figure is the German philosopher Gottfried Wilhelm Leibniz (1646–1716), whose interest in the *Yijing* was inspired by readings of missionary reports and the great respect that was devoted to it by Jesuit writers.[15] Notably, Lévi himself mentions the Jesuits and their endeavour to understand China, which he portrays as unfortunately having failed. This is a clear allusion to the extensive conflicts that were part of the Christian missionary attempts in China in the sixteenth and seventeenth centuries.[16] According to Lévi's interpretation, those discords caused to follow the wrong track, as the Jesuits 'who were right in substance' (*qu'avaient raison pour le fond*) 'were convinced of being wrong in form' (*furent convaincus d'avoir tort pour le forme*), and therefore the whole mission had no chance to succeed (Lévi 1860: 411).

After alluding to this debate Lévi turns his attention to the actual object of interest in this chapter, that is, away from China to Europe and, particularly, eighteenth-century France. As indicated earlier, this introductory section on Chinese matters might serve as an attempt to put the following information in a more global context by introducing the specific link between Chinese and European traditions – together with the fact that both countries were apparently tormented by what Lévi refers to as 'an enormous anxiety' (*une immense inquiétude*; Lévi 1860: 411) with a reference to major religious and societal upheavals. This would be a proper explanation of the seemingly awkward placing of the Chinese information and could even offer the opportunity to interpret it as an aspect of an intended global trajectory.[17] What follows is an exposition of authors who caused exactly such turmoils, starting with the revelations of Emanuel Swedenborg (1688–1772) (Lévi 1860: 412–14) and the mesmerism of Franz Anton Mesmer (1734–1815) (Lévi 1860: 414–17), the latter being introduced as a beacon of a modern understanding of the connection between science and religion.

The most important aspect of this exposition is the reference to Fuxi and the *Yijing* as a master tool for the presupposed magic tradition that is more practically applied in Lévi's second most widespread publication, *Dogme et Rituel de la Haute Magie*. The publication of the two volumes was basically Lévi's coming out as a 'magician' (Otto 2015: 421) and the books are conceptualized as a practical guide to magic (whose epistemological and historical basis is more or less explained in the better known *Histoire* afterwards). In spite of its later great influence, the text of the *Dogme et Rituel* is difficult to comprehend. It is replete with vague reasoning, a constant change of subjects and a volatile style which often makes it impossible to follow the argumentation (Strube 2016a: 491–2).

However, it is at least possible to isolate some major concepts that are also relevant for understanding Lévi's take on Chinese materials. One of the pillars of his magical world view is the doctrine of polarity: he deems the cosmos as being built around complementary forces that stand in opposition, and one of the main tasks of the true magician is to reconcile them as everything is based on 'the magic law of universal equilibrium' (*la loi magique de l'équilibre universel*; Lévi 1860: 55).[18] In Lévi's interpretation, the *Yijing* mirrors this world view and is therefore accompanied by other concepts that allegedly witness this presupposed basic polarity. In the first volume of the *Dogme et Rituel*, devoted to the 'dogma', which is built up (as the second volume) in twenty-two parts following the order of the Hebrew alphabet, an allusion to the basis of 'Fohi's' – that is, Fuxi's – trigrams is included in the exposition of the Hebrew letter *beth*: the broken or unbroken line of the *Yijing* trigrams (that are also depicted in the text) are directly connected to the concept of *yin* 陰 and *yang* 陽: 'the unity' (*l'unité*) – that is, the unbroken line – representing *yang*, and 'the binary' (*le binaire*) – that is, the broken line – referring to *yin* (Lévi 1861a: vol. 1, 124). This reference makes up part of the description of the aforementioned polarity model that is connected to other instances of Lévi's historical trajectories related to it, such as the 'Kabbalistic' interpretation of the columns at the temple of Salomo, named Bohas and Jakin, or specific interpretations of letters of the Hebrew alphabet (which is the dominating reference tool in *Dogme et Rituel*). The polarity is basically interpreted as sexual imagery: the 'active' male *versus* the 'passive' female principle, with the *yang* and *yin* concept ideally fitting in this scheme (Lévi 1861a: vol. 1, 124–5).

However, these musings on binary polarity are supplemented with a tripartite structure in the following exposition of the *Dogme et Rituel* (on the Hebrew letter *gimel*) since only the 'ternary' (*le ternaire*) would be the perfect structure, 'the universal dogma' (*le dogme universel*; Lévi 1861a: 137), which is visualized in the image of the 'triangle' of Salomon, one of the emblems Lévi is referring to quite often (see the image in Lévi 1861a: vol. 1, 124). Once again, the trigrams of the *Yijing* fit the argumentation according to Lévi and are mentioned in this context. An actual connection to the male-female polarity is added, since 'the superior ternary is composed of three *yang* or masculine figures' (*le ternaire superieur se compose de trois yang ou figures masculines*; Lévi 1861a: vol. 1, 140). This follows the traditional order of the Chinese trigrams, with the one composed of three unbroken lines ☰ (called *qian* 乾) having the superior position and representing father and heaven, opposed to the trigram *kun* 坤 with three broken lines ☷ representing mother and earth (on this imagery, see Schilling 2009: 260–5). This basic structure gives Lévi the legitimization to parallel it with the triangle of Salomo (Lévi 1861a: vol. 1, 141). Consequently, the trigrams of the *Yijing* are presented as one example of the 'ancient pantacles' (*anciens pantacles*) and an outflow of the magic tradition as is stated in a summarizing paragraph in the second volume of the *Dogme et Rituel* (Lévi 1861a: vol. 2, 122).

In order to underline this kind of interpretation, Lévi also refers to the interpretation of the Tarot card deck. As a matter of fact, his exposition of the images of the traditional Tarot became highly influential and is probably Lévi's most lasting impact on various cultural levels (Strube 2016a: 14; see also 442–5, 475–9 for the development of his Tarot interpretation; on Lévi's importance for the further reception of the Tarot, see Piegeler 2020: 266; Laurant 2006b: 111).[19] In this context, the well-known combined symbolic representation of the *yin-*

Figure 2.1 The Sacerdotal Demonic Hand with the *taijitu* above it, from Lévi, *Dogme et rituel de la haute magie. Deuxième édition très augmentée*, vol. 1, 103.

yang dyad, the *taijitu* 太極圖, is found in its best-known – but historically rather later – form ☯,[20] in a depiction of a 'sacerdotal hand' that in the *Dogme et Rituel* is interpreted as representing a devilish curse because its shadow shows 'the figure of the demon' (*la figure du démon*; see Figure 2.1). In the description, the *taijitu* is interpreted as the (Chinese version of the) 'as de deniers'[21] of a presupposed 'Tharot chinois'.

The Tarot as a master key for the interpretation of a globally relevant pool of imagery is also relevant in some cursory mentioning of an alleged 'Chinese Tarot', which is also a good example for Lévi's superficial use of material and his interpretation. In the second volume of the *Dogme et Rituel*, he cursorily points to the existence of this 'Tarot chinois' (Lévi 1861a: vol. 2, 362–3) in the French *Bibliothèque nationale* and identifies some of its cards with the traditional Tarot. The major source in this regard is the book *Les Cartes a jouer et la cartomancie* (Playing Card Decks and Cartomancy) by the prolific French writer Paul Boiteau d'Ambly (1830–86), which is basically a thorough presentation of different types of card decks with a keen interest into their origin and their function in the history of cartomancy. 'Oriental' card decks are a component and, consequently, Boiteau d'Ambly also included Chinese card systems and even gave examples of them although he stated that our knowledge of them is rather vague and therefore any attempt to find parallels is problematic.[22] This *caveat* did not prevent Lévi to refer to the 'Chinese Tarot' as an additional example of his transculturally relevant card imagery system, although he himself had problems to identify the full Tarot imagery in them.[23]

Another probable source for this information on a Chinese Tarot might also have been the excessive, yet unfinished volumes entitled *Monde primitif analysé et comparé avec le monde moderne* (The Primitive World Analyzed and Compared to the Modern World) by the former Huguenot pastor, polymath, Freemason and prolific writer Antoine Court de Gébelin (1719 or 1725–85), who is often credited with the launch of the modern esoteric interpretation of the Tarot (Piegeler 2020: 51–142; Davies 2009: 169–70; Mercier-Faivre 2006: 280).[24] In the first part of the eighth volume, a whole section is 'about the game of the Tarots' (*du jeu des Tarots*) and therein a reference to a Chinese pre-version or parallel that serves the all-encompassing comparative trajectory of this monumental work (Mercier-Faivre 1992) is prominently put to the fore (Court de Gébelin 1781: 387–8).[25]

Scanning some further magical and some earlier Catholic-cum-socialist musings on China

The passages in the *Histoire* and the *Dogme et Rituel* are actually the most concise treatment of China in Lévi's writings. There are some further references, most of them cursorily though, that take Chinese contexts into consideration without going into more detail. In most cases China is mentioned together with India, Egypt or other cultural contexts as part of the presupposed stream of wisdom and its outflows: for instance, in *La science des esprits* (1865), where Lévi mentions the existence of the Tarot in India or Egypt alongside with China and 'among the Hebrews' (Lévi 1865: 161).[26] Another instance would be the posthumously published *Le Grand Arcane ou l'occultisme devoilé* that also contains a comparable cursory list (Lévi 1898: 136).[27] However, other major key texts of his occult writing phase, such as *La clef des grands mystères* (Lévi 1861b), do not contain any reference to China.

As indicated earlier, the occult phase of Lévi's work should not be separated from the Catholic-*cum*-socialist Constant before that, as it was common in the academic approach for a rather long time (and thereby following emic histories as introduced by the occult tradition). Already in earlier writings, before 1848, he exposed the idea of a stream of real Catholicism that he was determined to present. In *La Bible de la liberté* (1841a), he delineates a trajectory that begins with Moses and Henoch and continues by Hermes and Orpheus, Socrates and Pythagoras, Plato and Aristotle, Homer and Virgil as intermediaries in order to bring everything together in the finalized version, namely, Christianity and Jesus Christ, who would amalgamate the orient and the occident.[28] In the same vein, a reference to China is found in the short pamphlet entitled *Doctrines religieuses et sociales* (Religious and Social Teachings; 1841b), wherein a list of 'sacred books' (*livres sacrés*) includes 'the books of Moses, of Salomon and other prophets, collected and revised by Esdras, what we refer to as *the Bible*, *the Zend-Avesta* of Zoroaster, *the classics* of Confucius [*les King* de Confucius][29], *the Vedas* [*les Védas*] of the Brahmans and the Quran of Muhammad' (Constant 1841b: 10; emphasis in the original).

Interestingly, these early texts sometimes place India in a high and esteemed position when Constant is enthusiastically referring to the Indian god Brahma (as equated with the Roman god Jupiter), the 'wonderful stories' of the Indian god Vishnu (*les fables merveilleuses de Wischnou*) and religious concepts such as the 'mystique *trimurti*' (*la mystique Trimourti*) (Constant 1841a: 93; on the background of these references in other authors of his time, see Strube 2016a: 343–4). What is quite obvious with these references is that Chinese contexts had at least a certain place in his early musings, and this obviously opened up a path of further interest that was deepened by the then available material. China, though, did not play a major role.[30]

Concluding remarks: Éliphas Lévi, the Jesuit missionaries and the Figurist penchant for the *Yijing*

As was shown in detail in the exposition, most of the materials Lévi is citing can be traced back to European sources on China that were accessible since the eighteenth century in France. Most of it was – naturally – informed by the Jesuit missionary reports that are responsible for introducing major aspects of this early reception of Chinese religious and cultural lore (Mungello 1999: 88–104). In this context, Lévi obviously follows some important prioritizations that are intrinsically related to the way the early Jesuit missionaries tried to implant Christianity within the multifaceted religious landscape of China at the time of their arrival by applying an all-encompassing cultural and religious trajectory and searching for presupposed connection points in the new context. This was a major aspect of the so-called Figurist tradition, which developed into a short-lived but – from a cultural-historical point of view – highly influential current that became relevant for many aspects of the further history of reception, particularly among European intellectuals. As was shown, Lévi mainly relied on this particular strand and its publications in his own take on things Chinese as primary sources, including the guiding principles and trajectories. One important aspect would be the focus on the *Yijing* as a kind of master key for understanding China. As a matter of fact, it was mainly the Figurist missionaries who developed a fascination about this curious text and then introduced it to Europe as a crucial source for the understanding of Chinese culture and religion, thereby provoking sincere interest in this text, with the philosopher Gottfried Wilhelm Leibniz as the most prominent example (Wei 2020; von Collani 2007). Yet, this fascinating history of reception had a bumpy start: the earliest missionaries to China rejected the text because of its seemingly 'superstitious' character (von Collani 2007: 230), and it was only later and within the Figurist branch of the Jesuit missionary endeavours that the *Yijing* occupied centre stage. As a matter of fact, Joachim Bouvet (1656–1730), who is credited with the foundation of this particular 'school' of mission, is responsible for the *Yijing*'s first introduction to European intellectuals with his essay *Idea generalis doctrinæ libri ye kim* (A General Sketch of the Doctrine of the Book *Yijing*; 1712).[31] It is worth noting that the European take on the *Yijing* remained convoluted throughout the subsequent history of encounters with it as it was also a major aspect of the so-called rites controversy that had a devastating effect on the Jesuit mission – and particularly on the Figurist interpretative school (Smith 2012: 171–7; Smith 2015; von Collani 2007: 238–41). As a consequence of this development, the first full translation (into Latin) of the *Yijing* that was offered by the French Jesuit Jean-Baptiste Régis (1663/1664–1738) was only published at the beginning of the nineteenth century. Although it was finished already a hundred years earlier, it was 'discovered' by the German orientalist Julius Mohl (1800–76) who arranged the edition in two volumes in 1834 and 1838,[32] respectively (von Collani 2007: 230–1).³³ The *Yijing*, however, remained a text whose interpretation was controversial throughout,³⁴ and Lévi's interest might have been triggered by its reputation as a curious and difficult-to-interpret, superstitious text. An additional factor was, beyond doubt, the early perception by Leibniz who is even mentioned explicitly by Lévi in exactly this context.

In this regard, it is worth highlighting that there are some other connections between Lévi and the Figurist tradition. One example is the interest for the connections between the (Jewish-)Christian Kabbalah and Chinese materials (von Collani 2007: 286 and n. 307; see also Wei 2020: 142). This suggestion can be traced back to the already mentioned Joachim Bouvet, who wrote a treatise to demonstrate the 'conformity of the primeval hieroglyphic wisdom of the Chinese with the more ancient and sincere Kabbalah of the Hebrews'.³⁵ With this interpretative frame, Bouvet was an heir to the immensely influential but highly convoluted work of the eminent Jesuit scholar Athanasius Kircher (1602–80),³⁶ whose monumental publications are responsible for the high esteem of the Kabbalah and who more or less gave birth to the specific (Jewish-)Christian Kabbalah tradition in early modern Europe.

Another instance is Lévi's view on India, and particularly Buddhism, that obviously followed some ideas that are quite prominent in early Jesuit writings. In the aforementioned more elaborate presentation of the fate of the *Yijing*, there is a clear allusion to the idea that it was soon misunderstood – a problem that began already with Confucius but was emphasized by the introduction of the 'worship of *Fo*'. This is in line with the historical accounts of the history of Buddhism in China that was eventually interpreted as the natural foe of the Christian missionaries. This has very much to do with a major shift in the early Jesuit mission generated by its archegete, Matteo Ricci (1552–1610), who was initially close to Buddhism but later switched to Confucianism as a natural ally in his endeavours and began to use its anti-Buddhist argumentation thoroughly (Liu 2011: 372–3; 2015).

To sum up, Lévi clearly shows a certain indebtedness to Jesuit interpretations of Chinese lore (that is mostly owed to important intermediary authors such as de Prémare or Court de Gébelin) and he follows a specific narrative and even alludes to the failure of the missionary endeavour as a kind of outcome of inner-Christian struggles. This proximity is further amplified when considering the general interpretative frame of the Figurist tradition, which can be summarized by the following three characteristics (following the suggestions by von Collani 2001: 668–9): (1) the so-called typological exegesis, which is bound to reveal alleged hidden meanings in the Old Testament; (2) a *prisca theologia* frame, which presupposes the idea of a kind of 'divine revelation' by non-Christian figures (with Melchizedek, Pythagoras, Plato, Orpheus or Zoroaster as some of the 'usual suspects', a list that could be supplemented if necessary); and (3) a reference to the Christian Kabbalah as an overarching concept or interpretative tool. Two of these argumentative strategies, namely, the *prisca theologia* and the interweaving with the Kabbalah, are obviously close to Lévi's approach towards the material and, to a certain extent, Lévi seems to be an heir to this interpretative frame: what the Figurists did within their all-encompassing Catholic interpretation of Chinese lore is transformed into his occult focus on magic as the representation of a hidden stream of knowledge through the ages and across all cultural boundaries. With that new bent he was apparently sailing into uncharted waters, which, although seemingly far off the original sources, were depending on those sources, trying to transfer China and its philosophical and religious traditions into a new-old frame.

Notes

The author wishes to thank Lukas K. Pokorny, Nickolas Roubekas and Julian Strube for their most valuable comments on previous versions of this paper.

1 A lot has been written on magic, its history, the various definitions and the conceptual and epistemological frames for distinguishing it from 'religion' or 'science'. For a recent overview of the academic literature, see Otto 2011: 1–31 and particularly 39–134 (for the modern discourse on magic); Davies 2012; Dubuisson 2016; Stein and Stein 2010: 136–60; Styers 2004; Cunningham 1999; the edited volumes with various contributions from different angles by Assmann and Strohm 2010; Kippenberg 1995; Petzoldt 1978 (who put together crucial texts from twentieth century religious studies and ethnology scholars in chronological order). For a recent view on the usage of the term in antiquity, see Frankfurter 2019 (and, more particularly, the methodologically orientated contributions in section 4, pp. 605–774).

2 The English versions have different titles: in his 1896 translation, Arthur E. Waite's opted for *Transcendental Magic: Its Doctrine and Ritual*, whereas the recent translation by John Michael Greer and Mark Mikituk (Lévi 2017) is more precise: *The Doctrine and Ritual of High Magic: A New Translation*.

3 Julian Strube is following a couple of academic studies before him that pointed to this kind of prehistory (such as Webb 1974: 262–6; see also Goodrick-Clarke 2008: 193), most of them, though, not sufficiently connecting both spheres.

4 A characteristic excerpt of his publications exposing some of his ideas might be found in a translated passage of the *Bible de la liberté* in Corcoran 1983: 220–3.

5 His better-known *nom the plume* was used after 1854 (Strube 2016b: 371–2).
6 This was upheld in the highly influential publication on Lévi by Cristopher McIntosh ([1972] 2011: 96–104) and has its origin in the biography of Lévi by Paul Chacornac ([1926] 1989). See Strube 2016b: 372–3 with further examples in the literature on Lévi.
7 The notion of Lévi as *rénovateur* was prominently propagated in the already mentioned influential biography by Chacornac ([1926] 1989), whom McIntosh ([1972] 2011) follows when introducing the idea of an occult 'revival' allegedly following the publications of Lévi.
8 'It [i.e., magic] reconciles perfectly and incontestably those two terms, so opposed on the first view – faith and reason, science and belief, authority and liberty [*foi et raison, science et croyance, autorité et liberté*]' (Lévi 1860: 2; Waite's translation). In the following, all translations are mine, unless otherwise indicated.
9 The common translation for *haute* in Waite is 'transcendental', which is a little bit misleading as it applies a concept not relevant to the writings of Lévi.
10 'The high science, the absolute science is assuredly Magic . . .' (Lévi 1860: 3).
11 On the multifaceted approach to the term Kabbalah in Lévi, see Strube 2016a: 393–401; for a summary, see Strube 2016b: 376.
12 See Schmitt 1922: 43–6, where the earliest interpretations of the Ethiopic book of Enoch in the course of its discovery and interpretation history is analyzed as a typical example for this kind of historico-archaeological approach.
13 For a common version of the story, see the chapter on 'the invention of the trigrams' in Dehai and Dinghuo 2018; see also Simon 2014: 581–2; Smith 2012: 19–21; Schilling 2009: 273–86; and more particularly the introduction. For a concise list of Chinese mythological and historical texts referring to Fuxi and their evaluation, see Le Blanc 2008.
14 'Vay-Ky' responding to *waiji* and 'Léon-Tao-Yuen' to be interpreted as a muddling up of 'Liu' (which became the French name León) and Daoyuan. I am indebted to Lukas K. Pokorny for this valuable information and identification that is also proven by the material I shall present as follows.
15 On Leibniz and his take on China, which culminated in the famous *Novissima Sinica* (Latest News from China; 1697) and was highly influenced by his contact with the Jesuit missionaries, see Mungello 1999: 98–104; also Perkins 2001. A collection of Leibniz's correspondence with the Jesuits is provided by Widmaier and Babin 2006; Lodge 2004: 141–61. His specific interest in the *Yijing* is portrayed in Smith 2012: 177–9.
16 See the following for further information.
17 This goes against other interpretations that clearly struggle with this passage. In Waite's English translation of the *Histoire* there is even an explanatory footnote maintaining that 'the lucubration on China is a curious preamble to a study of remarkable authors of the eighteenth century, who had nothing to do with

China' (Lévi 1913: 394 n. 1). This is probably an aspect of the interpretative frame used by Waite to isolate Lévi from major societal debates of his time by understanding him as the actual revelator of the presupposed occult, that is, magic tradition due to his initiation. On this general problem in interpreting Lévi, see above.

18 See also Lévi 1860: 144: 'this universal law of equilibrium' (*cette loi universelle de l'équilibre*) and 'the science of equilibrium' (*la science de l'équilibre*); Lévi 1860: 77: "the unchangeable law of equilibrium" (*la loi immuable de l'équilibre*); Lévi 1860: 171: 'the eternal laws of equilibrium' (*les lois éternelles de l'équilibre*). In addition, a whole introductory chapter of the second volume is devoted to the 'magic equilibrium' *(l'équilibre magique)* (Lévi 1861a: vol. 2, 47–59).

19 On the importance of the Tarot, whose origin can be traced back to fourteenth century Italy and which developed into one of the most widely used instruments of cartomancy in the eighteenth century and particularly in France, see Auger 2016: 41–52, and the extensive study by Piegeler 2020; see also Laurant 2006b. It is noteworthy that among the many publications of the main translator of Lévi's magic books into English, Arthur Edward Waite, his Tarot pack (that was conceptualized together with Pamela Colman Smith [1878–1951] and is usually referred to as the Rider-Waite-Tarot) and the accompanying *Pictorial Guide to the Tarot* (1910) were the most successful (see Piegeler 2020: 243–4; Davies 2009: 181–2).

20 The representation of the *taijitu* ('diagram of the great ultimate') has a long and convoluted history in China that goes at least back to the tenth century. The popularized version, the ☯, probably relates to the Ming 明 period (1368–1644) and is also the version the Jesuit missionaries encountered (see Robinet 2008, with some examples from the traditional representations).

21 The *as de deniers*, that is, the 'ace of coins', is a very important card of the Tarot deck carrying a variety of supposed meanings and interpretations. For a classical interpretation in the wake of Lévi, see Waite 1911: 199–200.

22 Boiteau d'Ambly 1859: 24–6: 'We have to say that we know them (sc. Chinese cards) very little (*nous les connaissons très-mal*) and that we can only speak of them from a few mismatched pieces (*d'après quelques pièces dépareillées*).' He then points to the fact that the 'designs' are 'incomprehensible' (*dessins incompréhensibles*) which does not give the opportunity to evaluate them correctly. About the images 'that the sinologists were not able to decipher' (*que les sinologues n'ont pu déchiffrer*), see Boiteau d'Ambly 1859: 159 n. 1.

23 The Chinese Tarot is said to show traces of the 'primitive images' (*emblèmes primitifs*) of the Tarot and he is even able to distinguish the 'denarii' and 'swords' (which are types of the Tarot cards), but he misses the 'cups' and the 'sticks' (*on y distingue très bien les deniers et les épées, mais il serait plus difficile d'y retrouver les coupes et les batons*). See Lévi 1861a: vol. 2, 363.

24 On Court de Gébelin, see the chapter by Julian Strube in this volume.
25 The work of de Gébelin and his musings on the Tarot are mentioned by Lévi in some instances of his Tarot interpretation. See Lévi 1861a: vol. 1, 234, 255, 258; vol. 2, 69, 337, 339, 350; see also Lévi 1860: 81.
26 See also Lévi 1865: 274, where China is mentioned in the same relation to the aforementioned countries regarding their alleged 'ancient' knowledge about magnetic forces.
27 See also Lévi 1898: 234, where China and Confucius are mentioned (but only in contrast to Europe and without any further information).
28 Constant 1841a: 88: 'Christianity is the fruit of all meditations of the oriental wise men [*toutes les meditations des Sages de l'Orient*], that resurge in Jesus Christ [. . .] the Christ has conquered the occident and the soft rays of the Asian sun [*le soleil de l'Asie*] has touched the blackest icicles in the North [*les plus noires glaçons du Nord*].'
29 I am translating here the plural according to the French text, 'the classics' (with *king* being *jing* 經), and considering it a reference to the idea that Confucius was credited with the introduction of a canonical list of 'classics' for his tradition as was purported in the European literature on China. In doing so I do not suggest a sole reference to the *Yijing* as proposed by Strube 2016a: 242 in his translation of the passage ('. . . das Zend-Avesta des Zoroaster, das *I Ging* [*les King*] des Konfuzius, die Veden der Brahmanen und der Koran Mohammeds . . .'). However, it is important to note that this is just a cursory reference which does not show any deeper acquaintance with the material and its background.
30 Other important texts of the pre-occult phase, such as the emotional pamphlet *La voix de la famine* (Constant 1846), do not contain any reference at all.
31 The full Latin text along with an introduction, a summary and an English translation is provided by von Collani 2007: 277–88.
32 Eventually, it was edited as Régis 1834/1839.
33 Even this early Latin translation remained rather unnoticed and it was only with the English translations at the end of the nineteenth century – by two Protestant missionaries to China, namely, Canon McClatchie (181485) (*A Translation of the Confucian Yi King or the 'Classic of Changes' with Notes and Appendices*, Shanghai 1876), and the more important and better known James Legge (1815–97) (*The Yi King*, London 1882; initially a volume within *The Chinese Classics* collection which became part of the influential *Sacred Books of the East*) – that a real appreciation appeared. Its contemporaneous popularity was stirred immensely by the even more influential translation by the German Protestant missionary Richard Wilhelm (1873–1930) (first published in 1924), whose English translation was published with a foreword by Carl Gustav Jung (1875–1961) (Wilhelm 1977) and attracted enormous interest. On Jung's interest in the esoteric reception of China, see the chapter by Karl Baier in this volume.

34 This remained as such through the subsequent history of reception. See, for instance, Alfred Forke ([1964] 2010: 9–13), who in his general history of ancient Chinese philosophy refers to the text as a mere "divination text" (*Wahrsagebuch*) whose 'philosophical value' is to be regarded as 'low' and whose content made it into a 'playground of the wildest speculations' (*Tummelplatz der wildesten Spekulationen*). Consider also Legge's verdict, who found the *Yijing* to be a 'a farrago of emblematic representations, albeit a highly influential one' (Legge 1882: 25; see also p. 17, where the *Yijing* is characterized as 'an important monument of architecture, [but] very bizarre in its conception and execution').

35 This is taken from the full title of a manuscript of Bouvet's *Pro expositione figurae sephiroticae Kabalae Hebraeorum et generatim demonstranda mira conformitate primaevae Sinarum sapientiae hieroglyphicae, cum antiquiore et sincera Hebraeorum Kabala, ab ipso mundi primordio, per sanctos patriarchas et prophetas successive propagata*. On this curious text, see von Collani 2017; Secret 1979; a description is also provided in Löwenthal 1946: 357.

36 On the importance of the symbolic imagery of the Kabbalah in Kircher, see Stolzenberg 2013: 132–5.

References

App, U. (2010), *The Birth of Orientalism*, Philadelphia: University of Pennsylvania Press.

Assmann, J. and H. Strohm, eds (2010), *Magie und Religion*, Paderborn: Wilhelm Fink Verlag.

Auger, E. E. (2016), *Cartomancy and Tarot in Film*, Bristol: Intellect Books.

Beecher, J. (2001), *Victor Considerant and the Rise and Fall of French Romantic Socialism*, Berkeley: University of California Press.

Beecher, J. (2021), *Writers and Revolution: Intellectuals and the French Revolution of 1848*, Cambridge: Cambridge University Press.

Boiteau d'Ambly, P. (1859), *Les Cartes à jouer et la cartomancie*, London: John Camben Hotten.

Camus, Y. (2007), 'Jesuits' Journeys in Chinese Studies', Macau Ricci Institute. Paper presented at the World Conference on Sinology. Available online: https://web.archive.org/web/20150924090942/http://www.riccimac.org/doc/JesuitsJourneys.pdf (accessed 3 March 2022).

Chacornac, P. ([1926] 1989), *Eliphas Lévi: Rénovateur de l'occultisme en France (1810–1875)*, Paris: Chacornac frères.

Constant, L'abbé (1841a), *La Bible de la liberté*, Paris: Le Gallois.

Constant, L'abbé (1841b), *Doctrines religieuses et sociales*, Paris: Le Gallois.

Constant, L'abbé (1846), *La voix de la famine*, Paris: Ballay Aîné.

Corcoran, P. E., ed. (1983), *Before Marx: Socialism and Communism in France, 1830–48*, London: MacMillan Press.
Court de Gébelin, A. (1781), *Monde primitif analysé et comparé avec le monde moderne*, Vol. 8, part 1, Paris: Valleyre/Sorin.
Cunningham, G. (1999), *Religion and Magic: Approaches and Theories*, Edinburgh: Edinburgh University Press.
Davies, O. (2009), *Grimoires: A History of Magic Books*, Oxford: Oxford University Press.
Davies, O. (2012), *Magic: A Very Short Introduction*, Oxford: Oxford University Press.
de Mailla, J.-A.-M. de Moyriac (1777), *Histoire générale de la Chine, ou Annales de cet Empire, traduites du Tong-kien-kang-mou. Publiées par M. L'abbé Grosier*, Vol. 1, Paris: P.D. Pierres, Clousier.
de Prémare, J. (1770), 'Discours préliminaire ou recherches sur les tems antérieurs à ceux dont parle le Chou-king, & sur la Mythologie Chinoise', in A. Gaubil (ed.), *Le Chou-king, un des livres sacrés des Chinois, qui renferme le fondemens de leur ancienne histoire, les principe de leur gouvernment & de leur morale. Revu et corrigé sur la texte chinois … par M. de Guignes*, xliv–cxxxviii, Paris: Tilliard.
du Halde, J.-B. (1735), *Description geographique, historique, chronologique, politique et physique de l'empire de la Chine et de la Tartarie chinoise*, Vol. 1, Paris: Le Mercier.
Dehai, J. X. and Z. Dinghao (2018), *Illustrated Myths and Legends of China: The Ages of Chaos and Heroes*, New York: Better Link Press.
Dubuisson, D. (2016), *Religion and Magic in Western Culture*, Leiden and Boston: Brill.
Fernandes, E. G., J. F. Rodriguez de Sá, and M. Gansohr (2013), 'Aterradora transcendência? Uma análise simbólica do Bafomé de Éliphas Lévi', *Horizonte (Belo Horizonte, Brazil)*, 11 (31): 1129–49.
Forke, Alfred ([1964] 2010), *Geschichte der alten chinesischen Philosophie*, Berlin: De Gruyter.
Frankfurter, David, ed. (2019), *Guide to the Study of Ancient Magic*, Leiden: Brill.
Goodrick-Clarke, N. (2008), *The Western Esoteric Traditions: A Historical Introduction*, Oxford: Oxford University Press.
Hanegraaff, W. J. (2010), 'The Beginnings of Occultist Kabbalah: Adolphe Franck and Eliphas Lévi', in B. Huss, M. Pasi, and K. von Stuckrad (eds), *Kabbalah and Modernity. Interpretations, Transformations, Adaptations*, 107–28, Leiden: Brill.
Kippenberg, H.-W. (1995), *Magie. Die sozialwissenschaftliche Kontroverse über das Verstehen fremden Denkens*, 2nd edn, Frankfurt am Main: Suhrkamp.
Laurant, J.-P. (2006a), 'Éliphas Lévi', in W. J. Hanegraaff (ed.), *Dictionary of Gnosis and Western Esotericism*, 689–92, Leiden: Brill.
Laurant, J.-P. (2006b), 'Tarot', in W. J. Hanegraaff (ed.), *Dictionary of Gnosis and Western Esotericism*, 1110–12, Leiden: Brill.
Le Blanc, C. (2008), 'L'invention du mythe de Fuxi et Nügua', in C. Le Blanc and R. Mathieu (eds), *Approches critiques de la mythologie chinoise*, 249–307, Montréal:

Presses de l'Université de Montréal. Available online: http://books.openedition.org/pum/19036 (accessed 21 March 2022).

Legge, J. (1882), *The Sacred Books of China: The Book of Changes*, London: Clarendon Press.

Lévi, É. (1860), *Histoire de la magie, avec une exposition claire et précise de ses procédés, de ses rites et de ses mystères*, Paris: Germer Baillière.

Lévi, É. (1861a), *Dogme et rituel de la haute magie. Deuxième édition très augmentée*, Paris: Germer Baillière (originally published 1854–1856).

Lévi, É. (1861b), *La clef des grands mystères suivant Hénoch, Abraham, Hermès Trismégiste, et Salomon*, Paris: Germer Baillière.

Lévi, É. (1865), *La science des esprits. Révélation du dogme secret des kabbalistes, esprit occulte des évangiles, appréciation des doctrines et des phénomènes spirites*, Paris: Germer Baillière.

Lévi, E. (1896), *Transcendental Magic: Its Ritual and Doctrine*, translated by A. E. Waite, London: George Redway.

Lévi, É. (1898), *Le Grand Arcane: Ou l'occultisme dévoilé*, Paris: Chamuel.

Lévi, E. (1913), *The History of Magic: Including a Clear and Precise Exposition of Its Procedure, Its Rites and Its Mysteries*, translated by A. E. Waite, London: Wiliam Rider & Son.

Lévi, E. (2017), *The Doctrine and Ritual of High Magic: A New Translation*, translated by J. M. Greer and M. A. Mikituk, New York: Tarcher Perigee.

Liu, Y. (2011), 'The True Pioneer of the Jesuit China Mission: Michele Ruggieri', *History of Religions*, 50 (4): 362–83.

Liu, Y. (2015), 'The Dubious Choice of an Enemy: The Unprovoked Animosity of Matteo Ricci against Buddhism', *The European Legacy, Toward New Paradigms*, 20 (3): 224–38.

Lodge, P. (2004), *Leibniz and his Correspondents*, Cambridge: Cambridge University Press.

Löwenthal, R. (1946), 'The Early Jews in China: A Supplementary Bibliography', *Folklore Studies*, 5: 353–98.

Lundbaek, K. (1991), *Joseph de Prémare (1666–1736), S. J.: Chinese Philology and Figurism*, Aarhus: Aarhus University Press.

McIntosh, C. ([1972] 2011), *Eliphas Lévi and the French Occult Revival*, Albany: State of New York University Press (reprint of the original edition New York: Samuel Weiser Inc.).

McIntosh, C. (2014), 'Eliphas Lévi', in C. Partridge (ed.), *The Occult World*, 220–30, London: Routledge.

Mercier-Faivre, A.-M. (1992), 'Le *Monde primitif* d'Antoine Court de Gébelin, ou le rêve d'une encyclopédie solitaire', *Dix-Huitième Siècle*, 24: 353–66.

Mercier-Faivre, A.-M. (2006), 'Court de Gébelin, Antoine', in W. J. Hanegraaff (ed.), *Dictionary of Gnosis and Western Esotericism*, 279–81, Leiden: Brill.

Mungello, D. E. (1999), *The Great Encounter of China and the West, 1500–1800*, Lanham: Rowman & Littlefield.

Mungello, D. E. (2019), *The Silencing of Jesuit Figurist Joseph de Prémare in Eighteenth-Century China*, Lanham: Lexington Books.

Nilsson, J. (2020), 'As a Fire Beneath the Ashes: The Quest for Chinese Wisdom within Occultism, 1850–1949', PhD diss., Centre for Theology and Religious Studies, Lund University, Lund.

Otto, B.-C. (2011), *Magie: Rezeptions- und diskursgeschichtliche Analysen von der Antike bis zur Neuzeit*, Berlin: De Gruyter.

Otto, B.-C. (2015), 'A Catholic "magician" historicises "magic": Éliphas Lévi's *Histoire de la Magie*', in J. Rüpke, S. Rau, and B.-C. Otto (eds) (with the support of Andrés Quero-Sánchez), *History and Religion: Narrating the Religious Past*, 419–44, Berlin: De Gruyter.

Perkins, F. (2001), *Leibniz and China: A Commerce of Light*, Cambridge: Cambridge University Press.

Petzoldt, L. (1978), *Magie und Religion. Beiträge zu einer Theorie der Magie*, Darmstadt: Wissenschaftliche Buchgesellschaft.

Piegeler, H. (2020), *Tarot. Bilderwelten der Esoterik*, Leiden: Brill.

Régis, J.-B (1834/1839), *Y-king, antiquissimus Sinarum liber quem ex latina interpretatione P. Regis aliorumque ex Soc. Jesu p.p. edidit Julius Mohl, I et II*, Stuttgart: Cotta.

Robinet, I. (2008), 'Taiji tu. Diagram of the Great Ultimate', in F. Pregadio (ed.), *The Encyclopedia of Taoism A–Z*, 934–6, Abingdon: Routledge.

Schilling, D. (2009), *Yijing. Das Buch der Wandlungen*, Frankfurt am Main: Verlag der Weltreligionen.

Schmitt, N. (1922), 'Traces of Early Acquaintance in Europe with the Book of Enoch', *Journal of the American Oriental Society*, 42: 44–52.

Secret, F. (1979), 'Quand la Kabbale expliquait le "Yi king" ou un aspect oublié du figuratisme du P. Joachim Bouvet', *Revue de l'histoire des religions*, 195 (1): 35–53.

Silva, F. (2009), 'Mathers' Translation of the Clavicula Salomonis: The Relationship between Translator, Text and Transmission of a "Religious Text"', PhD diss., University of Manchester, Manchester.

Simon, R. (2014), *Yijing. Das Buch der Wandlungen*, Leipzig: Reclam.

Smith, R. (2012), *The "I Ching": A Biography*, Princeton: Princeton University Press.

Smith, R. J. (2015), 'Collaborators and Competitors: Western Translators of the *Yijing* in Eighteenth and Nineteenth Centuries', in L. W. Wong and B. Fuehrer (eds), *Sinologists as Translators in the Seventeenth to Nineteenth Centuries*, 385–434, Hong Kong: The Chinese University of Hong Kong Press.

Standaert, N. (2016), *The Intercultural Weaving of Historical Texts: Chinese and European Stories About Emperor Ku and His Concubines*, Leiden: Brill.

Stein, R. L. and P. L. Stein (2010), *The Anthropology of Religion, Magic, and Witchcraft*, 3rd edn, London: Routledge.

Stolzenberg, D. (2013), *Egyptian Oedipus: Athanasius Kircher and the Secrets of Antiquity*, Chicago: University of Chicago Press.

Strube, J. (2016a), *Sozialismus, Katholizismus und Okkultismus im Frankreich des 19. Jahrhunderts. Die Genealogie der Schriften von Eliphas Lévi*, Berlin: De Gruyter.

Strube, J. (2016b), 'Socialist Religion and the Emergence of Occultism', *Religion*, 46 (3): 359–88.

Strube, J. (2017), 'The "Baphomet" of Eliphas Lévi: Its Meaning and Historical Context', *Correspondences*, 4: 37–79.

Styers, R. (2004), *Making Magic: Religion, Magic and Science in the Modern World*, Oxford: Oxford University Press.

von Collani, C. (2001), 'Figurism', in N. Standaert (ed.), *Handbook of Christianity in China: 635–1800*, Vol. 1, 668–79, Leiden: Brill.

von Collani, C. (2007), 'The First Encounter of the West with the *Yijing*', *Monumenta Serica*, 55 (1): 227–387.

von Collani, C. (2017), 'Cabbala in China', in C. von Collani and R. Malek (eds), *From Kaifeng ... to Shanghai: Jews in China*, 527–58, London: Routledge.

Waite, A. E. (1911), *A Pictorial Guide to the Tarot, being Fragments of a Secret Tradition under the Veil of Divination*, London: William Ryder & Son, Ltd.

Webb, J. (1974), *The Occult Underground*, La Salle: Open Court Publishing Co.

Wei, S. L. (2020), *Chinese Theology and Translation: The Christianity of the Jesuit Figurists and their Christianized Yijing*, London: Routledge.

Widmaier, R. and M.-L. Babin (2006), *Leibniz, Gottfried Wilhelm. Der Briefwechsel mit den Jesuiten in China (1689–1714). Französisch, lateinisch – deutsch*, Hamburg: Meiner.

Wilhelm, R. (1977), *The I Ching or Book of Changes. The Richard Wilhelm Translation rendered into English by Cary F. Baynes. Foreword by C. G. Jung. Preface to the Third Edition by Hellmut Wilhelm*, Princeton: Princeton University Press.

Winter, F. (2018), 'Searching for the Hidden "One": Muslim and Early European Interpretations of the Upanishad', *Numen*, 65 (1): 28–61.

Zander, H. (2008), *Anthroposophie in Deutschland: Theosophische Weltanschauung und gesellschaftliche Praxis, 1884–1945*, 2 Vols, Göttingen: Vandenhoeck & Ruprecht.

3

The Theosophical *Daodejing*
The beginnings

Lukas K. Pokorny

Introduction

An enigmatic and succinct text, the *Daodejing* 道德經 has a central place in the Euro-American esoteric reception of East Asia. Ridiculed and vilified at first by most clerical commentators of Chinese religions, nineteenth-century scholars 'discovered' the book's mystical message. A Chinese expression of a universal Divine Wisdom (*Gottweisheit*), the *Daodejing* penned by 'the mystic' Laozi 老子 was seen to be 'theosophic' (*theosophisch*) in nature; that is, being directed at the illumination of this very Divine Wisdom, as one of its first translators, Viktor von Strauß (1809–99), put it (von Strauss 1870: xxvii–xxix). This line of argument was happily adopted by many Theosophical writers who credited the *Daodejing* to be a verbalization of the perennial truth as systematically unearthed by Helena P. Blavatsky (1831–91). Notably, a number of Theosophists were actively participating in the early stages of the wider *Daodejing* translation endeavor: Walter Richard Old (1864–1929) in 1894; Franz Hartmann (1838–1912) in 1896–7; Johan van Manen (1877–1943) from June 1898 to July 1901;[1] Charles Spurgeon Medhurst (1860–1927) in 1905; Johannes Assuerus Blok (1867–1955) in 1910; Isabella Mears (1853–1936) in 1916/1922; and Charles Henry Mackintosh in 1926.[2] Many more provided and continue to offer their Theosophical ruminations on the 'ancient wisdom' contained in it. To many Theosophists today, the *Daodejing* is mandatory reading, and indeed – as the high-ranked American Theosophist Richard W. Brooks (1931–2013) once observed – 'Many Theosophists have fallen in love with the little Chinese classic . . . We see in it an echo of many familiar Theosophical ideas' (Brooks 2001: 18).

This chapter traces the use of the *Daodejing* in the first some two decades following the foundation of the Theosophical Society (1875–1896/1897). It (1) examines which translations (and *Daodejing* verses) were used in the Theosophical literature, (2) explores what (Theosophical) role the authors ascribed to the *Daodejing* and (3) takes a look at the first two Theosophical translations by Old and Hartmann. To give a glimpse of the pool of translations (several of which early Theosophical writers consulted) crafted before Old and Hartmann, a brief outline of the Western translation history of the *Daodejing* from its Jesuit beginnings is given as follows.

The *Daodejing* in translation

The beginnings of the Western translation history of the *Daodejing* was an exclusively Jesuit project. The earliest partial (i.e. one verse each) Latin translations date back to the Austrian Martino Martini (1614–61) and the Belgian Philippe Couplet (1623–93) in 1658 and 1687, respectively. The first two complete (Latin) translations were crafted several decades later. Of these only one is extant today,[3] namely, that by the French Figurist Jean-François Noëlas (1669–1740) produced in the 1720s (von Collani 2015). However, these handwritten translations did not reach a wider public and thus had virtually no impact.

In 1842, the first full rendition by an academically trained sinologist was published – *Lao Tseu Tao Te King. Le livre de la voie et de la vertu* (Lao Tseu Tao Te King: The Book of the Way and the Virtue) by Stanislas Aignan Julien (1797–1873), professor of Chinese at the Collège de France (Zhang and Xie 2022). Four years prior, the French orientalist Guillaume Pauthier (1810–73) had translated the first nine verses into French and Latin in his *Tao-te-King* (1838). Julien's translation proved to be a template for many subsequent translations, starting with the first English rendering *Tau Tĕh King. The Speculations on Metaphysics, Polity, and Morality of 'The Old Philosopher' Lau-tsze* by the Scottish missionary John Chalmers (1825–99) in 1868. Heavily criticizing Julien's translation, the German astronomer and hobby sinologist Reinhold von Plänckner (1820–84) published his own in 1870, entitled *Lao-Tse Táo-Tĕ-King. Der Weg zur Tugend* (Lao-Tse Táo-Tĕ-King: The Way to Virtue), which in turn received very unfavourable reviews due to its lack of philological rigour (see e.g. Legge 1883: 78). The first such being voiced by the German poet, China specialist and fellow *Daodejing* translator Viktor von Strauß in his *Laò-Tsè's Taò Tĕ Kīng* (1870: xiii–xiv) published shortly after that of von Plänckner.[4]

The 1880s saw four further translations: *Taoist Texts: Ethical, Political and Speculative* (1884) by the Shanghai-based English sinologist Frederic Henry Balfour (1846–1909); a partial rendition in his article 'The Remains of Lao Tzŭ' (1886) by the English professor of Chinese at the University of Cambridge Herbert Allen Giles (1845–1935);[5] and two renditions largely unknown to Theosophical writers: the German *Taòtekking von Laòtsee* (1888) published by one Friedrich Wilhelm Noak,[6] and the Spanish 'Tao-Te-King de Yan-Tsu' (1889) written by the Spanish Dominican Bishop of Hauara and former Vicar apostolic of Fujian 福建 Salvador Masot (1845–1911).

A seminal translation was subsequently produced by the former Scottish missionary and professor of Chinese Language and Literature at the University of Oxford James Legge (1815–97) with his *Tâo Teh King* (1891), published as part of Friedrich Max Müller's (1823–1900) *Sacred Books of the East* series. The same year, the Belgian Orientalist Charles Joseph de Harlez de Deulin (1832–99) published his *Textes Tâoïstes* (Daoist Texts; 1891).

These were the chief translations in European languages more or less available prior to Old's rendition of 1894. Further translations up until the publication of Hartmann's rendition of 1896–7 include 'Le Tao de Laotseu' (1894) by the French Martinist Eugène-Albert Puyou de Pouvourville (1861–1938),[7] Тао те кингъ (Конисси 1894) by the Japanese Russicist Konishi Masutarō 小西増太郎 (1862–1940) and *Lâo-Tzse: The Great Thinker* (1895) by the British major-general turned writer George Gardiner Alexander (1821–97). As will be indicated later, Theosophists also occasionally drew on additional translations, which were included in other works not exclusively dealing with the *Daodejing*.

The Theosophical *Daodejing*

Whereas Laozi and the *Daodejing* were but a footnote in the earliest Theosophical writings,[8] interest slowly but gradually increased from the late 1880s onwards – concomitant to the surge of translational work. One of the first Theosophical writers emphatically recognizing the importance of the *Daodejing* as the nucleus of a 'Chinese Theosophy' was Marie, Countess of Caithness (1830–95).[9] In her *The Mystery of the Ages, Contained in the Secret Doctrine of All Religions*, she determined that the teachings of the 'Tao-Sse' (i.e., *daoshi* 道士) chiefly represent the Chinese manifestation of Theosophy. Their 'Tao-Te-King' would be a work of Theosophy 'adapted to the Chinese mind' and indeed 'should be studied by every Theosophist' (Countess of Caithness 1887: 193–8). While Lady

Caithness repeatedly referenced Balfour,[10] the four unnumbered *Daodejing* verses she added in translation (Fifteen, Sixteen, Twenty-Five, Forty-Seven) are her English renderings of the Julien version.

Another early aficionado of the 'mystical school of Lao-tzeu' (*école mystique de Lao-tzeu*) and the *Daodejing* was the French Edouard J. Coulomb (pen name: Amaravella), who was a chief figure of early French Theosophy (Godwin 1989), founding member of the Blavatsky Lodge and prolific translator of Theosophical writings. With his self-reported sinological background, he appeared amid his peers as the first Theosophist connoisseur of 'Chinese esotericism'. The 'great "Lao-Tseu" also, the Founder of Taoism' would have retired to the supposed hub of Chinese mystical and alchemical learning, the Kunlun Mountains, 'after having written his "*Tao-TE-King*"' (Amaravella 1889b: 372). Coulomb views the *Daodejing* as to confirm the notion of *ganying* 感應 (resonance or moral retribution), which he attempted to corroborate by abbreviated translations (Verses One, Five and Six) based on the Pauthier rendition (1838) of the *Daodejing* (Amaravella 1889a: 147). Pauthier's translation of Verse One and commentary snippets alongside Julien's translation of Verses Fifty and Fifty-Two also served Coulomb in his perennialist *magnum opus Le Secret de l'Absolu* (The Secret of the Absolute) to highlight the inherent complementarity of *dao* 道 as a paradigm of the 'absolute' (Coulomb 1892: 16–19).

At one point also Blavatsky, albeit posthumously, addressed the *Daodejing* more elaborately,[11] namely, in her *The Theosophical Glossary*. Following the entries on 'Lao-tze' ('A great sage, saint and philosopher who preceded Confucius'; Blavatsky 1892: 186) and 'Tao' ('The name of the philosophy of Lao-tze'; Blavatsky 1892: 319), in the one on the 'Tao-teh-king' she stated (Blavatsky 1892: 320):[12]

> 'The Book of the Perfectibility of Nature' written by the great philosopher Lao-tze. It is a kind of cosmogony which contains all the fundamental tenets of Esoteric Cosmogenesis. Thus he says that in the beginning there was naught but limitless and boundless Space. All that lives and is, was born in it, from the 'Principle which exists by Itself, developing Itself from Itself', *i.e.*, *Swabhâvat*. As its name is unknown and its essence is unfathomable, philosophers have called it *Tao* (*Anima Mundi*), the uncreate [sic], unborn and eternal energy of nature, manifesting periodically. Nature as well as man when it reaches purity will reach *rest*, and then all become one with Tao, which is the source of all bliss and felicity. As in the Hindu and Buddhistic philosophies, such purity and bliss and immortality can only be reached through the exercise of virtue and the perfect quietude of our worldly spirit; the human mind has to control and finally subdue

and even crush the turbulent action of man's physical nature; and the sooner he reaches the required degree of moral purification, the happier he will feel. (See *Annales du Musée Guimet*, Vols. XI. and XII.; *Etudes sur la Religion des Chinois*, by Dr. Groot.[13]) As the famous Sinologist, Pauthier, remarked: 'Human Wisdom can never use language more holy and profound.'[14]

Her translation of *Daodejing* as 'The Book of the Perfectibility of Nature' is based on de Groot's rendition 'Le Livre de l'excellence de la Nature'. Inner Group member and Blavatsky's private secretary George Robert Stow Mead (1863–1933) in his 1892 essay 'The World-Soul' also drew on de Groot (1886) (besides Balfour 1892).[15] He gives the title of the *Daodejing* slightly differently as 'The Book of the Perfection of Nature'. His discussion, which is largely a collection of quotations from de Groot and especially Balfour (1892), revolves around the notion of 'Tao' as the Daoist expression of 'that supreme intuition of Humanity, the essential Unity of all things' (Mead 1892b: 121). To Mead, Daoism 'is the most mystical of the creeds of the far East' (Mead 1892a: 30; cf. Anonymous 1881: 9) and Laozi a 'great Chinese Mystic' (Mead 1893: 12).

The rising interest in Daoism and the *Daodejing* in particular is captured by another of Blavatsky's Inner Group disciples, Alice Leighton Cleather (1846–1938), in a correspondence (June 1892) for *The Theosophist*, writing that the 'awakening of a general interest in Tàoism seems just now to be widespread' (Cleather 1892: 703). She then mentions two recent, related and very well-received publications, Legge's *Tâo Teh King* and the French Japanologist Léon de Rosny's (1837–1914) *Le Taoïsme* (de Rosny 1892). Before, Cleather reports on the upcoming Annual Convention of the Theosophical Society in London, attended by key exponents of Theosophy, including, among others, the likes of Judge, Mead, Coulomb, Annie Besant (1847–1933), the president of the Madrid Lodge Josef Xifre (1856–1920)[16] and Walter Richard Old (1864–1929), who was also scheduled to deliver a lecture entitled 'On Tao' in the course of the weekly Blavatsky Lodge meetings two months later.

Also known by his nom de plume 'Sepharial', Old was an Inner Group member and Assistant Secretary of the European Section, the chief Theosophist astrologer and the first Theosophist translator of the *Daodejing*. Born in Birmingham and slated to become a pharmacist, as an adolescent Old rather immersed himself in Swedenborgianism, the Kabbalah, numerology and astrology. In addition, he professed to have turned to studying ancient languages, such as Hebrew, Sanskrit and literary Chinese, which, however, must have been at an elementary level. In his early twenties, he started a career as an astrologer, later becoming indeed one of the most eminent practitioners of his days. In 1887, he published a first small booklet entitled *Astrological Judgment upon the Great Solar Eclipse of 1887* and would subsequently take up the pen name 'Sepharial' in many of his writings. The same year, he started a correspondence with Blavatsky, became Fellow of the Theosophical Society in Birmingham in January 1888 and moved to the London headquarters in April upon Blavatsky's invitation who appointed him vice-president of the Blavatsky Lodge in 1889 and general secretary of the British Theosophical Society in 1890. Closely working with Blavatsky at the time, she asked him to preface her *Gems from the East* (Blavatsky 1890). The following year, he published *What Is Theosophy?* (Old 1891), prefaced by Besant for her 'friend' Old. Notably, Daoism or the *Daodejing* were not mentioned. When Blavatsky died of influenza, the 'Astral Tramp' (how Blavatsky had nicknamed him) was reportedly at her side, '[h]olding her hand and kneeling at the foot of her chair' (Farnell 1998: 35). Old kept himself busy becoming the chief Theosophist librarian in 1891 and secretary of the European Section Convention held in July 1892.

His Blavatsky Lodge lecture from September 22 was published with the simple title 'Tao' in the November issue of *Lucifer*, the organ of the Blavatsky Lodge. The article was republished as 'The Tao' as postscript to his *Daodejing* translation (Old 1894: 33–46). Therein Old outlines basic Daoist tenets, not outing himself as being proficient with the Chinese language or Chinese religions overall. Yet, he already assigns to the 'Tao-te-King' the translation of the title used in his rendition – *The Book of the Path of Virtue*. The 'Tao' he describes as 'a mystical term ... among the Tao-tze', meaning 'Supreme Reason, and Nature, the Alpha and Omega of all things' and representing the '"diversity in Unity" of Nature and the "Unity in diversity" of God' (Old 1892: 207). Old also subscribed to the common view at the time that 'the pure Tao of Lao-Tze' degenerated in the later use of 'the sect of the Tao-tze'[17] (Old 1892: 209). Only twice in the essay does Old effectively cite a passage in translation from the *Daodejing*. However, he does not do so based on any existing complete translation. First, he adopts a passage (Kenealy 1866: 36) from *The Book of God: The Apocalypse of Adam-Oannes* by one of his early favourite authors, the Irish barrister Edward Vaughan Kenealy (1819–90), which apparently draws (and very liberally so) on Verse Forty-Two as given by Julien. Shortly thereafter, he quotes (again with reference) a translation of Verse Twenty-Five made by Friedrich Max Müller in his *Introduction to the Science of Religion* (Müller 1873: 249–50).[18] Müller's rendition was not from the original Chinese but from the French version by Julien. These quotes aside, Old throughout draws on the *Zhuangzi* 莊子 in Herbert Allen Giles's translation

(Giles 1889) when citing Laozi.[19] This is surprising and suggests (all the more because of the citation of the deficient rendering or paraphrasing by Kenealy) that Old at the time was unfamiliar with any existing *Daodejing* translations.

The article was lauded by Old's best friend Sydney V. Edge as an 'extremely interesting and a useful *résumé* for students who have not time to read authorities, first hand' in the January issue of *The Theosophist* (Edge 1893: 242). Edge had left London in August 1892 to become assistant secretary of the India Section of the Theosophical Society. His best friend Old would join him to Adyar in December. With his arrival commenced in earnest what was to be called the 'Judge affair', that is, the struggle for power following the passing of Blavatsky between Besant and Henry Steel Olcott, the president of the Theosophical Society, on the one side and William Quan Judge, General Secretary of the American Section, on the other. By siding with his friend Olcott against Judge (but later turning against Besant), Old was involved at the very heart of the controversy. It was in the midst of these difficult times – which would ultimately entail a lasting schism within the Theosophical Society and Old's ousting in 1894 – that he committed to his translation of the *Daodejing*, a book he reportedly deemed most superior in its 'philosophical depth and subtlety of wit', even eclipsing the *Bhagavadgītā* and the *Dhammapada* (Anonymous 1894: 463).

Old finished his work in early 1894 and left for England in late March[20] after the book was put into print. His *The Book of the Path of Virtue* was meant to be the second volume in a series entitled 'Studies in Theosophy'[21] with the aim to 'supply the members of the Section from time to time with [freely disseminated] publications of matter which might be of use to them in their studies', as it was announced in the April issue of *The Theosophist* (Anonymous 1894: 463). As soon as the book was released, Olcott himself penned an amiable review in the May issue of *The Theosophist* of this 'very charming monograph', whose translator thanks to his 'theosophic studies' could catch the 'spirit of … Laotze, the Theosophist of China' (Olcott 1894). He further informs the readers that Old 'has utilized the several translated editions of the *Tao-teh-king* in the Adyar Library for the purpose of compiling the present version' and to bring 'contradictory passages in the several translations into accord with the spirit of Taoist philosophy' (Olcott 1894). Olcott eventually calls on scholars of Chinese to see whether Old's version would be 'warrantable'. Another Theosophical reviewer, the then assistant general secretary of the American Section Alexander Fullerton (1841–1913), writing for *The Path*, the organ of the American Section, while praising Old's 'ever-pleasing style' is somewhat baffled by the mostly 'superficial and commonplace' wisdom the *Daodejing* would have to offer and wonders how this 'could form the basis of a national school of philosophy' (Fullerton 1894: 102).[22]

Old's translation, which is otherwise unannotated save for one remark,[23] is introduced with a brief three-and-a-half pages text in which he casts a glance at the supposed origin of the *Daodejing*, the development of Daoism in subsequent centuries and 'the use of the terms *Tao*, *Teh* [*de* 德] and *Tien* [*tian* 天]' (Old 1894: ii). His historical outline is undoubtedly informed by (in fact partly a mere summary of) portions of Legge's introduction (1891: 4–8) to his 1891 *Daodejing* translation. In addition, he paraphrases (with a wrong dating) from Müller's preface to the same volume (1891: xi–xii). Old's reflections on the Daoist key terminology are likewise largely drawing on Legge (1891: 12–19) with some of his own Theosophically minded conclusions, when he takes, for example, the 'Tao of Heaven' (*tian zhi dao* 天之道) to mean 'the Path of God' (Old 1894: iii). Finally, Old notes that his rendition 'has been adapted after careful reading of the several translations extant, aided by such intuitions as have arisen from familiarity with theosophical and mystical speculations' (Old 1894: iv).

Old adds a title to every verse. Whereas he points out that he follows one of the *Daodejing*'s 'numerous commentators', he indeed does do so primarily via Chalmers and lesser so via Legge (who both provide a translation of the titles given to the verses by the major commentator Heshang Gong 河上公), essentially rephrasing the translation and occasionally adjusting it with a view to the verse translation or the 'chapter' outline in Legge. Notably, Old's translation of the *Daodejing* is in its entirety likewise a rephrasing of the Chalmers version with the occasional help of Legge. Needless to say that Old did at no point express his indebtedness to these two scholars. The 'several translations carefully read' by Old were indeed only these two. Old did not employ the Balfour or Giles versions nor any German and French ones available at the time.

Despite its endorsement by Olcott and *The Theosophist* as well as its alleged Theosophical-cum-mystical imprint, Old's translation exerted little influence at first. This might have been connected to Old turning into a veritable *persona non grata* for many Theosophists shortly after the publication due to his crucial involvement in the Judge affair and specifically the bad press it caused, for which he was deemed responsible. The impact of his translation at first was indirect, as will be briefly discussed further below with respect to the *Daodejing* translation into German by the German Theosophist Franz Hartmann (1838–1912). Only with the re-publication of his *The Book of the Path of Virtue* ten years later in a new guise did Old's translation reach a substantial audience (including Theosophists and fellow esotericists). Distributed by large publishing houses in the United

States and England, now equipped with annotations – the translation itself largely remained untouched – and an extended introduction (which absorbed the postscript on the *Zhuangzi* of the 1894 version), *The Book of the Simple Way of Laotze* by Walter Gorn Old[24] (Old 1904) saw at least eight re-prints from 1905 to 1943. Facsimile editions circulate to this day.

Even if the Old translation of 1894 was at first only sparsely used by Theosophists,[25] it echoed a wider reclamation of the *Daodejing* as a natural part and the foremost Chinese expression of global Theosophical knowledge. Indeed, interspersed quotes from the *Daodejing* started to become more frequent in the Theosophical literature around the time.[26]

A Theosophist who later came to appreciate Old's translation, himself gaining the reputation of a Theosophical authority of Daoism specifically due to his publication of *The Inner Life and the Tao-Teh-King* (1912; a collection of previously published essays), is the Danish-American librarian Carl Henrik Andreas Bjerregaard (1845–1922).[27] His first notable step to become a well-regarded connoisseur of Daoism within Theosophist circles dates back to 1895 and his essay 'Tao the Chinese "Being"'. To Bjerregaard, the 'Tao-te-King' was reestablishing the mystic connection 'with the abyss', that is, the transcendent realm or 'the Deity' (Bjerregaard 1887).[28] Being 'one of the few remarkable books in the world', the *Daodejing* would be a manual on the esoteric and exoteric dimensions of 'Being', which is Bjerregaard's idiosyncratic translation of *dao* (Bjerregaard 1895: 410). In the essay, he assembles a number of quotations from the *Daodejing* to give account of each dimension (Bjerregaard 1895: 411–14). He does not indicate the respective verse numbers, nor does he disclose which translation he uses. To the contrary, his concluding statement that '[i]n all the above quotations the term [Tao] has been left untranslated in accordance with common custom' (Bjerregaard 1895: 415) might be read to insinuate that this is Bjerregaard's own rendition after all. In fact, what Bjerregaard does is to largely stack together portions from the *Daodejing* translations of Chalmers (1868) and Balfour (1884) with his own modifications. For the esoteric teachings, for example, he so starts with Verse One, bringing together (slightly modified) portions from Chalmers,[29] Chalmers's translation of Julien,[30] and a mixture of Balfour and Chalmers. Next come selections from Verse Four, again largely based on Chalmers with a brief Balfour insertion; Verse Six combining Chalmers and Balfour; Verse Fourteen with Balfour first while also picking up a note by Chalmers (which is perhaps even further informed by von Strauss 1870: 61–2) and then once again Chalmers; Verse Fifteen is based on one sentence by Chalmers only; Verse Twenty-One comprising of Balfour and a modified ending of Chalmers; and Verse Thirty-Two which is yet another combination of Balfour and Chalmers.[31] At the time, Bjerregaard apparently had not taken notice of the Old version yet. He would do so later at least with respect to Old's slightly revised rendition (Old 1904) (see e.g. *The Inner Life and the Tao-Teh-King*).

Another early Theosophist commentator on Daoism and the *Daodejing* is Annie Besant who was to become long-term president of the Theosophical Society, Adyar (1907–33). In her essay programmatically entitled 'The Unity Underlying All Religions',[32] Besant unsurprisingly discovers Theosophy to be 'the origin and basis of all religions' (Besant 1896a: 405). She subsequently tries to locate its chief characteristics in the Daoist tradition, especially drawing on the Tang Dynasty (618–907) *Qingjing jing* 清靜經 (Classic of Purity and Quietness)[33] as 'a fragment of an ancient scripture' from the days of the 'great Fourth Race'[34] settling in what is today China. To bolster her argument, Besant also adds passages from the '*Tâo Teh King*' exclusively according to the Legge translation[35] (1891) – in order of appearance: Verses One, Twenty-Five, Forty, Forty-Two, Thirty-Four and again One – with which she tries to give evidence of the first four (of altogether five) 'spiritual verities of religion', namely: 'i. One eternal infinite incognizable real Existence. ii. From That the manifested God, unfolding from unity, from duality to trinity. iii. From the manifested Trinity many spiritual Intelligences, guiding the kosmic order. iv. Man a reflexion of the manifested God and therefore a trinity fundamentally, his inner and real Self being eternal, one with the Self of the universe' (Besant 1896a: 406).[36] Across the ages, Besant avers (Besant 1896b: 488–9), Theosophy had its 'definite custodians'. The *Daodejing* would confirm that with a view to the Daoist tradition, an argument Besant anchors in a collection of verses relating to those following the *dao* such as the 'sage' (Forty-One, Seven, Twenty-Two, Forty-Six, Forty-Nine, Fifty-Five, Sixty-Seven).

Whereas Besant shunned Old's translation, another chief exponent of Theosophy (and, incidentally, an avid translator of Besant's works) embraced it wholeheartedly – the famous German Theosophist Franz Hartmann. A medical doctor, Hartmann immigrated to the United States in 1865 where he encountered Spiritualism and Theosophy. He joined the Theosophical Society via Olcott in 1882 and relocated to Adyar a year later where he became one of Blavatsky's closest aides, accompanying the latter back to Europe in 1885. He subsequently settled in Austria, embarking on a prolific occult publishing career and becoming the most eminent Theosophist in the German-speaking world. He eventually founded the short-lived *Theosophische Gesellschaft in Europa (Deutschland)* (Theosophical Society in Europe [Germany]) in 1896, which was a branch of Judge's US splinter group then led by Katherine Tingley (1847–1929), and a year later the *Internationale Theosophische Verbrüderung* (International Theosophical Fraternization) with the aim to end the Theosophical schism. In 1896, he commenced his translation of the 'Tao-Teh-King', which he published serially in his monthly *Lotusblüten* (Lotus Blossoms) from July 1896 to February 1897 (Hartmann 1896a–f; 1897a–b). The whole translation – yet without his two-page introduction contained in the first *Lotusblüten* installment – was published as a book carrying the same title, namely, *Theosophie in China. Betrachtungen über das TAO-TEH-KING* (Theosophy in China: Reflections on the TAO-TEH-KING) in Leipzig in 1897 (Hartmann 1897c). Several additional unrevised editions followed over the years (1900, 1903, 1910, 1920, 1922).[37] Hartmann's serialized publication of his German *Daodejing* rendition was continuously mentioned in various issues of *Le lotus bleu* and *Lucifer*. Moreover, the translation was well-received by German esotericists,[38] and led many subsequent generations of readers to believe that it was indeed crafted based on the Chinese original, since the subtitle of the book publication indicates: 'Aus dem Chinesischen des Lao-tze übersetzt' (Translated from the Chinese of Lao-tze). Instead, the translation is in fact essentially a verbatim rendition of Old's translation of 1894, supplemented with annotations by Hartmann meant to render the supposed Theosophical nature of the *urtext* explicit, for Laozi himself was a 'Chinese Theosophist' (1896a: 467). Evidently, Hartmann never gained the slightest proficiency of (literary) Chinese nor had he any actual knowledge of the contemporaneous scholarly literature on Chinese religions and Daoism in particular. In the introduction, he states that Laozi's teachings had developed into a religious system that had many followers especially among the higher strata of Chinese society. Next, he addresses the terms 'Tao', 'Teh' and 'King' (*jing* 經): whereas he gives 'Tao' as 'word' (*Wort*) and 'way' (*Weg*), his renderings for 'Teh' as 'truth' (*Wahrheit*) and 'law' (*Gesetz*) and 'King' as 'heaven' (*Himmel*) and 'light' (*Licht*) are peculiar. He ultimately translates the book title as 'The Way to the Knowledge of Truth' (*der Weg zur Erkenntnis der Wahrheit*), thereby referencing Old (Hartmann 1896a: 467–8), who does not give such (paraphrasing) translation himself. Hartmann seems to allude to Old's notion of 'the Path of God', which is meant as the Theosophical way to uncover the divinity within one's self, that is, one's alleged true self. Indeed, the German title mirrors Hartmann's Theosophical grasp of the *Daodejing*, which also represents the guiding thread of his whole commentary. Equipped with the Christian New Testament, Blavatsky's *Secret Doctrine*, the *Bhagavadgītā* and quotations by Christian mystics Thomas a Kempis (1380–1471), Jakob Böhme (1575–1624), Angelus Silesius (1624–77) and Miguel de Molinos (1628–96), Hartmann establishes the *Daodejing* as a wisdom text in line with his own distinct Theosophical soteriology where Christian mysticism is wed with Blavatskian Theosophy.

Concluding remarks

Clearly, among Asian religions, the *Daodejing* and Daoism or Chinese religions overall did not occupy the centre stage in the Theosophical discourse. This status was held by the Indian traditions. However, Theosophy's engagement with Comparative Religion and the surge of translations of the Chinese classics in the 1880s and 1890s entering the intellectual mainstream assigned the *Daodejing* and Laozi a firm place in the perennialist project of Theosophists and fellow occultists. Laozi and his Daoist following as code words for carriers of millennia-old Chinese mysticism came handy in Theosophical enumerations of a ubiquitous Ancient Wisdom. For most Theosophists, Laozi – let alone the *Daodejing* – were exactly this: an additional (and otherwise generally ignored) element in their itemization of the multifarious utterers/expressions of the one universal Truth. As part of the Theosophical narrative, however minor its significance at first, the mysticism of Laozi and 'his' *Daodejing* waited to be explored and appropriated to fit Theosophy's grand scheme. Indeed, a number of eminent Theosophists embraced this very agenda.

In their accommodation of Daoism, early Theosophists made use of several of the major translations of their time: Julien (1842) – also in partial translation by Müller (1873) – Chalmers (1868), Balfour (1884) and Legge (1891). Scattered (occasionally modified) quotations were also based on Pauthier (1838), von Plänckner (1870), Alexander (1890), Old (1894) and de Pouvourville (1894). In addition, some Theosophists knew the works of von Strauß (1870) and Giles (1886). With the increasing visibility of Daoism in the intellectual discourse at the time, Walter Richard Old provided the first 'Theosophically-inspired' translation in 1894. Franz Hartmann was to follow in 1896–7 with his German rendition. Yet, their Theosophical *Daodejing* was essentially a case of what would be called plagiarism today. Having only elementary proficiency in Chinese, Old copied vastly from the Chalmers version guided by Legge. Subsequently, and even more bluntly, Hartmann (lacking any knowledge of literary Chinese) copied verbatim from Old. But their translations – initial setbacks for that of Old notwithstanding – endured for many decades to come. They mark the inception of a 'Theosophical lineage' within the general translation history of the *Daodejing*.

Notes

1. A serialized translation with extensive commentary of parts of the *Daodejing* published in the Dutch Theosophical journal *Theosophia*. Van Manen calls it 'a Dutch approach' rather than 'a translation' (van Manen 1898: 25) since he draws on the existing renditions by Legge (1891), de Pouvourville (1894), Noak (1888), von Plaenckner (1870), von Strauss (1870) and Old (1894).
2. Knut Walf (b. 1936), a German theologian and scholar of the Western reception of Daoism, even suggests that Theosophical translators and editors were possibly 'the main cause for popularizing Laozi's book in the West' (Walf 1999: 126). Important as their contribution was, they were certainly not 'the main cause'.
3. The other one being a translation by the Belgian François Noël (1651–1729) done before 1711.
4. A third translation published in 1870, but having only a very limited audience, was a Spanish rendition based on Julien entitled *Lao-tseu-tao-te-king. Libro de la vía eterna y de la virtud* (Lao-tseu-tao-te-king: Book of the Eternal Way and of Virtue) by the Mexican poet Agustín de Bazán y Caravantes. Furthermore, in 1878, the Czech philosopher František Čupr (1821–82) published a Czech translation: *Tao-Tě-King. Cesta k Bohu a ctnosti* (Tao-Tě-King: The Path to God and Virtue).
5. In his article (which even featured in a brief review note in *The Theosophist*'s 1895 March issue), Giles gave a damning review of Balfour's translation, whose 'exegetical value' he considers to be on a par with – would it ever be written – a 'commentary of the fourth Gospel from Madame Blavatsky' (Giles 1886: 234).
6. That the Noak rendition was made accessible at least to some early Theosophists is indicated by a gratitude note of the Dutch Theosophical Society in April 1897, in which the receipt of the Noak volume alongside that of von Plänckner for their library collection is reported (Theosofische Vereeniging 1897: 232). Van Manen making use of this collection also consulted the Noak translation.
7. On de Pouvourville, see the chapter by Davide Marino in this volume.
8. Laozi is mentioned twice (qua 'the Chinese philosopher' Laotsen [*sic*] or Lao-tsi, as well Tissoo) in Helena P. Blavatsky's *Isis Unveiled* (Blavatsky 1877: 600, 159). In her story 'A Bewitched Life' she referred to the Japanese *yamabushi* 山伏 as '(the ascetics, or "hermits") who follow the doctrines of Lao-tze', the 'followers of Lao-tze' (Blavatsky 1885a: 267) and the 'initiates of Lao-tze' (Blavatsky 1885b: 285). Here Blavatsky apparently drew on a *The Theosophist* article of 1881 on 'The Religions of Japan', where account is given on 'the doctrines of Lao-Tye, the most mystical and spiritual of all' and their followers the '*Yamabusi* or the "Hermit-Brothers"' (Anonymous 1881: 9; for an early Dutch translation of this part, see Anonymous 1895: 495). Other early Theosophical writers, such as Henry Steel Olcott (1832–

1907), Alfred Percy Sinnett (1840–1921) and William Quan Judge (1851–96), left things Daoist unmentioned.

9 An ardent spiritist and early member (1876) of the Theosophical Society, she was the first president of the Société Théosophique d'Orient et d'Occident, which she founded in Paris in June 1883.

10 Yet, she does not reference Balfour's *Daodejing* translation but his earlier *The Divine Classic of Nan-hua* in which he remarked that contemporary Daoism would be 'one of the most degenerate systems of belief in the entire world' (Balfour 1881: xxix). Lady Caithness deridingly called this into question (Countess of Caithness 1887: 198).

11 Before that, Laozi is mentioned once (qua 'the predecessor of Confucius' Lao-tse) in Blavatsky's two-volume *The Secret Doctrine* (Blavatsky 1888a: xxv), in which she also alludes to Daoism as 'Lao-tse doctrine' (Blavatsky 1888a: xxv) and the 'esotericism of Lao-tse' (1888b: 37) and to Daoists as 'priests and followers of Lao-tse' (1888a: xxv) and 'Lao-Tze sect' (1888a: 173). She references the *Daodejing* ('*Tao-te-King*' or 'the sacred scriptures of the *Taosse*') twice, drawing on Julien's translation and Friedrich Max Müller, whom she quotes stating that 'the text is unintelligible without commentaries, so that Mr. Julien had to consult more than sixty commentators for the purpose of his translation' (1888a: xxv; see Müller 1873: 115; for an early Dutch translation of this part, see Blavatsky 1893: 206), as well as on Julien's teacher Jean-Pierre Abel-Rémusat (1788–1832) again through Müller (Blavatsky 1888a: 472; see Müller 1873: 332). Laozi ('Laotze' and 'Lao-Tze') and the *Daodejing* are also mentioned *en passant* in *The Key to Theosophy* (1889: 49, 117).

12 In two further entries (Blavatsky 1892: 224, 320) she also uses the term 'Taoist'.

13 The Dutch sinologist Jan Jakob Maria de Groot (1854–1921). Blavatsky draws on the brief description of Daoism in de Groot 1886: 691–706.

14 See Pauthier 1839: 118: 'La sagesse humaine n'a peut-être jamais exprimé des paroles plus saintes et plus profondes.' Blavatsky picked up the reference from de Groot 1886: 695.

15 The essay was reprinted alongside three others in Mead 1895.

16 Whereas Laozi was occasionally mentioned in the early Spanish Theosophical literature, *Daodejing* quotations are absent.

17 Here (as well as in the subtitle of his book) Old seems to use an early rendering of *daozi* 道子 in the sense of 'sons of the *dao*' (another meaning used in early Western texts is 'Master Dao' referring to Laozi) for 'Daoists'. The terms 'Tao-tze' and 'Tao-tse' in the sense of 'Daoists' was already largely obsolete at the time. Also, he might have simply taken 'Tao-tze' as being synonymous with the more common transcription 'Tao-sse' (i.e. *daoshi*). At any rate, this and the text at large do not necessarily suggest that Old had any (other than perhaps rudimentary) knowledge of Chinese at the time of writing.

18 This is from the same brief discussion of Müller on Daoism that had already been referenced before by Blavatsky (1888a: xxv).
19 Although not referenced, Old was also clearly informed by the Dutch religious historian Cornelius Petrus Tiele's (1830–1902) account on 'Religion among the Chinese' (Tiele 1877: 25–38). Moreover, he was also sympathetic to the philosophical note by English theologian Aubrey Moore (1848–1890), whom he references in Giles 1889: xviii–xxviii.
20 Notably, the same month a note in *Lucifer*'s 'Theosophical and Mystic Publications' section reports on a new French 'literal translation of *The Tâo* of Lao-tsze, which is at least an improvement on the paraphrase of M. Stanilas [*sic*] Julien' (T. 1894: 88). The said translation was published in four parts in the first few 1894 issues of the French esoteric journal *La Haute Science* (de Pouvourville 1894). The translator was the French Martinist and self-styled Daoist initiate Eugène-Albert Puyou de Pouvourville (pen name: Matgioi). In the introduction, de Pouvourville criticizes the paraphrasing of Julien, which would have urged him to produce an 'exact' rendering of the *Daodejing* based on his first-hand knowledge of the tradition. His (philologically inexact) translation was indeed well-received in French Theosophist circles. A very early quotation from his rendition (namely, that of Verse One) in the Theosophical literature can be found, for example, in the December 1896 issue of the French Theosophical monthly *Le lotus bleu* (Luxâme 1896: 394–5).
21 The first volume being *Theosophical Gleanings: Notes on 'The Secret Doctrine'* (Indian Section of the Theosophical Society, 1893).
22 Yet another brief review by George William Russell (1867–1935) in *The Irish Theosophist*'s June issue notes that the book 'is largely Ethical, and will . . . be welcomed by a large circle of readers' (Russell 1894: 135).
23 In his translation of Verse Fourteen Old takes up Abel-Rémusat's view that the Chinese characters *yi xi wei* 夷希微 would phonetically refer to the tetragrammaton (Abel-Rémusat 1823: 40–54). Curiously, he does not mention Abel-Rémusat but wrongly refers to Chalmers as suggesting this. In fact, Chalmers, although mentioning that 'some scholars have fancied [these] to be the syllables of the sacred name of God in Hebrew' (Chalmers 1868: 9), explicitly rejects this idea. Old must had effectively drawn on Legge's commentary to the verse that also gives the name of Rémusat (Legge 1891: 57–8).
24 Old had changed his name to 'Walter Gornold Old' in 1895.
25 The only early use of Old's translation up until Franz Hartmann's rendition I could trace is Julia van der Planck's – pen name: Jasper Niemand; the wife of the prominent English Theosophist Archibald Keightley (1859–1930) – reference to Verses Sixty-Three and Sixty-Four (in a slightly modified form) in an article for *The Irish Theosophist*'s June 1895 issue (Niemand 1895: 151).
26 For example, *The Path*'s March 1894 issue has a quote of Verse Seven according to the Legge translation on top of its cover page (Judge 1894a: 369). *Mercury*'s

September 1894 issue (Walters 1894: 44) concludes with an alleged Laozi quote, of which only portions are indeed based on the *Daodejing*, namely, Verses Seven (drawing liberally on Balfour) and Twenty-Two (drawing on Chalmers). The *Path*'s December 1894 issue (Judge 1894b: 265) front page starts with the beginning part of Verse Twenty-Five in Müller's rendering. The English Theosophist Ernest Temple Hargrove (1870–1939; alias Che-Yew-Tsăng), the founder of The Theosophical Society in America (1898), quotes parts of Verse Twenty-Eight (using Chalmers) in an article for *Lucifer*'s October 1893 issue (Tsăng 1893: 100; for a contemporaneous Dutch translation of the article, see Tsang 1894) as well as parts of Verse Thirty-Eight (again Chalmers but with modifications) in *The Path*'s January 1895 issue (Tsăng 1895: 304). Prior to the 1890s, *Daodejing* quotations were virtually absent in the Theosophical literature. Additional quotations from the early 1890s are found in *Lucifer*'s January 1891 issue, which contains a translation (Blavatsky and Besant 1891: 401) by George Gardiner Alexander taken from his *Confucius, the Great Teacher*, in which he also added several *Daodejing* verses in translation. The translation consists of Verse One (Alexander 1890: 305–6) and Verse Sixteen (Alexander 1890: 96) in a peculiar adaptation of a paraphrase by Pauthier; quotations by the German Theosophist Wilhelm Hübbe-Schleiden (1846–1916) in the February 1891 (Verse Thirty-Three) and March 1892 (a portion of Verse Seventy-Eight) issues of his journal *Sphinx* in which he cites von Plänckner's rendering (Hübbe-Schleiden 1891: 128; 1892: 96); an article by the American Theosophist Jerome A. Anderson (1847–1903) in the May issue of his journal *The New Californian* (Anderson 1892: 329) (made available to European readers through a reprint in *Theosophical Siftings* the same year) where he quotes parts of Verses Forty-Nine and Sixty-Three according to Chalmers; or an earlier article by the Vice-President of the Oakland Lodge Marie A. Walsh in the same journal's November 1891 issue (Walsh 1891: 187) where again Chalmers is used when quoting Verses Seven and Twenty-Two.

27 On Bjerregaard, see the chapter by Johan Nilsson in this volume.
28 Bjerregaard drawing on the Chalmers translation of Verse Fifteen: 'The skilful philosophers that were in the olden time had a mystic communication with the abyss' (Chalmers 1868: 10).
29 Bjerregaard generally replaces Chalmers's 'Tau' with 'Tao'.
30 In doing so, Bjerregaard accidentally adds two different versions of one sentence.
31 Regarding the supposedly exoteric teaching of the *Daodejing*, Bjerregaard, in the same vein, brings together jumbled portions of the Chalmers and Balfour translations with his occasional own interventions in terms of style: Verse Four (Chalmers/Balfour); Verse Six (Chalmers); Verse Twenty-Five (Chalmers and little bit Balfour); Verse Thirty (Chalmers/Balfour); Verses Thirty-One and Thirty-Two (modifications of Balfour); Thirty-Four (Chalmers with slight adaptions); Thirty-Five (Chalmers and a tad Balfour); Thirty-Seven (Balfour/Chalmers, partly

intermingled); Thirty-Eight (Chalmers); Forty-Two (Balfour); Forty-Six (modified Chalmers); Forty-Seven, Forty-Eight, Fifty-One, Fifty-Five and Sixty-Two (all Chalmers); Sixty-Three (modified Chalmers); Seventy-Three and Eighty-One (once again Chalmers). Eventually, Bjerregaard adds another selected collection of statements under the heading 'Moral aspect and uses of Tao', taken from Verses Twenty and Twenty-One (Chalmers), Twenty-Three (modified Chalmers), Twenty-Four, Thirty-Eight, Forty-One and Fifty-Two (Chalmers, adding an alternative translation from the Balfour version to the latter verse), Fifty-Seven (modified Chalmers), Fifty-Nine (mixing Balfour and Chalmers) and Sixty-Five (Chalmers).

32 Reprinted in her seminal *The Ancient Wisdom* (Besant 1897).
33 Besant uses Legge's translation of 1891.
34 Besant invokes Blavatsky's root race theory (see Lubelsky 2013).
35 Besant was indubitably aware of Old's rendition but most likely shied away from using it due to their enmity as a result of the Judge affair.
36 The fifth feature ('v. His evolution by repeated incarnations, into which he is drawn by desire and from which he is set free by knowledge and sacrifice, becoming divine in potency as he had ever been divine in latency') she discovers partly in *Daodejing* Verse One and partly (among others) in the *Zhuangzi*.
37 New facsimiled editions are circulating since 2010.
38 Notably, even some subsequent German translations of the *Daodejing* were informed by that of Hartmann.

References

Abel-Rémusat, J.-P. (1823), *Mémoire sur la vie et les opinions de Lao-tseu, philosophe chinois du VI.e siècle avant notre ère*, Paris: Imprimerie Royale.
Alexander, G. G. (1890), *Confucius, the Great Teacher: A Study*, London: Kegan, Paul, Trench, Trübner & Co.
Alexander, G. G. (1895), *Lâo-Tzse: The Great Thinker. With a Translation of His Thoughts on the Nature and Manifestations of God*, London: Kegan, Paul, Trench, Trübner & Co.
Amaravella (1889a), 'Remarks on the Above by a Sinologist', *Lucifer*, 4 (20): 145–8.
Amaravella (1889b), 'The Mahatmas through the Ages', *Lucifer*, 3 (17): 372.
Anderson, J. A. (1892), 'The World's Crucified Saviours', *The New Californian*, 1 (11): 321–9.
Anonymous (1881), 'The Religions of Japan. "Sadasad vikaram na sahate"', *The Theosophist*, 3 (1): 8–10.
Anonymous (1894), 'Theosophy in All Lands. India', *The Theosophist*, 15 (7): 462–3.
Anonymous (1895), 'De Godsdiensten der Japanners', *Theosophia*, 3 (34): 494–6.

Balfour, F. H. (1881), *The Divine Classic of Nan-Hua; Being the Works of Chuang Tsze, Taoist Philosopher. With an Excursus, and Copious Annotations in English and Chinese*, Shanghai: Kelly & Walsh and London: Trübner & Co.

Balfour, F. H. (1884), *Taoist Texts: Ethical, Political and Speculative*, London: Trübner & Co.

Balfour, F. H. (1892), 'Taoism', in South Place Institute (ed.), *Religious Systems of the World: A Contribution to the Study of Comparative Religion*, 3rd edn, 76–91, London: Swan Sonnenschein & Co and New York: Macmillan & Co.

Besant, A. (1896a), 'The Unity Underlying All Religions', *Lucifer*, 18 (107): 404–15.

Besant, A. (1896b), 'The Unity Underlying All Religions', *Lucifer*, 18 (108): 482–94.

Besant, A. (1897), *The Ancient Wisdom: An Outline of Theosophical Teachings*, London: Theosophical Publishing Society.

Bjerregaard, C. H. A. (1887), 'The Historic Position and Value of Neo-Platonism, &c.', *The Platonist*, 3 (1): 36–8.

Bjerregaard, C. H. A. (1895), 'Tao the Chinese "Being"', *The Metaphysical Magazine*, 1 (5): 410–21.

Bjerregaard, C. H. A. (1912), *The Inner Life of the Tao-Teh-King*, New York: The Theosophical Publishing Co. of New York.

Blavatsky, H. P. (1877), *Isis Unveiled: A Master-Key to the Mysteries of Ancient and Modern Science and Theology*, New York: J. W. Bouton.

Blavatsky, H. P. (1885a), 'A Bewitched Life. (As Narrated by the Voice of a Quill-Pen)', *The Theosophist*, 6 (11): 265–8.

Blavatsky, H. P. (1885b), 'A Bewitched Life. (As Narrated by the Voice of a Quill-Pen)', *The Theosophist*, 6 (12): 281–5.

Blavatsky, H. P. (1888a), *The Secret Doctrine: The Synthesis of Science, Religion, and Philosophy, Volume 1. Cosmogenesis*, London: The Theosophical Publishing Company.

Blavatsky, H. P. (1888b), *The Secret Doctrine: The Synthesis of Science, Religion, and Philosophy, Volume 2. Anthropogenesis*, London: The Theosophical Publishing Company.

Blavatsky, H. P. (1889), *The Key to Theosophy, Being a Clear Exposition, in the Form of Question and Answer, of the Ethics, Science, and Philosophy for the Study of which the Theosophical Society has been Founded*, London: The Theosophical Publishing Company.

Blavatsky, H. P. (1890), *Gems from the East: A Birthday Book of Precepts and Axioms*, London: The Theosophical Publishing Society.

Blavatsky, H. P. (1892), *The Theosophical Glossary*, London: The Theosophical Publishing Society.

Blavatsky, H. P. (1893), 'Inleiding tot de Geheime Leer', *Theosophia*, 2 (16): 206–7.

Blavatsky, H. P. and A. Besant, eds (1891), *Lucifer*, 7 (41): 353–440.

Blok, J. A. (1910), *Tao Teh King van Lao Tse in het hollandsch overgebracht*, Amsterdam: Theosofische Uitgevers-Maatschappy.

Brooks, R. W. (2001), 'The Theosophy of the Tao Te Ching', *Quest*, 89 (1): 18–21.
Chalmers, J. (1868), *Tau Tĕh King. The Speculations on Metaphysics, Polity, and Morality of "The Old Philosopher" Lau-tsze. Translated from the Chinese with and Introduction*, London: Trübner & Co.
Cleather, A. L. (1892), 'Correspondence: Theosophy in Western Lands', *The Theosophist*, 13 (11): 701–4.
Coulomb, E.-J. (Amaravella) (1892), *Le Secret de l'Absolu*, Paris: Société Théosophique.
Countess of Caithness (1887), *The Mystery of the Ages, Contained in the Secret Doctrine of All Religions*, 2nd edn, London: C. L. H. Wallace.
Čupr, F. (1878), *Tao-Tĕ-King. Cesta k Bohu a ctnosti. Staročinská kniha náboženská*, Praze: A. Urbánka.
de Bazán y Caravantes, A. (1870), *Lao-tseu-tao-te-king. Libro de la vía eterna y de la virtud*, Mexico: Imprenta del Gobierno.
de Groot, J. J. M. (1886), *Les fêtes annuellement célébrées à Émoui (Amoy). Étude concernant la religion populaire des chinois*, Paris: Ernest Leroux.
de Harlez, C. (1891), *Textes Tâoïstes. Traduit des originaux chinois et commentés*, Paris: Ernest Leroux.
de Pouvourville, A. (1894), 'Le Tao de Laotseu. Traduction exacte', *La Haute Science*, 1: 7–32; 258–70, 361–72; 385–95.
de Rosny, L. (1892), *Le Taoïsme*, Paris : Ernest Leroux.
Edge, S. V. (1893), 'Our Magazines and Publications', *The Theosophist*, 14 (4): 242–3.
Farnell, K. (1998), *The Astral Tramp: A Biography of the Astrologer Sepharial*, London: Ascella Publications.
Fullerton, A. (1894), 'Literary Notes', *The Path*, 9 (3): 100–2.
Giles, H. A. (1886), 'The Remains of Lao Tzŭ: Retranslated', *China Mail*, 14: 231–80.
Giles, H. A. (1889), *Chuang Tzu: Mystic, Moralist, and Social Reformer*, translated from the Chinese, London: Bernard Quaritch.
Godwin, J. (1989), *The Beginnings of Theosophy in France*, London: Theosophical History Centre.
Hartmann, F. (1896a), 'Theosophie in China. Betrachtungen über das TAO-TEH-KING. (Der Weg, die Wahrheit und das Licht.) Aus dem Chinesischen des Lao-tze', *Lotusblüten*, 8 (46): 467–84.
Hartmann, F. (1896b), 'Theosophie in China. Betrachtungen über das TAO-TEH-KING. (Der Weg, die Wahrheit und das Licht.) Aus dem Chinesischen des Lao-tze', *Lotusblüten*, 8 (47): 547–68.
Hartmann, F. (1896c), 'Theosophie in China. Betrachtungen über das TAO-TEH-KING. (Der Weg, die Wahrheit und das Licht.) Aus dem Chinesischen des Lao-tze', *Lotusblüten*, 8 (48): 633–45.
Hartmann, F. (1896d), 'Theosophie in China. Betrachtungen über das TAO-TEH-KING. (Der Weg, die Wahrheit und das Licht.) Aus dem Chinesischen des Lao-tze', *Lotusblüten*, 8 (49): 726–43.

Hartmann, F. (1896e), 'Theosophie in China. Betrachtungen über das TAO-TEH-KING. (Der Weg, die Wahrheit und das Licht.) Aus dem Chinesischen des Lao-tze', *Lotusblüten*, 8 (50): 800–19.

Hartmann, F. (1896f), 'Theosophie in China. Betrachtungen über das TAO-TEH-KING. (Der Weg, die Wahrheit und das Licht.) Aus dem Chinesischen des Lao-tze', *Lotusblüten*, 8 (51): 892–914.

Hartmann, F. (1897a), 'Theosophie in China. Betrachtungen über das TAO-TEH-KING. (Der Weg, die Wahrheit und das Licht.) Aus dem Chinesischen des Lao-tze', *Lotusblüten*, 9 (52): 33–50.

Hartmann, F. (1897b), 'Theosophie in China. Betrachtungen über das TAO-TEH-KING. (Der Weg, die Wahrheit und das Licht.) Aus dem Chinesischen des Lao-tze', *Lotusblüten*, 9 (53): 139–48.

Hartmann, F. (1897c), *Theosophie in China. Betrachtungen über das Tao-Teh-King (Der Weg, die Wahrheit und das Licht). Aus dem Chinesischen des Lao-tze übersetzt*, Leipzig: Verlag von Wilhelm Friedrich.

Hübbe-Schleiden, W., ed. (1891), *Sphinx. Monatschrift für die geschichtliche und experimentale Begründung der übersinnlichen Weltanschauung auf monistischer Grundlage*, 11 (62): 65–128.

Hübbe-Schleiden, W., ed. (1892), *Sphinx. Monatschrift für die geschichtliche und experimentale Begründung der übersinnlichen Weltanschauung auf monistischer Grundlage*, 13 (73): 1–96.

Indian Section of the Theosophical Society (1893), *Theosophical Gleanings: Notes on 'The Secret Doctrine'*, Madras: Thompson and Co.

Judge, W. Q., ed. (1894a), *The Path*, 8 (12): 369–400.

Judge, W. Q., ed. (1894b), *The Path*, 9 (9): 265–96.

Julien, S. (1842), *Lao Tseu Tao Te King. Le livre de la voie et de la vertu. Composé dans le VIe siècle avant l'ère chrétienne. Par le philosophe Lao-Tseu; traduit en français, et publié avec le texte chinois et un commentaire perpétuel*, Paris: Imprimerie Royale.

Kenealy, E. V. (1866), *The Book of God: The Apocalypse of Adam-Oannes*, London: Reeves & Turner.

Конисси Д. П. (1894), *Тао те кингъ. Лаоси*, Москва: типо-лит. т-ва И.Н. Кушнерев и К.

Legge, J. (1883), 'The Tâo Teh King', *The British Quarterly Review*, 78 (155): 74–107.

Legge, J. (1891), *The Sacred Books of China: The Texts of Tâoism, Part I. The Tâo Teh King. The Writings of Kwang-dze Book I–XVII*, Oxford: Clarendon Press.

Lubelsky, I. (2013), 'Mythological and Real Racial Issues in Theosophy', in O. Hammer and M. Rothstein (eds), *Handbook of the Theosophical Current*, 335–55, Leiden: Brill.

Luxâme (1896), 'Sur l'arbre Bodhi. Théosophe et théosophiste, théosophie et théosophisme', *Le lotus bleu: Revue theosophique mensuelle*, 7 (10): 393–7.

Mackintosh, C. H. (1926), *Tao: A Rendering into English Verse of the Tao Teh Ching of Lao Tsze (B.C. 604)*, Chicago: Theosophical Press.

Masot, S. (1889), 'Tao-Te-King de Yan-Tsu', *El correo Sino-Annamita ó correspondencia de las misiones del sagrado órden de predicadores en Formosa, China, Tung-king y Filipinas*, Manila: Real Colegio de Sto. Tomas, 23: 100–58.

Mead, G. R. S. (1892a), 'The World-Soul', *Lucifer*, 10 (55): 24–34.

Mead, G. R. S. (1892b), 'The World-Soul', *Lucifer*, 10 (56): 118–27.

Mead, G. R. S. (1893), 'Notes on Nirvana', *Lucifer*, 12 (67): 9–16.

Mead, G. R. S. (1895), *The World-Mystery: Four Essays*, London: Theosophical Publishing Society.

Mears, I. (1916), *Tao Teh King by Lao Tzŭ: A Tentative Translation from the Chinese*, Glasgow: William McLellan & Co.

Mears, I. (1922), *Tao Teh King by Lao Tzŭ: A Tentative Translation from the Chinese*, London: Theosophical Publishing House.

Medhurst, C. S. (1905), *The Tao Teh King: A Short Study in Comparative Religion*, Chicago: Theosophical Book Concern.

Müller, F. M. (1873), *Introduction to the Science of Religion. Four Lectures Delivered at the Royal Institution, with Two Essay. False Analogies, and The Philosophy of Mythology*, London: Longmans, Green, and Co.

Niemand, J. (1895), 'Letter to a Lodge', *The Irish Theosophist*, 3 (9): 149–52.

Noak, F. W. (1888), *Taòtekking von Laòtsee. Aus dem Chinesischen*, Berlin: Carl Duncker's Verlag.

Olcott, H. S. (1894), 'The Book of the Path of Virtue', *The Theosophist*, 15 (8): 521.

Old, W. R. (1891), *What is Theosophy? A Handbook for Enquirers into the Wisdom-Religion; Being an Outline of Theosophical Teaching Relating to Man and the Universe, Occultism, etc.*, London: Hay Nisbet & Co.

Old, W. R. (1892), 'Tao', *Lucifer*, 11 (63): 204–14.

Old, W. R. (1894), *The Book of the Path of Virtue or A Version of the Tao-Teh-King of Lao-tze, the Chinese Mystic and Philosopher: with an Introduction & Essay on the Tao as Presented in the Writings of Chuang-tze, The Apostle of the Tao-Tze*, Madras: The Indian Section of the Theosophical Society.

Old, W. R. (1904), *The Book of the Simple Way of Laotze. The Contemporary of Confucius, China, B.C. 604: A New Translation from the Text of the Tao-Teh-King with Introduction and Commentary*, London: Philip Wellby.

Pauthier, G. (1838), *Tao-te-King, ou le Livre révéré de la Raison suprême et de la Vertu, par Lao-Tseu; traduit en français et publié pour la première fois en Europe, avec une version latine et le texte chinois en regard, accompagné du commentaire complet de Sie-Hoëï, d'origine occidentale, et de notes tirées de divers autres commentateurs chinois*, Paris: F. Didot/Leipzig: Brockhaus et Avenarius.

Pauthier, G. (1839), *Chine ou description historique, géographique et littéraire de ce vaste empire, d'après des documents chinois. Première partie, comprenant un résumé de l'histoire et de la civilisation chinoises depuis les temps les plus anciens jusqu'à nos jours*, Paris: Firmin Didot Frères.

Russell, G. W. (1894), 'Notes about Books', *The Irish Theosophist*, 2 (9): 134–6.

T. (1894), 'Theosophical and Mystic Publications', *Lucifer*, 14 (79): 85–8.

Theosofische Vereeniging, ed. (1897), *Theosophia*, 5 (12): 213–32.

Tiele, C. P. (1877), *Outlines of the History of Religion to the Spread of the Universal Religions*, translated by J. E. Carpenter, Boston: James R. Osgood and Company.

Tsăng, C. Y. (1893), 'Some Modern Failings', *Lucifer*, 13 (74): 97–100.

Tsang, C.-Y. (1894), 'Eenige verkeerde opvattingen van den modernen tijd', *Theosophia*, 2 (21): 274–7.

Tsăng, C. Y. (1895), 'Our Overwhelming Virtues', *The Path*, 9 (10): 304–6.

van Manen, J. (1898), 'Tao Te King. Een Nederlandsche benadering', *Theosophia*, 7 (2): 25–8.

von Collani, C. (2015), 'The Manuscript of the Daodejing in the British Library', in L. W. Wong and B. Fuehrer (eds), *Sinologists as Translators in the Seventeenth to Nineteenth Centuries*, 39–86, Hong Kong: The Chinese University Press.

von Plaenckner, R. (1870), *Lao-Tse Táo-Tĕ-King. Der Weg zur Tugend. Aus dem Chinesischen übersetzt und erklärt*, Leipzig: F. A. Brockhaus.

von Strauss, V. (1870), *Laò-Tsè's Taò Tĕ Kīng. Aus dem Chinesischen ins Deutsche übersetzt, eingeleitet und commentirt*, Leipzig: Verlag von Friedrich Fleischer.

Walf, K. (1999), 'Christian Theologoumena in Western Translations of the Daoists', in I. Eber, S.-K. Wan and K. Walf (eds), *Bible in Modern China: The Literary and Intellectual Impact*, 123–34, Sankt Augustin: Monumenta Serica.

Walsh, M. A. (1891), 'The Children's Hour', *The New Californian*, 1 (6): 184–8.

Walters, W. J., ed. (1894), *Mercury*, 1 (3): 29–44.

Zhang, C. and P. Xien (2022), 'Challenge and Revolution: An Analysis of Stanislas Julien's Translation of the Daodejing', *Religions*, 13 (8): 1–13.

4

The Daoist who wasn't

Albert de Pouvourville, Matgioi, Nguyễn Văn Cang and the problem of Indochinese masters in *fin de siècle* occultism

Davide Marino

Introduction

This chapter is about three people and their names. Describing the first of them, Eugène-Albert Puyou de Pouvourville (1861–1939), would require a book-length study.[1] De Pouvourville, almost unknown today, was a prominent figure of French *fin de siècle* intellectual life. Born into an aristocratic military family, he received an elite education. In his youth, de Pouvourville developed a keen interest in Asian culture and occultism and, in 1887, he decided to leave France and partake in three military missions in French Indochina, the modern-day Vietnam (Laurant 1982). It is in this context that de Pouvourville met the two other protagonists of this story: Nguyễn Văn Luật 阮文律 (*c*.1850–1930) and his younger son, Nguyễn Văn Cang 阮文亢 (*c*.1870–?).

According to de Pouvourville's later accounts, Văn Luật had been his master and taught him the foundations of Daoism while his son was serving in de Pouvourville's regiment as his personal assistant. It is commonly believed that after his resignation from the army (1892), de Pouvourville returned to France and, together with Nguyễn Văn Cang, participated in the Parisian Occultist milieu, where he illustrated to the French public the heights of 'Far-Eastern metaphysics'. In this chapter, I intend to look closely at the interaction between these three figures. On the one side, there is the esotericist/adventurer de Pouvourville, with his spiritual thirst and his fascination for the exotic Orient. On the other side, there are the two 'real Orientals', who are said to have cooperated with de Pouvourville's depiction of Asian religion.

The agency of Asian believers in the European esoteric discourse is a theme of utmost importance in the current debate about the qualifier 'Western' in Western esotericism (Strube 2021; Granholm 2013; Pasi 2010). The outcomes of this chapter illustrate a result of the encounter between 'Western' and 'Eastern' esotericism but, evidently, they only represent one of the possible trajectories of such interaction. Against the scholarly consensus, my analysis will conclude that Văn Cang was never in France and that almost certainly, all the texts published under his authorship were instead written by de Pouvourville himself.

The encounter with the master

Non hic piscis omnium. Placed in a cartouche under a portrait of a seductive siren,[2] this motto introduced to the *fin de siècle* French audience the esoteric journal *La Haute Science* (High Science). The Latin frontispiece (literally, 'this fish is not for everyone') set the tone for the publication. As indicated by its cover art, *La Haute Science* was not intended for the general public but targeted a cultivated readership with an interest in occult themes. The proponents of *La Haute Science* intended to maintain a high scholarly profile and wished to differentiate themselves from the 'occultism-spectacle' (Laurant 1982) centred on paranormal phenomena and extraordinary experiences. Over the course of its existence (between 1893 and 1894), *La Haute Science* offered to its readers French translations of classics of the esoteric tradition, such as the *Zohar*, the *Upanishads*, Porphyry's *De Antro Nympharum* and Agrippa's *De Occulta Philosophia*.

It is within this project that, in the 1894 January issue, we can find an 'exact translation' of the 'Tao de Laotseu', intended as a translation of the first part of the *Daodejing* 道德經.[3] The author of this 'exact translation' was an important occultist of his time, Albert de Pouvourville (better known by his Vietnamese *nom de plume* 'Matgioi').[4] Presenting his work, de Pouvourville informed the reader that someone else had helped him with 'the interpretation of the ideographic characters'. His collaborator is identified as 'the Xuat Doi Nguyen Van Hi, younger son of Doctor Ng. The Duc, Luat, Tongsang[5] of the Rite of Laotseu' (de Pouvourville 1894a: 10). In the same year, de Pouvourville's translation was republished in two separate volumes by *La Haute Science*'s publisher, the Parisian *Librairie de l'art indépendent*, inaugurating a collection of religious texts of the Far East, titled *L'esprit des races jaunes* (The Spirit of the Yellow Races). On this occasion, de Pouvourville corrected the name of his assistant, now indicated as 'Nguyen Van Cang, Hi' (de Pouvourville 1894b: i). The collaboration between these two authors continued with the publication of another 'exact translation', that of *Le Traité des Influences Errantes*[6] (The Treatise on Wandering Influences, 1896a).

In order to know more about de Pouvourville's mysterious helper, French readers had to wait over ten years. In 1904, de Pouvourville began a new publication, *La Voie* (The Path), which was intended as a sort of spiritual successor to *La Haute Science* and was especially remarkable for its emphasis on East Asian religions (the title of the journal is meant as a translation of the Chinese term *dao* 道). In the May 1904 issue, the editor's note announced:

> We are pleased to inform our readers that we were able to obtain the direct collaboration of Far-Eastern *literati*, who, knowing how to remain cautious, have no reason to remain anonymous. The first is the *xuâtdoï*, Nguyen van Cang, younger son of the *thay-thuoc*[7] Nguyen The Duc Luat, Tongsang of the Laotseu school. Luat, who occupies a high rank in the Daoist hierarchy and important functions in the scholarly caste, is one of the five *tiensi*[8] of southern China. It was Luat and his son Cang, in the house of the latter, who powerfully helped Matgioi in the only esoteric translation that exists of the three great Daoist texts ... which once appeared in *La Haute Science*.

This introduction marked the beginning of Nguyễn Văn Cang's contributions to *La Voie*, which consisted of ten articles dating from May 1904 to February 1906, most of them falling under one of two categories: *Correspondance d'Extrême-Orient* (Correspondence from the Far East) and *Lettre de Chine* (Letter from China).

The presentation of Văn Cang is extremely interesting. First of all, we understand that Văn Cang and his father were two religious savants of 'southern China'. Second, we learn that the two Vietnamese and de Pouvourville/Matgioi had entertained a personal relationship that culminated in the translations of the Daoist Classics that appeared in *La Haute Science*. Lastly, we know that Văn Cang was a 'xuatdoi', a Vietnamese word that may indicate, in a military context, the rank of sergeant.[9]

The representation of Văn Cang as a Vietnamese soldier is confirmed by what we know about de Pouvourville's life. Born in Nancy, de Pouvourville decided to abandon his rank in the French Army and to enrol as a simple soldier in the Foreign Legion. In 1887, he was sent to French Indochina as a soldier in the context of France's colonial wars (Laurant 1982). De Pouvourville spent most of the years between 1887 and 1892 in Tonkin (modern Northern Vietnam) with various military and administrative duties. There, in 1890, he had undertaken the role of second-class inspector of *La Garde Civile Indigène* (the Indigenous Civil Guard), a paramilitary organization that recruited the local population who served as local auxiliaries for the police under the commanded of a French officer (Rivers and Deroo 1999). It was during his term as second-class inspector of the Civil Guard that de Pouvourville met Nguyễn Văn Cang.

Two independent sources confirm this version of the event. The first is visual: there are two photographs (probably taken in 1891) in which Văn Cang stands next to de Pouvourville in uniform (Laurant 1982: 36–7). In both pictures the uniforms confirm the common service in the Indigenous Civil Guard and allow us to guess Văn Cang's age. Considering that de Pouvourville was around thirty years old at the time, Văn Cang looks considerably younger, surely not older than twenty.

A second record, which was found in de Pouvourville's archive after his death, further testifies to the relationship between Văn Cang, his father and de Pouvourville and provides some additional details about his identity. This document, signed by Nguyễn Văn Luật (Văn Cang's father), is a type of certificate that attests that his son moved from the division where he was previously serving[10] to a safer post in the Indigenous Civil Guard commanded by de Pouvourville. Due to this document, we know that Nguyễn Văn Cang was originally from Huyện Phúc Thọ, a village near the French posts in the 'soldier town' of Sơn Tây, not far from Hà Nội. This is the full translation of the document:

> Nguyễn Văn Cang is from Huyện Phúc Thọ, Phủ Quảng Oai, Tỉnh Sơn Tây.[11] He was originally a conscripted soldier in the Third Regiment. Between 1886 and 1889, he served as a *Lính tập*.[12] He was fortunate enough to be accepted by the Second-Class Inspector [i.e., de Pouvourville] and became his subordinate. It is better that you, Nguyễn Văn Cang, treat others as parents and brothers and stay peaceful in mind and calm in temper.
>
> Noted by his father, Nguyễn Văn Luật.[13]

A last source of information about Nguyễn Văn Cang is de Pouvourville's novel *Le maître des sentences* (The Master of Maxims). The 'master' mentioned in the title is a literary version of Nguyễn Văn Cang's father, 'Nguyen Luat, also known as the Masters of Maxims' (de Pouvourville 1899: 95). The protagonist of *Le maître des sentences*, Jacques Ayriès, 'a soldier of fortune, enrolled in the Foreign Legion, [who] left for Tonkin' to escape the 'Lorraine melancholy' (de Pouvourville 1899: 31) is clearly based on de Pouvourville himself. In the novel, Ayriès befriends Nguyễn Văn Luật and 'his youngest son, Thang, a former sergeant in the *Tirailleurs*' (de Pouvourville 1899: 105). Thang spoke enough French to become Ayriès's interpreter and he is described as 'well-educated, a knowledgeable clerk, and a fine horseman' (de Pouvourville 1899: 112). In the novel, Thang helps the French soldier 'to understand the Yellows and to live without boredom in loneliness' (de Pouvourville 1899: 105). Thus, it seems safe to say that the character of Nguyen Van Thang was based on the real Nguyễn Văn Cang that de Pouvourville had met during his sojourn in Tonkin.[14] Although written in literary form, *Le maître des sentences* is the most comprehensive of our sources. De Pouvourville's portrait of a young Vietnamese cavalryman, son of a local healer, who enlisted in the French army and was later the personal assistant and friend of a French colonial administrator matches with what the available primary sources say about Nguyễn Văn Cang.

Le maître des sentences contains a lot of information about Văn Cang (including that he was 'well-educated') but it does not say much about his ideas.[15]

The teachings of the master

As noted earlier, Văn Cang was active in French occultism in two ways: his contribution to de Pouvourville's translation of Chinese texts and the series of articles published in *La Voie*. Here, I will focus my attention on the texts published under Văn Cang's sole authorship, that is, his articles for *La Voie*[16] written between 1904 and 1906. Despite the fact that Văn Cang was introduced to his readers as an 'Indo-Chinese *literatus*', most of his texts do not deal with Southeast Asian topics. Instead, they indulge in many theories about Tibet and its religion that draw primarily on nineteenth century European sources.

The cradle of humanity

The first of Văn Cang's articles for *La Voie*, a short text titled *Signe de reconnaissance des sociétés secrètes chinoises* (The Sign of Recognition of Chinese Secret Societies), is the kind of contribution that one might expect to read from a Daoist initiate. Therein, Văn Cang discusses the signs of recognition of the members of the '*Thien dianhien* (literally: Heaven-Earth-Man)[17] which, in Western translations, is indifferently called the Society of the True or the Triad' (Van Cang 1904a: 174). According to Văn Cang, at the moment of their initiation, the members of this society received a triangle-shaped token made of bamboo paper that contained the maxims of the organization[18] and the 'identification number of the adept'.

Given the nature of the informant – that is, by a member of a 'Chinese' secret society[19] – one can be inclined to take Văn Cang's description at face value.

It is difficult to maintain this same trust in Văn Cang's role of an insider with regard to the second of his contributions, *Le berceau de l'humanité* (The Cradle of Humanity). One of the three-part series entitled *Correspondance d'Extrême-Orient*, this article is the first instance of Văn Cang discussing Tibetan matters. In particular, Văn Cang affirmed that a very advanced ancient civilization had existed centred around 'the Tchertchen oasis, in the north of the Viceroyalty of Tibet'. (Van Cang 1904b: 567). Some 'curious Tibetan students' decided to carry out excavations where this civilization had ceased to exist some 3,000 years ago and they found 'more than three thousand almost entire skeletons of human beings, who belonged to the races that populated these cities' (Van Cang 1904b: 567). According to Văn Cang, when the Dalai Lama was informed of such a discovery, he decided to forbid further digging.

One may wonder how our Vietnamese author could acquire such secret information about this remote region of Asia. Văn Cang affirmed that in the Tchertchen oasis 'several of my relatives received a Russian explorer, General Prjevalsky'. Nikolay Mikhaylovich Prjevalsky (1839–88) was a renowned Russian explorer who entered northern Tibet during one of his expeditions (Rayfield 1976) and, if we are to believe Văn Cang's account, he was received there by some members of the Nguyễn family.

It should be noted that this was not the first time that Prjevalsky and his adventures were mentioned by an occultist author. Sixteen years before Văn Cang's article, Helena Petrovna Blavatsky (1831–91) had published her monumental *The Secret Doctrine*, in which, discussing the possibility of now forgotten ancient civilizations, she had written that (Blavatsky 1888: xxxiii):

> the oasis of Tchertchen . . . is surrounded with the ruins of archaic towns and cities in every direction. There, some 3,000 human beings represent the relics of about a hundred extinct nations and races, the very names of which are now unknown to our ethnologists.

Blavatsky did not claim to have obtained this information from Tibetan relatives. More modestly, she appealed to a public lecture held by 'The Russian traveller, Colonel (now General) Prjevalsky' who 'found quite close to the oasis of Tchertchen, the ruins of two enormous cities, the oldest of which was, according to local tradition, ruined 3,000 years ago' (Blavatsky 1888: xxxiv). This passage contains the essence of Văn Cang's 1904 article. There is such a similarity between the two texts that one may conclude that, despite our

Vietnamese author's alleged familial ties in Tibet, in order to write his *Berceau de l'Humanité* he could have simply relied on the hugely influential *Secret Doctrine*.

The Dalai Lama and his palace

Văn Cang's discussion of Tibetan religion would continue in the following months with two more articles, *Le Palais du Dalé-Lama* (The Dalai Lama's Palace) and *Le Dalé-Lama* (The Dalai Lama). The occasion for these contributions was the occupation of Tibet by the (British) Indian Army, led by Colonel Sir Francis Edward Younghusband (1863–1942). The event was remarkable since it was the first time that a European military had occupied the proverbially inaccessible Lhasa. Even more dramatically, upon the arrival of the British troops, the thirteenth Dalai Lama Thubten Gyatso (1876–1933) had fled to Urga (modern Ulan Bator, Mongolia), and these events 'aroused much sadness and anguish among those who thought that Tibet had been forced to conclude a disadvantageous treaty and that the invisibility of the sacred person of the Dalai Lama had been violated' (Van Cang 1904d: 271). Văn Cang reassured all people concerned about the Dalai Lama by claiming that (Van Cang 1904c: 177):

> the Dalai-Lama's residence [is] known to very few people; pilgrims from all nations who make the journey to Lhasa are not allowed inside; and not even the English conquerors, these pilgrims of a new kind, dared to enter it.

In order to deny the success of the British invasion, Văn Cang fabulously described the powers of the Dalai Lama by insisting that (Van Cang 1904c: 272):

> the person of the Dalai Lama appears only on the floor of the Great Sacred Palace of Buddha-La, when the twelve great Nomekhans are gathered there under certain conditions . . . The presence of another man, whoever he may be, would be enough for the Dalai Lama not to appear. And there is more than a material impossibility of profaning the presence of the Dalai Lama. He cannot be where his enemies or simple strangers are.

As we will see, this passage impressed the young esotericist René Guénon (1886–1951),[20] who applied this theory about the Dalai Lama's intangibility to the 1910 Chinese invasion of Tibet.[21] On that occasion, Guénon quoted the following conclusion of Văn Cang's *Correspondance* (Van Cang 1904d: 179):

> the Pope of the East, as the believers of the Pope of the West say,[22] is not one of those who can be despoiled or coerced, for he is not here under human power or control.

Even more remarkably, Guénon agreed with Văn Cang, who had argued that the Dalai Lama

> is always the same, today as on that rather distant day, when he revealed himself to that prophetic Lama, whom the Tibetans call Issa, and whom the Christians call Jesus. (Van Cang 1904d: 272)

This unusual designation further testifies to Văn Cang's familiarity with *fin de siècle* French occult literature. In fact, the story of a 'Saint Issa' circulated widely after the publication of a famous and controversial book, *La vie inconnue de Jésus-Christ* (The Unknown Life of Jesus Christ), which was published in 1894. The author of this volume was a Russian journalist, Nicholas Notovitch (1858–1916), who claimed he had found documents in a Tibetan Buddhist monastery that described Jesus's life in India. In the scrolls allegedly discovered by Notovitch, when Jesus

> had reached the age of thirteen, the age when an Israelite must take a wife ... he secretly left his father's house, left Jerusalem and, with merchants, headed for Sindh in order to perfect himself in the divine word and to study the laws of the great Buddhas. (Notovitch 1894: 89)

According to this account, Jesus/Issa had travelled to Kashmir and Tibet, where he mastered the Buddhist Scriptures and performed miracles before returning to Palestine to end his career as an itinerant preacher (Rice 2017).

Despite having been received with skepticism by several European intellectuals (Joseph 2012),[23] Notovitch's book enjoyed major commercial success and was read widely in esoteric circles. The presence of the story of Saint Issa in Văn Cang's *Correspondance* proves (besides the persistence of the influence of *La vie inconnue* in the occult milieu) how 'Nguyễn Văn Cang' was well versed in the French literature of his time.

Letters from China

Tibet remained the focus of many of Văn Cang's articles after the end of his *Correspondance*. Between 1905 and 1906, his articles appeared under the title *Lettre de Chine*. In one of these letters, we find a polemic against those Asian religious figures who

> do not have the patience to reach the highest degree of Science; they gladly stop on the steps which are dazzling and advantageous; they spread through the cities and the countryside, less to gain followers than to amaze the people; and with

what they know of natural laws they make shows capable of enchanting the multitude, and above all of earning for themselves a living, and of making them live by travelling a lot and studying nothing. (Van Cang 1906: 89)

The article continues by informing us that in Tibet this type of spectacle was the exclusive prerogative of 'mediocre or undisciplined lamas' who were frowned upon by the 'higher masters', although 'sages do not stop these shows'.

Despite his disdain for such popular practices, Văn Cang illustrated to his readers some of these 'spiritual performances'. In particular, he reported two of the most profitable kinds of spectacle, 'the temporary burial, and the painless opening of the bowels'. *La Voie*'s readers are also informed about 'the exact text of the formula they pronounce just before their exhibition', known as 'Siéfa'. The formula reported in the article goes as follows:

> I know you, you know me; do, my elder friend, what I ask you . . . What is this for your great power? I know very well that what I am asking you is burdensome. But do it anyway because you will be paid for your effort, and you will have all that is due to you. (Van Cang 1906: 90)

Once more, this comprehensive information about minute details of Tibetan religious life can lead us to think that Văn Cang has had some insider knowledge. However, even in this case, it seems that all the information contained in Văn Cang's letter was already available to the French public.

Several decades before *La Voie*, in 1850, a Catholic missionary named Évariste Régis Huc (1813–60) published his *Souvenirs d'un voyage dans la Tartarie, le Thibet et la Chine* (Recollections of a Journey through Tartary, Thibet and China). This hefty publication (two volumes for a total of over 900 pages) was the report of Huc's mission to Tibet from 1844 to 1846. During his journey, Huc encountered the 'Sié-fa' mentioned by Văn Cang in 1906. The French missionary recalled having witnessed several of these bloody spectacles, including a Lama who 'slits open his stomach, in one long cut' (Huc 1850: 322).

Huc also remarked that the Lamas who were 'in the high ranks of the Lamaic hierarchy' disdained such spectacles, and he argued that those who partook in these rituals were 'low-rank Lamas, little esteemed by their comrades'. More strikingly, Huc reported the 'Siéfa formula' (Huc 1850: 324–5):

> I know you, you know me; Come old friend, come do what I ask of you. . . . what is that for your vast power! I know you charge dearly . . . but do what I ask you nevertheless. . . . One day we will come to a reckoning: on the appointed day you shall receive what is due.

The parallel between Văn Cang and Huc can also be shown by reading the last article about Tibet left out of our analysis, a text published in February 1905 entitled *Khaldan*. Khaldan is described as a city 'four leagues east of Lhasa' that hosted an important lamasery. The popularity of this site was due to the preaching of master Tsongkhapa, who established a temple there in 1409. After Tsongkhapa's death, the lamasery enjoyed an influx of new believers, attracted by the fame of the deceased master. Văn Cang informs us that, at the time of his article, 'fifteen thousand lamas are installed in the immense cloisters of Khaldan' (Van Cang 1905: 468).

As in his previous articles, Văn Cang embellished his account with a vivid description of Tibetan religious life. In particular, we are told that Tsongkhapa's body was still preserved in an underground tomb and, after 480 years, 'has remained fresh and incorruptible'. Over the centuries, this tomb became the object of veneration and frequent miracles:

> during the annual pilgrimage, this body becomes wonderful, dazzling and luminous: the lips move; emitting incomprehensible sounds, and sometimes, when the most numerous crowds surround Khaldan and prostrate themselves, the body of Tzong-Kaba leaves its bed, rises and remains in the air, with nothing visibly supporting it. (Van Cang 1905: 468)

This account, exactly as in the case discussed before, can be found in Huc's *Souvenirs*. In fact, Huc reported that Khaldan 'was founded in the year 1409 of our era, by the famous Tsong-Kaba' (Huc 1850: 236) and that, at the time of his Tibetan journey (1846), it 'contain[ed] nearly 15,000 Lamas'. Huc (1850: 238) also described that

> the Tibetans pretend that they still see his [Tsong-Kaba's] marvellous body there, fresh, incorruptible, sometimes speaking, and, by a permanent prodigy, always holding itself in the air without any support.

The textual analysis of Nguyễn Văn Cang's articles for *La Voie* clearly shows that, despite the alleged 'oriental' status of the author, they mainly rely on secondary sources, both orientalist (Huc) and esoteric (Notovitch, Blavatsky).

Accepting the master

Văn Cang's writings left a trace in the Parisian occultist milieu. As already mentioned, in 1910, from the pages of the new journal *La Gnose* (Gnosis), young Guénon quoted several excerpts of Văn Cang's writings for *La Voie* in his discussion of the Chinese invasion of Tibet and the subsequent flight of the Dalai Lama. Guénon denounced as 'fake news' both the invasion and the Dalai Lama's escape and, to support his claims, he resorted to a 'highly authoritative source', the *Correspondance d'Extrême-Orient* that Nguyễn Văn Cang had published a few years prior.

The fact that the soon-to-be-famous Guénon considered Văn Cang a reliable source of information on Asian religious matters would have an enormous influence on the subsequent discourse on the Vietnamese master. In fact, in the years following Guénon's article, Văn Cang's ideas remained authoritative in Traditionalist circles. In 1930, Marcelle Clavelle (1905–88) – one of Guénon's closest associates – appealed to Văn Cang's authority on the occasion of his review of Alexandra David-Néel's (1868–1969) book *Mystiques et magiciens du Thibet* (Mystics and Magicians of Tibet) (1929).[24] Clavelle showed some distrust about David-Néel's affirmation of having met the Dalai Lama in 1912 and, to counter her claim, he resorted to 'an eminent Chinese [*sic*] scholar, Nguyen Van Cang, *tongsang* of the Laotseu rite' who had written that the Dalai Lama 'cannot be where his enemies or simple strangers are' (Clavelle 1930: 208).

Văn Cang's name appeared again over two decades after Clavelle's review. The occasion was one of utmost importance: the first biography of Guénon, written by his closest friends. In fact, Guénon's sudden death in January 1951 had left many of his followers shocked and puzzled about the nature of his teaching. In this general confusion, Guénon's legacy was disputed by followers of different bents, and rumours began circulating among Traditionalist readers. In an attempt to rectify this situation, Paul Chacornac (1884–1964), the publisher and editor of the Guénonian journal *Études Traditionnelles* (Traditional Studies), began collecting biographical material which resulted in the publication of *La vie simple de René Guénon* (The Simple Life of René Guénon) – a sort of 'Traditionalist-authorized biography' of the great French esotericist. Discussing the origin of Guénon's expertise in Daoism, Chacornac (1958: 43) affirmed that

> with regard to Daoism, it seems plausible to formulate a conjecture. It seems that a preliminary knowledge of Far Eastern metaphysics reached Guénon through the channel of Matgioi, and it is possible to suppose that the oral teaching was imparted by the youngest son of the 'Master of Maxims', the tong-sang Luat, who lived in France for some time and who had collaborated in the translation of the Chinese texts.

In the following decades, authors who studied these events took Chacornac's conjecture at face value. For instance, one of the pioneers of the academic study of Traditionalism, Marie-France James (1981a), reported Chacornac's information about the French sojourn of 'the enigmatic Nguyen V. Cang', and insisted that 'the son of the Tong-Song [*sic*] Luat, passing through France, [helped with] the translation of Chinese texts' (James 1981b: 221). Laurant (1982: 91) argued that Guénon acquired his first rudiments of the Chinese language in the company of Nguyễn Văn Cang. Massimo Introvigne (2007: 304) repeated this information, affirming that 'Nguyen Van Cang, younger son of the Daoist initiator of Matgioi in Vietnam, the Master Nguyen Van Lu, who had become a French soldier, had come to France and even collaborated with journals of the esoteric milieu'. For Introvigne, Văn Cang's presence in Paris allowed Guénon to receive 'information (and an initiation) directly from this character, without passing through Matgioi' (2007: 304). Erik Sablé (2018: 29) also insisted that Guénon was 'introduced to Daoism through Nguyễn Văn Cang'. Similarly, David Gattegno (2001: 53) and Jean Robin (1978: 68) contended that 'the son of the "Master of Maxims", Nguyễn Văn Cang, stayed for a while in Paris' and Guénon's knowledge of Daoism came 'only through the intermediary of Tong-Sang Luat with whom we know he was acquainted'. A nice summary of this narrative about Nguyễn Văn Cang can be found in the 2010 issue of the journal *Péninsule* (Laurant 2010: 112):

> Nguyễn Văn Cang . . . [was] the son of the village chief, Nguyễn Văn Của.[25] Mat Gioi succeeded in bringing this twenty-year-old young man to France, and he became both Mat Gioi's and Guénon's informant. The latter in 1905-1906 was able to secure for himself one of the rare Vietnamese who frequented the Parisian social and occult circles of the time.

To sum up, it is possible to divide all the information about Văn Cang in three groups. First, the facts confirmed by direct sources, according to which Nguyễn Văn Cang was born in Vietnam, probably near modern-day Hanoi, around 1870. His father, Nguyễn Văn Luật, was a healer, a religious expert and probably some sort of community leader who cooperated with the occupying French army.[26] Being the youngest son, Văn Cang did not inherit his father's profession but was enlisted in the Third Regiment of Tonkinese Rifles in 1886. In the three years he served in this corps, the young Vietnamese soldier learned some French, at least to a level necessary to understand the orders of a French officer. In 1889 he left the army (he probably deserted)[27] and returned to his family's home. In 1890 Văn Cang (possibly through his father) met the second-class inspector of the Indigenous Civil Guard de Pouvourville. In fact, de Pouvourville was acquainted with Văn Cang's father Nguyễn Văn Luật. De Pouvourville and Văn

Cang befriended one another, and the latter decided (in 1891, with his father's blessing) to join the Civil Guard as de Pouvourville's assistant/translator.

In addition to these facts, a second set of information was provided by de Pouvourville who, however, is not always a reliable source. De Pouvourville argued that in the period he was serving as an official in the Civil Guard he had worked together with Văn Cang on a translation of the *Daodejing* and of the *Traité des influences errantes*, later published in the occultist journal *La Haute Science*. The collaboration between the two friends continued in the years 1906–8 when Văn Cang contributed to de Pouvourville's new editorial project *La Voie* with ten articles about 'Far-Eastern' themes. These writings (especially those concerning Tibet) impressed the young Guénon so much that he extensively quoted Văn Cang's work in one of his articles published in 1910.

The third set of information about Văn Cang stems from Guénon's most loyal followers (more particularly, Chacornac). According to this narrative, which is accepted unreservedly by many modern scholars, the relationship between Văn Cang and Guénon was much deeper than mere intellectual admiration. Many have insisted that Văn Cang and Guénon began a fruitful personal relationship after the latter moved to France. According to this view, Guénon has learned the rudiments of the Chinese language and he received secret information and initiation into Daoism via Văn Cang, who operated in Paris as the intermediary of his father, the 'Master of Maxims'. Thus, from this perspective, Văn Cang was one of the few 'authentic Orientals' active in the occultist milieu that flourished in *fin de siècle* France. In this guise, that is, as one of the few living Daoists in Europe at the time, he is said to have played a pivotal role in the spiritual formation of important esotericists such as Guénon and the intellectual movement that originated from his thought, namely, Traditionalism. As I will show in the following pages, this version of the story is untenable.

Questioning the master

In his popular *Misquoting Jesus*, the New Testament scholar Bart Ehrman warns his readers of the risks of misreading the different sources about Jesus's life (Ehrman 2005: 214):

> If they [the four Gospels] are not saying the same thing, it is not legitimate to assume they are –for example, by taking what Mark says, and taking what Luke says, then taking what Matthew and John say and melding them all

together, so that Jesus says and does all the things that each of the Gospel writers indicates. Anyone who interprets the Gospels this way is not letting each author have his own say; . . . anyone who does this is not reading the Gospels themselves – he or she is making up a new Gospel consisting of the four in the New Testament, a new Gospel that is not like any of the ones that have come down to us.

Văn Cang's portrait at the end of the previous section is the product of a method suspiciously similar to that brilliantly criticized by Ehrman. But what happens if we apply a different method? For instance, what story do our sources tell us once we read them horizontally?[28] Rather than integrating them in a single narration, let us see what every source has to say on the topic.

A chronological analysis of our sources seems to indicate a noteworthy trend. For a visual representation of such a trend, see Table 4.1.

The table clearly indicates that, in the oldest sources available, Văn Cang is described as a soldier and the son of a religious specialist (the 'Master of Maxims', Tong-Sang Nguyễn Văn Luật) that helped de Pouvourville in Tonkin and with his translation of some Chinese texts. In these sources, all written in the last decade of the nineteenth century (it should be remembered that de Pouvourville met Văn Cang and his father around 1890), the real protagonist is Văn Luật. Văn Cang is a secondary character in the story, a young and brilliant soldier able to facilitate de Pouvourville's Asiatic sojourn.

The situation changed at the turn of the century. Once de Pouvourville was back in France, Văn Cang's language skills were not important for daily

Table 4.1 The Development of French Sources about Nguyễn Văn Cang

Characteristics \ Source[29]	A. 1891	B. 1894	C. 1899	D. 1904	E. 1930	F. 1958	G. 1981	H. 2006	I. 2010
Soldier	✓	✓	✓	✓	✗	✗	✗	✓	✓
Son of a religious specialist (Tong-Sang Luat)	✓	✓	✓	✓	✗	✓	✓	✓	✓
Assistant Translator for Chinese Texts	✗	✓	✓	✓	✗	✓	✓	✓	✓
Far Eastern *literatus*	✗	✗	✓	✓	✓	✓	✓	✓	✓
Religious specialist (Tong-Sang)	✗	✗	✗	✗	✓	✓	✗	✗	✗
Lived in France for a period	✗	✗	✗	✗	✗	✓	✓	✓	✓
Guénon's Daoist initiator/informant	✗	✗	✗	✗	✗	✓	✓	✓	✓

life but they could be profitably utilized by *La Haute Science* as a key for the interpretation of the Chinese characters. Once de Pouvourville founded the journal *La Voie*, his young Vietnamese friend (or at least his *name*) proved useful once more. The information provided by *La Voie* on the occasion of the first of Văn Cang's articles is fundamentally the same as that we encountered in the previous sources.

As noted earlier, Văn Cang's contributions to de Pouvourville's journal were well received by Guénon, who deemed them a 'highly authoritative source'. The fact that one of Văn Cang's articles was cited positively by Guénon was enough to ignite the interest of his followers for the Vietnamese author. It is in this context that we found Văn Cang mentioned by Clavelle. Surprisingly, for Clavelle (1930: 208), it was Văn Cang and not his father that was a '*tongsang* of the Laotseu rite'. In Traditionalist circles, Văn Cang's original identity as soldier and de Pouvourville's brilliant assistant was gradually erased and replaced by the image of a '*noble voyageur* sent from the centres of the "eternal oriental wisdom"' (Laurant 2010: 106).

The turning point of this process is the 1958 and the publication of Chacornac's 'conjecture'. Therein, Chacornac offered a piece of information I was not able to find anywhere else prior to 1958: that Nguyễn Văn Cang had 'lived in France for some time'.[30] This detail would be crucial. In the years following *La vie simple*, every Traditionalist author would repeat this part of Chacornac's 'conjecture', highlighting the importance of Văn Cang for Guénon's intellectual formation.

It is easy to understand the reason for this interpretational shift. After Guénon's death, his followers began to look for the roots of his knowledge. In fact, the problem of Guénon's 'Masters' was the object of intense debate among Traditionalists, divided between those who believed that Guénon was a quasi-prophetic figure, someone whose work 'was and will be the "Infallible Compass" and the "Impenetrable Armor"' (Vâlsan 1951: 255), and those who 'just' saw him as a profound thinker capable of making errors and using bad sources like every intellectual.[31] Chacornac belonged to the first group: for them, it was crucial to demonstrate that Guénon's sources were 'authentic oriental masters'. Văn Cang, the son of 'the Master of Maxim', was an ideal candidate for the role of Guénon's Daoist informant (and initiator).

In the following decades it appears that those scholars who were laying the groundwork for the academic study of Traditionalism tended to read the sources 'vertically', lumping together all the information available, and creating a portrait of Nguyễn Văn Cang that included both the young soldier/assistant of de Pouvourville and the Paris-dwelling instructor of Guénon. As we will see,

I am not convinced that this method can give us a faithful portrait of the real Nguyễn Văn Cang.

Inventing the master

The cornerstone of the image of Nguyễn Văn Cang described earlier is found in Chacornac's conjecture. In fact, only if Văn Cang had 'lived in France for some time' could have met Guénon and, subsequently, become his Daoist informant. But what evidence do we have of this fact? There are several arguments that can be brought against Chacornac's case.

First of all, none of the sources before 1958 makes such a claim. This is significant, since if Văn Cang was ever in Paris meeting with Guénon, this should have occurred between 1908 (the year in which Guénon and de Pouvourville met) and 1910 (the year of Guénon's article mentioning Văn Cang). Thus, it appears that the first mention of a friendship between Guénon and Văn Cang comes fifty years after the alleged event, when both the protagonists were dead. This periodization opens up a whole new set of questions. For instance, if Văn Cang was in Paris, why didn't he contribute to other journals (e.g. *La Gnose*, initiated by de Pouvourville and Guénon in 1909)? In fact, over the course of its short existence (1909–12), *La Gnose* constantly struggled to find valued contributors and Văn Cang's knowledge of Daoism would have been surely appreciated in a 'monthly journal devoted to esoteric and metaphysical studies'.[32]

Furthermore, if we accept Văn Cang's presence in France in the first decade of the twentieth century, we should ask: when did he arrive? Considering that he served as de Pouvourville's assistant in Tonkin, it is reasonable to speculate that the two friends returned together once de Pouvourville completed his service in the French colony. We know the exact date of de Pouvourville's resignation: 29 October 1892. If he brought his assistant to Paris with him, where the two worked together on a series of translations (first published in 1894) and in *La Voie* (where Văn Cang published in the period 1904–6), then we should accept that the young Vietnamese was in France for over fifteen years,[33] which is definitely longer than what suggested by Chacornac.

There are two further problems with this interpretation of the events. First of all, it is hard to believe that an 'authentic Daoist initiate' could have passed unnoticed in an environment such as the Parisian occultist milieu, which was always thirsty for exotic wisdom. I believe that in a world of many made-up

'Oriental Masters', a real representative of the 'Daoist hierarchy' would have been extremely popular.[34] Hence, if Văn Cang lived in France for more than a decade, then why isn't his name mentioned in any source until May 1904, that is, the year of his first article for *La Voie*?

Lastly, those who followed Chacornac's conjecture ignored a crucial detail. The only text contemporary to Văn Cang's alleged stay in Paris is *La Voie*'s introduction to his first contribution. As we saw in the first section, the journal announced to its readers 'the direct collaboration of Far-Eastern *literati*'. The nature of this 'direct collaboration' can be deduced from the titles given to Văn Cang's contributions (*Correspondence d'Extrême-Orient* and *Lettres de Chine*) which seems to clearly indicate that Nguyễn Văn Cang's 'direct collaboration', if ever occurred, has been of an epistolary nature.

Therefore, it seems fair to assume that it is highly unlikely that Văn Cang was ever in France, a conclusion that falsifies Chacornac's conjecture. Moreover, if Văn Cang never lived in Paris, he could have never met Guénon and surely could not have been his privileged Daoist source and – even less – his initiator. At this point, one question still stands: if the popular interpretation of the sources regarding Nguyễn Văn Cang is unsatisfactory, how should we read them? What can actually be said about our Vietnamese Daoist?

Killing the master

Having repeatedly criticized Chacornac's interpretation, it is now time to create my own 'conjecture', hoping that it will be as persuasive and possibly more grounded than that elaborated by the Traditionalist author.

I am going to start with the two indisputable facts:

1. Nguyễn Văn Cang and his father Nguyễn Văn Luật were two people that de Pouvourville met during his second mission in Indochina (1890–1).
2. The names of Nguyễn Văn Cang (in a few variants) and of his father Nguyễn Văn Luật appeared as authors or co-authors of different texts published by de Pouvourville.

Note that in point 1 I refer to three people, whereas in point 2 to their *names* (in particular, the Vietnamese ones). This distinction is the starting point of my theory. As taught in the text deeply treasured by the protagonists of this story, the *Daodejing*, 'Having names – this is the mother of the ten-thousand things' (I, 3).

Thus, my conjecture begins exactly with this necessity, that of 'having names' on one's side.

Surely de Pouvourville met the two Vietnamese, the younger of whom served as his assistant and probably they taught him something about Vietnamese religious life, about which de Pouvourville was very interested. Once in France, the former French soldier began publishing on Asian religious subjects and desperately needed 'names' that could give authority to his theories. This phenomenon is typical of those initiates/adventurers of the turn of the century, those 'seekers of truth' in need of authority. Blavatsky had pioneered this approach in the 1870s, claiming that her theories were not the product of her readings, but 'from living spiritual masters of Oriental origin' (Hammer 2003: 60). Those 'Oriental masters' became an essential ingredient in the esoteric discourse of the following decades. As summarized by Laurant (2010: 118):

> the potential initiate waited for the *noble voyageur* ... either because he was sent by a hidden centre or because when the future initiate was ready, the initiator presented himself spontaneously. The spiritual thirst of the West summoned Nguyễn Văn Cang, led by Mat Gioi, like the Sikh Hardiji Scharipf had come into contact with Saint-Yves d'Alveydre.

The parallelism between Văn Cang and Hardjji Scharipf is extremely pertinent since it is one of the many examples of (semi)fictional 'Oriental Masters' invented by Western esotericists in the attempt of legitimizing their religious theories.[35] In this particular case, there are several reasons to believe that the names Nguyễn Văn Cang and Nguyễn Văn Luật were two powerful means of legitimation of de Pouvourville's theories, but their personal contribution to his work was, at best, negligible.

This first possible argument for my thesis is, again, a matter of 'names'. As seen in the presentation of our sources, the name of the son of the 'Master of Maxims' was Nguyễn Văn Cang. However, once his name was associated with de Pouvourville's translations, he was first mentioned as 'Nguyen Van Hi', then 'Nguyen Van Cang, Hi', before the final form 'Nguyen Van Cang'. The fact that we are told that Nguyễn Văn Luật had another son, named 'Hi' (de Pouvourville 1899),[36] made me think that once in Paris, de Pouvourville maybe began to rework his Tonkinese memories in the attempt to find an 'oriental' who could lend authority to his 'exact translations'. For reasons that are not entirely clear, in a later moment that coincided with the establishment of his journal *La Voie*, de Pouvourville's choice fell not on the eldest son of his old master but, rather, on the younger Văn Cang. To my knowledge, nobody has noticed this revealing discrepancy. However, it is hardly plausible that de Pouvourville did not know the name of his own co-author, especially if Văn Cang was in Paris with him.

De Pouvourville's inconsistency did not end here. In 1914, a curious book was published with the title *Physique et psychique de l'opium* (Physics and Psychics of Opium). The volume was authored by no less than 'Nguyen Te Duc Luat', who was introduced in the preface (not surprisingly written by Albert de Pouvourville) as 'a physician, a tongsang of the Daoist rite and . . . a sage', a seventy-four-year-old who 'has had twenty-two children and has smoked thirty opium pipes daily since the day of his puberty' (Nguyen Te Duc Luat 1914: 3). It is very unlikely that anyone other than de Pouvourville actually wrote the book, especially if we consider that *Physique et psychique de l'opium* is a reworking of another volume, published in 1903, under de Pouvourville's most famous pseudonym 'Matgioi' (de Pouvourville 1903). Thus, the authorship of *Physique et psychique de l'opium* demonstrates de Pouvourville's habit of borrowing the authority of his Vietnamese friends in support of his own ideas. Even further, to increase the authority of the author of the volume, de Pouvourville informs us that the translations of several Chinese texts that had been published years before were translated by 'Nguyen Te Duc Luat and Albert de Pouvourville'![37]

To sum up, if we take into consideration the information provided by de Pouvourville, the person who helped him with the translation of Chinese Classics in 1894 was 'Nguyen Van Hi' (or 'Nguyen Van Cang, Hi'). In 1904, his assistant's name changed, becoming 'Nguyen Van Cang'. In 1925, a different occasion required a different kind of authorship, this time attributed to 'Nguyen Te Duc Luat'. This continuous shift between the names of the members of the family he met in Vietnam is, in my opinion, sufficient evidence of the unreliability of de Pouvourville's claims about his 'Oriental' sources.

It seems logical therefore to conclude that all the Vietnamese names listed in this article were nothing but different personas of the same author: that of Albert de Pouvourville himself. The advantage of my conjecture lies in the fact that it also gives a more credible explanation of the content of the articles signed as penned by 'Nguyen Van Cang'. Rather than posit that a young Vietnamese soldier could have had – together with expertise in Daoism – a strong background in European occultist and orientalist literature, it seems much safer to theorize that a French author with the taste of the exotic like de Pouvourville could be hidden behind an 'Oriental' mask.

Concluding remarks: The resurrection of the master

As we have seen throughout the chapter, the world of occultism can sometimes take the shape of a hall of mirrors. Authors like de Pouvourville enjoyed hiding behind multiple personas, each fulfilling a specific function.

After a detailed analysis of all the sources available, it seems that all the Vietnamese names mentioned in this work need to be added to the known list of his pseudonyms.[38] In fact, according to the theory proposed in this chapter, there has never been an enigmatic Vietnamese soldier, translator and Daoist authority who, while spending over a decade in Paris unnoticed, wrote articles for *La Voie* filled with references to French occultist literature and initiated Guénon into Daoism. Instead, all the texts that were attributed to Nguyễn Văn Cang were probably the production of de Pouvourville, who, looking for legitimation, borrowed the authority of his 'Oriental' friend. This is the most plausible hypothesis considering the timeline of the events, the content of Văn Cang's articles and the inconsistency of their attribution. If this conclusion is accurate, it disproves the arguments of all those authors who, following Chacornac's 'conjecture', have argued that Văn Cang played a role in Guénon's formation, either by teaching him the Chinese language or by initiating him into Daoism.

Unlike other authors of his time, de Pouvourville had really come into contact with 'the Orient' (French Indochina). Because of his experience, he deemed his knowledge of Asian religion superior to that of the academics, whose comprehension of the sacred is irredeemably limited by their secular perspective. However, because of the short and discontinuous nature of his stays in Tonkin (three sojourns for a total of less than five years), de Pouvourville was never able to make up for his lack of formal training in Asian languages and cultures and had to rely, especially in his books about the 'metaphysics of the East', on second-hand accounts or on problematic sources like Blavatsky and Notovitch.

In his impossible quest for authenticity, de Pouvourville tried to mobilize as many names as possible, no matter if real ('de Pouvourville', 'Poyou'), invented ('Matgioi', 'Mogd'), or borrowed from others ('Nguyen Van Cang', 'Nguyen Van Luat'). The consequences of this choice went beyond de Pouvourville's time and aims. Văn Cang's name was saved from oblivion and reached the second half of the twentieth century, being used by other people (the Traditionalists) with different agendas (such as to justify Guénon's exceptionality). Văn Cang's name has even reached the twenty-first century when secular scholars are using his story to reflect on Asian agency in Western esotericism.

Notes

I wish to thank all those who supported my work in the time of great displacement in which this chapter was composed. Mark Sedgwick, Lukas K. Pokorny and Franz Winter for their insightful suggestions on the first draft of this work and Fabrizia Agnesone for the many discussions about the psychology of the Traditionalists. A special thanks to Andrea, Matteo and Desirée for offering me a comfortable environment for writing and to Derek Paylor and Jaret Rushing for proofreading the manuscript.

1 To date, the only scholarly book entirely dedicated to de Pouvourville is a short volume entitled *Matgioi, un aventurier taoïste* penned by Jean-Pierre Laurant (1982). Recently, two PhD dissertations have discussed some aspects of de Pouvourville's work (Nilsson 2020; Suwanwattana 2020).
2 The picture was *Poisson rare* (Rare Fish) by the Belgian symbolist painter Félicien Rops (1833–98).
3 De Pouvourville's translation.
4 Since de Pouvourville never used diacritics in his writings, it is occasionally difficult to understand which Vietnamese word he is referring to. According to his friend Léon Champrenaud (1870–1925), 'Matgioi' means 'literally eye (Mat), day (gioi), and designates the sun, in other words the eye of the sky during the day' (Champrenaud 1910: 6). However, the Vietnamese word for the Sun, *mặt trời* or *mặt giời* 柵丕, is composed of the two Sino-Vietnamese terms *mặt* 柵 (face) and *trời* or *giời* 丕 (heaven/sky) and it means, literally, 'the face of the sky/heaven'. Thus, it seems that de Pouvourville confused *mắt* 眛 (eye) with *mặt* 柵 (face). This detail alone may well indicate that despite what is commonly believed, de Pouvourville had no real proficiency of the Vietnamese language.
5 According to de Pouvourville, the word 'tongsang' literally means 'men who see clearly' and indicates those 'who deal with metaphysics and the problems raised by the teaching of Laotseu, imparting the classical teaching of Daoism' (de Pouvourville 1896b: 9). I was not able to identify these 'tongsang' in the Vietnamese religious context. 'Tong' could refer to *tong* 宗 (lineage). The second part of the word, 'sang', may perhaps be *sáng* 灯 or 燗 (enlightened). In this case, 'tongsang' may, for example, indicate the leader of some kind of kinship association. However, I was not able to find the combination of these two characters in any Vietnamese source, so the term may be simply a fabrication of de Pouvourville.
6 In his *Bibliotheca Sinica*, Henri Cordier (1849–1925) considers this work as a partial translation of the Warring States period collection of texts conventionally known as *Guanzi* 管子 (Cordier 1922: 3803). However, both the title's mention of the 'wandering influences' and the first sentence of the book ('A spirit, my Master, descended from heaven and explained to me clearly what I am writing') give the

impression of a recent scripture produced via 'spirit writing'. Spirit writing or
   'automatic writing' is a practice very common in Southeast Asia. It is a mode of
   scriptural production 'via the body of a spirit-medium (đồng tử) . . . also known as
   cơ bút (jibi 机笔, the divine brush) or phò loan (fuluan 扶鸾, to hold the phoenix)'
   (Jammes 2021: 115).
7 Thầy thuốc, a physician, a healer.
8 Perhaps tianshi 天師 (heavenly master). The title of tianshi is normally attributed
   to the leader of Tianshidao 天師道 (Way of the Heavenly Master), a movement
   established in the mid-second century in Sichuan by the semi-legendary Zhang
   Daoling 張道陵 (Goossaert 2021). Nguyễn Văn Luật did not hold this hereditary
   title. However, it is not impossible that he used such designation loosely.
9 Assuming that 'xuâtdoï' stands for suất đội.
10 Les Tirailleurs Tonkinois (The Tonkinese Rifles), a corps of colonial infantry
   composed of soldiers recruited from the local population and led by a French official.
11 Today's Huyện Phúc Thọ, Thành phố Hà Nội.
12 The Vietnamese name of the Tirailleurs Indochinois.
13 成泰叁年肆月拾壹日山西省廣威府福壽縣甘蔗盛總甘蔗盛社阮文亢原後雄
   (雄)奇叁隊揀兵同慶年摘為習兵蒙得率隊式圈官應取為臣子具如父母兄弟平
   心安順為妥茲筆⌐父阮文律記。My thanks to Jean-Pierre Laurant for showing
   me a copy of this document in his possession.
14 Also, 'Thang' is homophonic with 'Cang'.
15 In the novel, the role of the master is played by Thang's father.
16 Since Văn Cang does not appear as the main author but only as a helper in de
   Pouvourville's translation, I am not going to consider these texts. Also, as I will
   discuss later, it was the articles and not the translations that left a trace in the later
   French esoteric milieu.
17 In Vietnamese: thiên địa nhân.
18 According to Văn Cang, these are: 'The strength is in the union of Kouang and Shi';
   'whoever speaks will die and will not be buried'; 'the lamp shines, blind the man
   who does not see it' (Van Cang 1904b: 174).
19 La Voie never makes such a claim explicit, but the information is surely suggested to
   the reader.
20 Guénon was soon to become the inspirator of a very influential religious and
   philosophical movement today known as Traditionalism. About Guénon's biography,
   see Laurant 2006. On the relevance of Traditionalism, see Sedgwick 2004, 2023.
21 Being worried about the increasing influence of the British in the area, the Qing
   dynasty had decided to begin a military campaign to gain direct control of the
   region. On 12 February, the Chinese army occupied Lhasa and the thirteenth Dalai
   Lama Thubten Gyatso fled to India.
22 Guénon added that this was a 'very improper' definition.

23 Friedrich Max Müller (1823–1900) suggested that either the Tibetan monks had deceived Notovitch or that Notovitch himself was the author of these passages (Joseph 2012: 162). Colonel Younghusband remarked that 'Notovitch has recently published what he calls a new "Life of Christ"... No one, however, who knows M. Notovitch's reputation, or who has the slightest knowledge of the subject, will give any reliance whatever to this pretentious volume' (Younghusband 1896: 210).
24 It has been suggested that this review was 'clearly inspired by Guénon' (Laurant 1987: 78).
25 I was not able to confirm this version of Văn Luật's name. According to the documents I consulted, Văn Cang's father name was 阮文律 (Chinese: *Ruan Wenlü*; Vietnamese: *Nguyễn Văn Luật*).
26 This information is confirmed from the pages of *La Voie*, that informs its readers, in the November 1905 issue, that 'the Tongsang Nguyen the Duc Luat received... the rare distinction of "*Sapèque d'Or*"'.
27 This was not unusual. According to Bouinais and Paulus (1885: 190) '[t]he regiment of the *Tirailleurs Annamites*, or *linh-tap*, was created by decree of March 15, 1880.... The main offences for which the *linh-tap* are accused are theft and desertion; the latter is very common'.
28 'Horizontal reading' is a method of textual analysis used to compare multiple accounts of a similar event in order to find possible contradictions, opposed to 'vertical reading' that aims to create a metanarrative composed by the harmonized sum of different sources.
29 The sources considered in the table can be grouped in three categories: de Pouvourville and his entourage (A, B, C, D), Guénon and his entourage (E, F) and scholars (G, H, I).
30 'It seems that a first knowledge of Far Eastern metaphysics reached Guénon through the channel of Matgioi, and it is possible to suppose that the oral teaching was imparted by the youngest son of the 'Master of Maxims', the tong-sang Luat, who lived in France for some time and who had collaborated in the translation of the Chinese texts' (Chacornac 1958: 43).
31 Laurant (2019) extensively illustrates this debate.
32 This was the subtitle of *La Gnose*. Also, for several months, the journal had the Chinese character *dao* 道 on its front cover.
33 Guénon and de Pouvourville met in 1908, so the former could not have met Văn Cang earlier.
34 Moreover, all 'eastern' religious authorities who actually visited the West in this period – such as, only to mention the most famous one, Swami Vivekananda (1863–1902) – left multiple traces.
35 The most famous example of this dynamic was that of Blavatsky and her mysterious *Mahatmas* (Johnson 1994).

36 'And, if he [Master Luat] reserved the heritage of his science for his eldest son Hi, always immersed like him in books, he felt happy at the idea that his younger brother would one day be the family's shield against the whims or the demands of Europeans' (de Pouvourville 1899: 116).
37 This is a note written on the inside cover of the 1925 edition of the book.
38 Three of which are already known: 'Matgioi', 'Mogd' and 'Puyoo'.

References

Blavatsky, H. P. (1888), *The Secret Doctrine; the Synthesis of Science, Religion and Philosophy*, London: The Theosophical Publishing Society.

Bouinais, A. and A. Paulus (1885), *L'Indo-Chine française contemporaine, Cambodge, Tonkin, Annam*, Paris: Challamel Ainé.

Chacornac, P. (1958), *La vie simple de René Guénon*, Paris: Éditions Traditionnelles.

Champrenaud, L. (1910), *Matgioi et son rôle dans les sociétés secrètes chinoises*, Paris: Librairie Hermétique.

Clavelle, M. (1930), 'Mystiques et magiciens du Tibet (compte-rendu)', *Le Voile d'Isis*, 35 (123): 207–9.

Cordier, H. (1922), *Bibliotheca Sinica, Supplement et index, Fascicule 1er*, Paris: Librairie Orientaliste.

David-Néel, A. (1929), *Mystiques et magiciens du Thibet*, Paris: Plon.

de Pouvourville, A. (1894a), 'Le Tao de Laotseu. Traduction Exacte par Albert de Pouvourville (Matgioi)', *La Haute Science*, 2: 7–32.

de Pouvourville, A. (1894b), *Le Tao de Laotseu*, Paris: Librairie de l'art independent.

de Pouvourville, A. (1896a), *Le Traité des influences errantes de Quangdzu*, Paris: Bibliothèque de la Haute Science.

de Pouvourville, A. (1896b), 'Le Taoïsme et les Sociétés Secrètes Chinoises', *L'Initiation*, 9 (1): 4–34.

de Pouvourville, A. (1899), *Le Maître des sentences*, Paris: Paul Ollendorff.

Ehrman, B. D. (2005), *Misquoting Jesus: The Story behind Who Changed the Bible and Why*, New York: Harper.

Gattegno, D. (2001), *René Guénon: qui suis-je?* Grez-sur-Loing: Pardès.

Goossaert, V. (2021), *Heavenly Masters: Two Thousand Years of the Daoist State*, Honolulu: University of Hawai'i Press.

Granholm, K. (2013), 'Locating the West: Problematizing the Western in Western Esotericism and Occultism', in H. Bogdan and G. Djurdjevic (eds), *Occultism in a Global Perspective*, 17–36, London: Acumen Publishing.

Guénon, R. (1910), 'Le Dalaï Lama', *La Gnose*, 2 (3): 88–90.

Hammer, O. (2003), *Claiming Knowledge, Strategies of Epistemology from Theosophy to the New Age*, Leiden: Brill.

Huc, É. R. (1850), *Souvenirs d'un voyage dans la Tartarie, le Thibet, et la Chine pendant les années 1844, 1845 et 1846*, Paris: A. Le Clère & Co.

Introvigne, M. (2007), 'L'interprétation des sociétés secrètes chinoises. Entre paradigme ésotérique, politique et criminology', in J. P. Brach and J. Rousse-Lacordaire (eds), *Études d'histoire de l'ésotérisme*, 303–17, Paris: Cerf.

James, M. F. (1981a), *Ésotérisme et christianisme. Autour de René Guénon*, Paris: Nouvelles Éditions latines.

James, M. F. (1981b), *Ésotérisme, occultisme, franc-maçonnerie et christianisme aux XIX et XX siècles. Explorations bio-bibliographiques*, Paris: Nouvelles Éditions latines.

Jammes, J. (2021), 'Ethnography of the Homo Secretus: Inside Secret Societies and Societies with Secrets in Vietnam', in J. Jammes and V. T. King (eds), *Fieldwork and the Self: Changing Research Styles in Southeast Asia*, 103–36, Singapore: Springer.

Johnson, K. P. (1994), *The Masters Revealed: Madame Blavatsky and the Myth of the Great White Lodge*, Albany: State University of New York Press.

Joseph, S. J. (2012), 'Jesus in India?', *Journal of the American Academy of Religion*, 80 (1): 161–99.

Laurant, J. P. (1982), *Matgioï, un aventurier taoïste*, Paris: Dervy.

Laurant, J. P. (1987), 'Lecture de quelques textes politiques', *Politica Hermetica*, 1: 72–81.

Laurant, J. P. (2006), *René Guénon. Les enjeux d'une lecture*, Paris: Dervy.

Laurant, J. P. (2010), 'Autour de «Mat Gioi» le Passeur et l'empreinte des écrits occultistes du comte de Pouvourville en France et au Vietnam', *Péninsule*, 60 (1): 99–120.

Laurant, J. P. (2019), *Guénon au combat; des réseaux en mal d'institutions*, Paris: L'Harmattan.

Nguyen Te Duc Luat (1914), *Physique et Psychique de l'Opium*, Paris: éditeurs Associés.

Nilsson, J. (2020), 'As a Fire Beneath the Ashes: The Quest for Chinese Wisdom within Occultism, 1850–1949', PhD diss., Centre for Theology and Religious Studies, Lund University, Lund.

Notovitch, N. (1894), *La vie inconnue de Jésus-Christ*, Paris: Paul Ollendorff.

Pasi, M. (2010), 'Oriental Kabbalah and The Parting of East and West in The Early Theosophical Society', in B. Huss, M. Pasi and K. von Stuckrad (eds), *Kabbalah and Modernity*, 151–66, Leiden: Brill.

Rayfield, D. (1976), *The Dream of Lhasa: The Life of Nikolay Przhevalsky (1839–88), Explorer of Central Asia*, London: Elek Books.

Rice, B. (2017), 'The Apocryphal Tale of Jesus' Journey to India: Nicolas Notovitch and the Life of Saint Issa Revisited', in T. Burke (ed.), *Fakes, Forgeries, and Fictions: Writing Ancient and Modern Christian Apocrypha*, 265–84, Eugene: Cascade.

Rives, M. and E. Deroo (1999), *Les Lính tập: histoire des militaires indochinois au service de la France, 1859–1960*, Beychac-et-Caillau: Lavauzelle.

Robin, J. (1978), *René Guénon Témoin de la Tradition*, Paris: Guy Trédaniel.

Sablé, E. (2018), *René Guénon et l'Evangile*, Grenoble: Mercure Dauphinois.

Sedgwick, M. J. (2004), *Against the Modern World: Traditionalism and the Secret Intellectual History of the Twentieth Century*, New York: Oxford University Press.

Sedgwick, M. J. (2023), *Traditionalism the Radical Project for Restoring Sacred Order*, London: Pelican.

Strube, J. (2021), 'Towards the Study of Esotericism without the "Western": Esotericism from the Perspective of a Global Religious History', in E. Asprem and J. Strube (eds), *New Approaches to the Study of Esotericism*, 45–66, Leiden: Brill.

Suwanwattana, W. (2020), 'Decadent Indochina and French Colonial Literature, 1880s to 1920s', PhD diss., Merton College, University of Oxford, Oxford.

Vâlsan, M. (1951), *La fonction de René Guénon et le sort de l'Occident*, Paris: Editions Traditionnelles.

Van Cang, N. (1904a), 'Signe de reconnaissance des sociétés secrètes chinoises', *La Voie*, 2: 174–5.

Van Cang, N. (1904b), 'Le Berceau de l'Humanité', *La Voie*, 6: 383.

Van Cang, N. (1904c), 'Le Palais du Dalé-Lama', *La Voie*, 8: 271–2.

Van Cang, N. (1904d), 'Le Dalé-Lama', *La Voie*, 9: 177–9.

Van Cang, N. (1905), 'Khaldan', *La Voie*, 11: 467–9.

Van Cang, N. (1906), 'Les Siéfa', *La Voie*, 22: 88–91.

Younghusband, F. (1896), *The Heart of a Continent: A Narrative of Travels in Manchuria, Across the Gobi Desert, Through the Himalayas, the Pamirs, and Hunza (1884–1894)*, London: John Murray.

5

Turning further East

C. H. A. Bjerregaard and the esoteric enthusiasm for Daoism

Johan Nilsson

Introduction

Although known – and sometimes derided – for their fascination and enthusiasm for India, the esoteric movements of the late nineteenth and early twentieth century varied significantly in where they sought for traces of ancient wisdom. This is readily apparent in the works of figures like Helena P. Blavatsky (1831–91), who wrote not only about Tibet, but sometimes also about the wisdom of the Norse gods and the lore of the Rosicrucians (Blavatsky 1888). It is even more clear, however, in more obscure publications, like pamphlets and journals, in which less remembered writers championed their own interpretations of the esoteric teachings of the movement. Although India was doubtlessly the geographical and cultural locus most associated with wisdom in esoteric writings, like those of Theosophy, it is misleading to see esoteric movements as only a vehicle for the global popularization and modernist interpretation of South Asian religious traditions. The scholarly focus on the Theosophical Society and its engagement with India (or with things associated with India) is understandable. The cultural impact of Theosophy and its interpretation of Buddhism and Hinduism was significant. Still, to exclusively focus on this aspect of late nineteenth- and early twentieth-century esoteric movements and their relationships to other religious traditions would conceal some important aspects of their cultural impact. Such issues include (but are not limited to) Theosophy's and other esoteric movements' interactions with Christianity and Christian reform movements in the late nineteenth and early twentieth century, their popularization of interpretations of Norse paganism, their enthusiasm for features of Islam and, finally (the focus of this chapter), their engagement with East Asian culture and religious traditions. A reader of major esoteric authors and ideologues, like Blavatsky or Annie Besant (1847–1933), would be justified for thinking that China was of very little interest to the esoteric environment. China, however, was an object of interest to a number of Theosophical and other esoteric writers who were influential and important in their own regard. Among them were the ex-Baptist missionary Charles Spurgeon Medhurst (1860–1927), the French esoteric writer Albert de Pouvourville (1861–1939)[1] and the Danish-American writer and librarian Carl Henrik Andreas Bjerregaard (1845–1922). These figures should not be regarded as isolated exceptions. They were part of a small but vital current within the European and American esoteric environment of the late nineteenth and early twentieth century. This current was involved in a reinterpretation of Chinese culture in ways that would become increasingly familiar to students of the global understanding of East Asia in the intellectual, cultural and religious history of the twentieth century. In contrast to older notions of the Chinese state as an ideal of order and reason promulgated by the likes of Voltaire (1694–1778), or the presupposed decadence of the pagan empire decried by many missionaries, esoteric writers tended to see China as one of many homes of universal wisdom. But what was that wisdom and how truly homogenous was the esoteric understanding of China? In this chapter I will explore these questions by looking closely at Bjerregaard's writings.

Bjerregaard and his works

Carl Henrik Andreas Bjerregaard was a Danish immigrant to the United States. He studied at the University of Copenhagen in the mid-1860s and later worked as a librarian at the Astor Library in New York.[2] He had broad religious and esoteric interests, among them Transcendentalism and the Hermetic Brotherhood of Luxor.[3] Bjerregaard was associated for a time with the early Theosophical movement in New York but would later deny that he was a follower of Blavatsky (Rasmussen 2016; Bowen 2015: 98–105). He has not completely escaped scholarly attention, although, with the exception of his engagement with Sufism and Islam, his religious and esoteric ideas remain largely unexplored. Bjerregaard's interest in Islam has recently drawn the attention of scholars like Mark Sedgwick and Patrick D. Bowen, both of whom see Bjerregaard's interpretation of Islam as closely related to and influenced by the broader esoteric and religious environments in which he navigated.[4] As it seems, Bjerregaard was a significant representative of the turn of the century esoteric interest in these matters, and Sedgwick (2017: 147) calls him '[t]he most important American Theosophical writer on Sufism'. Bowen and Sedgwick also note that Bjerregaard was likely involved in at least one early American Sufi organization, the Order of Sufis, although little is known of this group (Bowen 2015: 104; Sedgwick 2017: 147). Sedgwick further notes that Bjeregaard's Sufism, as it appears in his writings in journals like *The Path* and *The Platonist*, relied on 'the main secondary sources then available in English, German, and French' (Sedgwick 2017: 147). Therein he presented a universalized form of Sufism that had significant similarities with the Theosophical self-image as anti-dogmatic and free from 'formalism and ritualism' (Sedgwick 2017: 147). As we will see, there are similarities between Bjerregaard's interpretation of Sufism and the ways in which he imagined Chinese religion.

Bjerregaard was a prolific writer who was extensively, but not exclusively, active in the Theosophical and esoteric press of his day. During the late nineteenth and early twentieth centuries a vibrant periodical culture existed focusing on esoteric subject matters. Periodicals like these were important for the emergence and popularization of organizations like the Theosophical Society and allowed the nurturing of authors whose specialized subject matter would interest sympathizers of the broad esoteric environment. Bjerregaard was published in several magazines, including *The Theosophist*, *The Path*, *The Metaphysical Magazine* and *The Word*. Sufism was by no means his only (or even predominant) interest, if measured by literary output. Bjerregaard wrote articles about, among other things, Norse mythology, esoteric historiography, elemental spirits and the philosophy of Søren Kierkegaard (1813–55). One of the recurring subjects of his work was Chinese religion, especially what he termed Daoism. According to his own account, Bjerregaard first came to 'engage with' the *Daodejing* 道德經 in 1877, making it an object of prolonged study (Bjerregaard 1912: 97). It was not until the mid-1890s, however, that he started to write with some frequency about related topics. He kept up this activity for about fifteen years, until the early 1910s. After that time, his interests (at least judged from his literary output) seem to have been more confined to subjects traditionally associated with European religion and philosophy. His writings on China appeared in the form of articles with titles such as 'The Mind of China, Japan, America and the New Age' and 'Tao: The Chinese "Being"' (Bjerregaard 1899, 1895). Most important, however, was the fifteen-part series published in *The Word* from 1908 to 1910. These articles were later collected in a book entitled *The Inner Life and the Tao-Teh-King*, which was published by the Theosophical

Publishing Company in 1912. These are the works that will be most relevant in the present context, although some of Bjerregaard's other writings, especially with regard to historiography and general mysticism, do offer some important insights to his understanding of China.

Like with Sufism, Bjerregaard's view of Chinese religion was likely (or almost) exclusively constructed from texts. The sources he openly referred to are (mostly academic) studies in European languages and a small number of translations of Chinese texts. Bjerregaard referred to a handful of sinologists, having a relatively good knowledge of the academic scholarship of his day, although he sometimes seemed to prefer what was at the time outdated research, like that of the important early nineteenth-century French sinologist Jean-Pierre Abel-Rémusat (e.g. Bjerregaard 1895: 411). It is quite likely that some of the approaches, biases and theoretical perspectives prevalent in these works shaped Bjerregaard's understanding of Daoism.

China in Bjerregaard's esoteric historiography

Representatives of late nineteenth- and early twentieth-century esotericism constructed a number of emic historiographies, some of which became quite influential even outside the movements and environments that gave rise to them. One such historical narrative, (mostly) popular in French esoteric movements, was the story of the universal Empire of Ram and the ancient traditions of wisdom the world had inherited from that forgotten culture (Saint-Yves d'Alveydre [1884] 1981). Even more well-known however is the Theosophical story of human and pre-human history flowing through a number of continents and so-called root races[5] leading up to present-day humanity. A number of scholars (Nilsson 2020; Hanegraaff 2014; Kilcher 2010; Trompf 2008, 1998) have argued that these narratives were important elements in post-Enlightenment esoteric literature. Although other geographical locations like Egypt, Chaldea and India, or emic and fictional realms like Atlantis or the underground land of Agarttha, figure more prominently in these narratives, China was often included. Most of the influential esoteric writers of the period incorporated China in their historiographies. Éliphas Lévi (1810–75), for example, seemed to argue that Confucius was a transmitter of inherited Chaldean wisdom (1860: 151).[6] The influential French esoteric writer Joseph Alexandre Saint-Yves d'Alveydre (1842–1909) stated that the important mythic figure and culture hero Fuxi 伏羲 preserved the true teachings of the empire of Ram, and Theosophical writers mention traces of Atlantean lore preserved in ancient Chinese texts (Lévi 1860: 151; Saint-Yves d'Alveydre [1884] 1981: 240; see also Nilsson 2020: 76–82). I have argued elsewhere that the incorporation of China in these narratives was one of the factors that helped shape a mode of understanding of Chinese culture that contained a type of spirituality that could and should be emulated (Nilsson 2020: 67–150).

The historical narrative that emerged out of Theosophy would be developed and reinterpreted by many authors in the late nineteenth and early twentieth century. It soon spread outside both Theosophy (e.g. to Anthroposophy) and esotericism (even involving the genre of academic historiography), where it came to exert an influence on the developing literary genres of science fiction and fantasy.[7] It tells of the development of human civilization and of the sinking of Atlantis. Furthermore, it explains how those Atlanteans who managed to survive this catastrophe preserved the knowledge of their civilization and spread it across the world. Considering Bjerregaard's relationship to Theosophy, we might have expected him to at least allude to this story. Nevertheless, Bjerregaard seemed disinterested in the root races, sunken continents and emigration patterns of Atlantean refugees that formed the building blocks of Theosophical lore. He did not, however, leave his readers without an alternative esoteric historiography and developed his own thoughts about history in several of his works. We know, for example, that he held a lecture on the subject of 'Historical Cycles' in New York on 25 March 1886, although the content seems not to have been preserved (Anonymous 1886: 30–2). Yet, the subject turns up in some of his published works. For example, it is discussed in his *Lectures on Mysticism and Nature Worship* (Bjerregaard 1897: 91–6). There is some overlap between the standard Theosophical historical narrative and the way in which Bjerregaard envisioned history as a cyclic and spiral motion. By this he meant that history repeated itself according to certain patterns and that it tended toward progress in the long term. 'Human history moves in cycles', he wrote, 'viz., at every turn of the upward or forward movement of the world-spiral we come to repetitions, but add a new element' (Bjerregaard 1897: 91). As stated earlier, however, the similarities are limited, and Bjerregaard generally restricted his narrative to the timespan of recognized recorded history. His examples in *Lectures on Mysticism and Nature Worship* included topics like the rise of Egypt and Greek civilizations, the birth of Jesus and what he saw as several periods of prosperity and unity for the Chinese empire.[8] The historical cycles can last between 250 and 1,000 years, and great catastrophes often occur when one cycle gives way to another.[9] When it comes to the role of Chinese culture in the flow of history, his thoughts can primarily be found in the sixth chapter of *The Inner Life and the Tao-Teh-King*. Supposedly about Laozi 老子, this chapter deals with a number of motifs relevant to historiography. It gives suggestions about how historical (religious) figures could be compared and classified. Therefore, like most esoteric historical narratives, it contains information about how their creators imagined the relationship between different religious traditions.

According to Bjerregaard, Laozi was the most prominent figure in Chinese history. He played a pivotal role as a preserver of tradition, but he was also an initiator of a new historical cycle. Bjerregaard wrote in *The Inner Life and the Tao-Teh-King* (Bjerregaard 1912: 96):

> I have claimed for Laotzse what a follower of Confucius will deny. I have claimed first place for him in China because he is the one who carries over into the New Age that begins with him, the contents, the inner value, the kernel of all the wisdom the previous ages had acquired, and, he is also the one who communicates to the New Age of China that begins with him, the virtue, or, the right principles of conduct, which the previous ages had discovered.

There is much to unpack in this short passage. I will however return below to the implied conflict between Laozi and (the followers of) Confucius and focus on the historical significance that Bjerregaard claimed for Laozi. In *The Inner Life and the Tao-Teh-King*, Laozi is regularly mentioned together with Buddha, Jesus and the *Bhagavadgītā*. These are all held to be 'teachers' of forms of wisdom that have contributed to the progress of humanity. Like Buddha and Jesus, Laozi has allegedly given humanity 'preparatory' revelations in order to guide its way to the coming age of 'God-Wisdom or Theo-Sophia', which he interestingly called 'New Age' (Bjerregaard 1912: 96). Nonetheless, Bjerregaard did not adopt a similarly positive view about all historical religious figures or traditions. In fact, these positive examples are often contrasted with negative ones. 'Brahmanism' – a religious category that according to Bjerregaard did not contain the *Bhagavadgītā* (Bjerregaard 1912: 94) – is said to be connected with 'priestcraft' and is explicitly said to be non-progressive. Likewise, Zoroastrianism is characterized as 'a dualism that contains no redemption' (Bjerregaard 1912: 94), and Confucius and his followers are associated with mere attention to ceremonies, a problematic preoccupation since 'ceremonialism has been the bane of China' (Bjerregaard 1912: 96). Along with Buddha and Jesus, then, Laozi's teachings are seen to be comparatively free from ceremonialism or ritualism, priestcraft and dualism.

Bjerregaard's view of history departed in several ways from influential tendencies in the esoteric movements of his time. His notion of how spiritual truth that has been preserved throughout history does not give any prominent position to secret societies or hidden masters. It does not even necessarily entail the preservation of *esoteric* truths in the sense of inner interpretations different from the surface meaning of sacred texts and the official doctrines of religious organizations. While Bjerregaard clearly felt unbound by traditional religious authorities when he interpreted texts held sacred by religious traditions like Christianity or Daoism, he did not give a prominent place to any explicit claim of representing a historical tradition preserving an inner truth, which exoteric authorities had tried to suppress or simply failed to understand. Furthermore, although we should be wary of forcing complex and often contradictory ideas about history into neat and simple models, Bjerregaard's understanding of historical development is closer to Wouter Hanegraaff's notion of *pia philosophia* than most esoteric writers of his time (Hanegraaff 2014: 6–12). In other words, Bjerregaard was more concerned with progress than with trying to regain a lost form of truth. Although, as Olav Hammer has pointed out, most late nineteenth- and early twentieth-century esoteric movements managed to combine these apparently contradictory positions in different ways, Bjerregaard presented a view of history that was more about a straightforward celebration of progress than trying to balance this notion with a wish to revive ancient truths (Hammer 2004: 198).

Preferring Old Tan

It is very clear that to Bjerregaard the teachings of Laozi and the *Daodejing* constituted the expressions of wisdom in Chinese culture. Although a few other Chinese texts are mentioned in his works, he retained the primary focus on Laozi and what he sometimes called 'Taoism'. In *The Inner Life and the Tao-Teh-King*, Bjerregaard wrote concerning the relationship between Laozi and Confucius (Bjerregaard 1912: 62):

> [Laozi] and Confucius met once and the following is part of a conversation that took place between them. Confucius is blamed for all the fuss he makes about laws, rules and regulations. It is reported by one of Laotzse's disciples that he spoke as follows to Confucius on the subject of Simplicity: 'The chaff from winnowing will blind a man. Mosquitoes will bite a man and keep him awake all night and so it is with all this talk of yours about charity and duty to one's neighbor, it drives me crazy'.

The quote about the chaff, although shortened, is drawn from Herbert Giles's (1845–1935) translation of the *Zhuangzi* 莊子 (Giles 1889: 184). Stories about Confucius and his interactions with a character often identified with Laozi occur in a number of classical Chinese texts. Their historical meaning is complex and vary depending on context. In late nineteenth-century European literary and esoteric sources, however, these stories became popular and were often quoted as a rebuke of the perceived moralism and superficiality of Confucianism (e.g. de Pouvourville 1905: 496). Almost without exception, the 'philanthropic and mundane doctrines' of Confucius were taken to be the exoteric surface of Chinese culture under which the true esoteric mysticism of Laozi was concealed (Old 1892). Writing in *The Theosophist*, Charles Spurgeon Medhurst (1909: 336) argued: 'Confucius and Lao Tzu represent divergent lines; the former is the practical man of affairs, the latter a mystic for mystics. It scarcely needs mentioning that the few who appreciate Lao Tzu are the leaders of Chinese spirituality.' The same distinction colored René Guénon's (1886–1951) understanding of the relationship between Daoism and Confucianism and likely had a significant impact on the way Confucianism was understood among enthusiasts of non-European religious traditions in Europe and elsewhere in the twentieth century (Guénon 1932). Bjerregaard did not develop his critique of Confucianism in detail. Only three things are clear: (1) He did not associate Confucius with any kind of ultimate truth. Although not altogether systematic in his terminology, concepts like 'mystic' and 'theosophical' are used to describe Laozi but not Confucius (see, e.g. Bjerregaard 1912: v); (2) Confucius was almost exclusively presented as a teacher of laws and duty (Bjerregaard 1912: 62–3); (3) He viewed the influence of Confucius as overwhelmingly negative, stating that 'Confusius' [sic] insistence upon laws, ordinances and rescripts had [a] fatal effect upon China, and, Confusianism [sic] no doubt is the cause of China's misery' (Bjerregaard 1912: 63).

Bjerregaard was very much a product of his time – and not only due to his preference for Laozi. The influence of the sinology of his day can also be seen in his understanding of the later religious traditions to which Laozi was associated. Although Bjerregaard used the term "Taoist" mostly in a positive sense, his concept of what constituted Daoism was largely limited to a small number of texts, mostly from the classical period and no later than the early Han dynasty. Like most of his contemporaries, he tended to see later Daoist traditions through a lens of degeneration. As he put it (Bjerregaard 1912: 97):

> A word or two about Taoism after Laotzse. Taoism as a system and in relation to Laotzse, is much like Christianity in its relation to Jesus: in both cases is

the founder ignored, his teachings shamefully perverted and a priestly system substituted for the founder's benevolent and sublime ideas. Taoism has temples and a pope. It is full of spiritism, superstitions and pretenses. It is a mixture of alchemy, polytheism and yoga practices. It is degeneration and disgrace.

Here we see a clear example of what Louis Komjathy has called the bifurcated interpretation of Daoism; that is, a division between what is sometimes called early (or philosophical) and late (or religious) Daoism (Komjathy 2014: 3–5). The former was primarily associated with the *Daodejing* and a handful of early texts, like the *Zhuangzi*. The latter was associated with the rise of Daoism in its institutional form, as a ritual tradition and hierarchical religious movement that had emerged with the Celestial Masters. The distinction was almost always emphatically normative. Influential sinologists like James Legge (1815–97) rejected later Daoist traditions, labelling them as 'degenerate' and 'nonsense' (Legge 1891). The influence of this way of understanding Daoism has been noted and explored by several modern scholars who have generally interpreted it as rising out of a combination of an elite Chinese perspective and some values current among nineteenth-century European scholars of religion (Komjathy 2014: 3–5; Kirkland 2004: 1–5, 1997; Girardot 2002: 443–4). Norman J. Girardot (2002: 12) puts it succinctly:

> In this sense . . . the standard emphasis on the early, pure, philosophical or classical Daoism associated with Laozi and Zhuangzi was in part a Ruist or Confucianized way of distinguishing the later ritualistic, corrupt, and heterodox Daoist religion, and in part a recasting of the overall Daoist tradition in the Müllerian, comparativist, Protestant, and Orientalist developmental pattern of world religions.

It is interesting, however, that this way of interpreting Daoism also exerted a strong influence on the esoteric understanding of that religion. It remains likely that the influence of this early esoteric interpretation to some degree colored the later popular understanding of Daoism in the twentieth century. Although few esoteric writers were as harsh as Legge, and some actually presented a mild form of criticism against the bifurcated interpretation of Daoism, most accepted the distinction and its implicit or explicit value judgements (Nilsson 2020: 228–36). Although Bjerregaard was repeating one of the most influential ideas about Daoism current in his day, his rejection of what he believed post-Classical Daoism to be was to a certain extent logical when considering his values and tastes. Both Bjerregaard and almost every authority on Chinese religion accessible to him understood later Daoism to be characterized by priestly hierarchies and a well-developed ritual tradition. That is, it was seen as characterized by things that Bjerregaard regularly condemned, even when associated with other religious traditions.

Simplicity, nature, non-action

As we have seen, Bjerregaard associated the ultimate truths of China primarily with the teachings of Laozi, which he sometimes called Taoism. We have also seen that Bjerregaard was careful to distinguish these teachings from the post-Classical Daoist traditions as well as from a number of negative tendencies current among religions, most importantly 'priestcraft' and 'ceremonialism'. But what were the teachings of Laozi? And, more importantly, which aspects of these teachings interested Bjerregaard the most?

The concept of non-action or *wuwei* 無為 is central to Bjerregaard's presentation of the teachings of Laozi. It is described as an inner emptiness and at the same time as an absorption into the Dao. Bjerregaard remarked that the concept of *wuwei* is frequently misunderstood, '[t]he method of "not-doing" is unfortunately always understood as doing nothing' (Bjerregaard 1912: 193). This, however, is incorrect. Instead, '"non-action" means having nothing to do with the incidental, the trivial, the "passing show," the phenomenal and devoting oneself exclusively and with energy to the essential and the real' (Bjerregaard 1912: 195). Bjerregaard insisted that non-action did not entail a withdrawal from the world. This, as we shall see, is an important distinction, which in Bjerregaard's mind distinguishes Daoism from Indian religions. 'Taoism by Wu Wei or non action', he wrote, 'is suitable for a practical world and makes wise men, who can be in the world and rule it and yet not be of it, nor lost in it' (Bjerregaard 1912: 193). Non-action is accomplished by suppressing the 'the noise of the senses and the clamorous desires' and by cultivating a form of childlike, non-reflexive absorption in daily life. Speaking of the sages revered by Laozi and his contemporaries, Bjerregaard wrote: 'Theirs was the simple life; they did not talk it, they lived it' (Bjerregaard 1912: 197). Simplicity, in fact, was an important consequence of non-action. It is not necessarily ascetic in an outward sense. As Bjerregaard put it, '[s]implicity does not necessarily mean a "Simple Life." Simplicity may be found in the midst of great abundance' (Bjerregaard 1912: 60). It is however, closely associated with nature and naturalness.

Bjerregaard in context

Many of the themes, notions and value judgements that shaped Bjerregaard's understanding of Chinese religion were also popular in the broader esoteric (and non-esoteric) engagement with Chinese culture. Some of his ideas and opinions existed comfortably in the mainstream of esoteric interpretations of China; others, although common, were not completely hegemonic among esoteric writers.

As Vincent Goossaert has shown in his study of the local and organizational expressions of Daoism, entitled *The Taoists of Peking* (2007), Daoism in China was highly shaped by religious specialists of different types at the time that Bjerregaard was writing. Temple clerics, mendicants and monks were inseparable from the way Daoism was practiced and organized as a whole (Goossaert 2007). This, however, is seldom the image we get from reading about Daoism in the works of esoteric writers. As we have seen, Bjerregaard had only distrust for 'priests' and imagined Daoism apparently consisting of solitary textual study and absorption in nature. Priests, temples and polytheism were signs of decline (Bjerregaard 1912: 97). This disregard for the organizations, social forms and types of specialists that were historically associated with Daoism was common among representatives of esoteric movements. There were some exceptions, but these were almost always associated with an interest in fraternal societies, like the Tiandihui 天地會 (literally, Heaven and Earth Society; an organization that was often seen as Daoist by esoteric writers), rather than the more traditional Daoist movements, like the Zhengyi 正一 (Orthodox Unity). This is of course interesting in itself and can likely be explained in part by what Karl Baier has called 'convergences', that is, perceived similarities between two cultural forms (Baier 2016: 318). Those European esoteric movements that were influenced by masonry tended to recognize and respond positively to highly formalized initiatory organizations like the Tiandihui. Some, like the French esoteric writer Albert de Pouvourville, were inclined to see these societies as central to Daoism (de Pouvourville 1896; Mundus 1900; de Commaille 1905) – although de Pouvourville was more or less unique in claiming to belong to one of them (de Pouvourville 1936). Still, the tendency did not extend to a more general interest in religious specialists or organizational forms, and most esoteric writers who took an interest in Daoism ignored this aspect of the religion. A related tendency in Bjerregaard's work was his complete disinterest in the pantheons of Daoism.[10] Like priests, polytheism is associated with decadence in his writings. However, the deep European cultural distaste for polytheism is not enough of an explanation for his views. Unlike others, Bjerregaard did not try to read monotheism in the *Daodejing*, and to him Laozi remained a human figure. There is no Lord Lao in *The Inner Life and the Tao-Teh-King*. In this regard, Bjerregaard's writings were typical of how Daoism was treated in the esoteric movements of the period. To a certain extent, this might have been a result of the texts that were available in translations accessible to most members of these movements. The available texts primarily associated with Daoism at the time – above all the *Daodejing* and the *Zhuangzi* – mention gods only sparingly. Still, some of the relevant esoteric writers had visited China. Moreover, the Protestant or modernist norms, like those underpinning the distaste for decadent 'religious Daoism', again do not offer a complete explanation. Although these norms fit quite well with Bjerregaard, individuals like Aleister Crowley (1875–1947) had no problems with gods, rituals or even priests outside the specific context of their interpretation of Daoism.[11] Likely a mix of all these explanations comes closest to clarifying the situation.

Concluding remarks

Although never in the majority, there existed a group of writers in the esoteric environment of the late nineteenth and early twentieth century who took a specific interest in Chinese religions. Among them was the Danish-American librarian C. H. A. Bjerregaard. He wrote about Chinese religion in several of the esoteric periodicals of the time and published a monograph entitled *The Inner Life and the Tao-Teh-King* in 1912. Bjerregaard was very critical of Confucius and saw Confucianism as exoteric teachings that had exerted a negative influence on Chinese culture. Instead, he focused on Laozi who he believed served an important historical function. Bjerregaard described history as a spiral motion moving in circles but also tending toward progress. This progress is, in part, made possible by influential religious ideas. Besides other influential religious founders, like Jesus and Buddha, the ideas of figures like Laozi have played a part. Thus, Bjerregaard participated in and contributed to a shift in the European and American understanding of Chinese religions. In a way that was typical of how Daoism was understood in the esoteric environment of the period, he associated the religion with a few early texts (primarily the *Daodejing*) and saw post-classical Daoism as degenerate. For Bjerregaard, Laozi's message was simplicity, non-action and a proper relationship to nature. Like most other representatives of Theosophy and other esoteric movements, he took no interest in religious specialists or organizations historically connected to Daoism. Similarly, he disregarded the pantheons of historical Daoist movements and regarded Laozi as simply a human being. Thus, he represented an early example of a way of interpreting Daoism that was to become common up to the present day.

Notes

1. On de Pouvourville, see the chapter by Davide Marino in this volume.
2. According to Bjerregaard's own account, he was hired as an assistant at the Astor Library in 1879. In 1882 he became a librarian (Rasmussen 2016: 155).
3. Transcendentalism was a movement which emerged in the first half of the nineteenth century. Partly influenced by European Romanticism, it valued individualism, self-reliance and the human connection with the natural world. Transcendentalism's impact remained in American culture and influenced later movements, like New Thought. The Hermetic Brotherhood of Luxor was an occult order active in the late nineteenth century and greatly influenced by the American occultist Paschal Beverly Randolph (1825–1975). The order is said to have emphasized ritual work and to have taught techniques for developing clairvoyance and astral travel. According to Patrick Bowen (2015: 100), Bjerregaard had been a member (Godwin, Chance and Deveney 1995).
4. It should be noted that Bjerregaard does not use the terms occultism or esotericism to refer to his own beliefs, preferring instead terms like mysticism or "the Inner Life." He is explicitly critical of occultism which he views as a potentially dangerous attempt to control hidden forces in nature in contrast to the inner cultivation of mysticism as he understands it (Bjerregaard 1912: 36). Nonetheless, I would argue that there are enough social and ideational connections between him and the esoteric environment of his time, as this is commonly understood today (Hanegraaff 2014; von Stuckrad 2005: 9–11), to make the early twentieth-century esoteric or occult milieu an important context for his work.
5. In Theosophy, the root races are major divisions of human physical and spiritual evolution. They supposedly proceed from one another and follow each other in a chain from the first to the seventh race, progressively becoming more evolved. Modern humanity belongs to the fifth root race (Santucci 2008).
6. On Lévi, see the chapter by Franz Winter in this volume.
7. See for example Antonin Artaud's (1896–1948) *Héliogabale ou l'anarchiste couronné* (1967) or H. P. Lovecraft's (1890–1937) *Call of Cthulhu* (1928).
8. It is not always self-evident which historical events are corresponding to Bjerregaard's changes in cycles. It is not unlikely, however, that he referred, among

other things, to the Western Han Dynasty, '[a]t about the beginning of our era', and the emergence of the Song Dynasty around the year 1,000 (Bjerregaard 1897: 95).

9   In other works by Bjerregaard, the historical cycles seem to be significantly longer. In *The Inner Life and the Tao-Teh-King* he stated that we are still in the same cycle instigated by Laozi more than two millennia ago (Bjerregaard 1912: 92). Elsewhere in the same text, the cycle instigated by Laozi is said to have ended with Greece and Rome, presumably in late antiquity (Bjerregaard 1912: 91).

10 For a short introduction, see Komjathy (2014: 79–100).

11 For a discussion of Crowley in this context, see Nilsson (2013), and the chapter by Gordan Djurdjevic in this volume.

References

Anonymous (1886), 'Theosophical Activities', *The Path*, 1 (1): 30–2.

Artaud, A. (1967), *Héliogabale ou L'Anarchiste Couronné, Oeuvres Complètes VII*, Paris: Éditions Gallimard.

Baier, K. (2016), 'Theosophical Orientalism and the Structures of Intercultural Transfer: Annotations on the Appropriation of the *cakras* in Early Theosophy', in J. Chajes and B. Huss (eds), *Theosophical Appropriations: Esotericism, Kabbalah, and the Transformation of Traditions*, 309–52, Beer Sheva: Ben-Gurion University Press.

Bjerregaard, C. H. A. (1895), 'Tao the Chinese "Being"', *The Metaphysical Magazine*, 1 (5): 410–21.

Bjerregaard, C. H. A. (1897), *Lectures on Mysticism and Nature Worship*, Chicago: M. R. Kent.

Bjerregaard, C. H. A. (1899), 'The Mind of China, Japan, America and the New Age', *The Metaphysical Magazine*, 9 (4): 243–50.

Bjerregaard, C. H. A. (1912), *The Inner Life and the Tao-Teh-King*, New York: The Theosophical Publishing Co.

Blavatsky, H. (1888), *The Secret Doctrine*, London: Theosophical Publishing Company.

Bowen, P. D. (2015), *A History of Conversion to Islam in the United States*, vol. 1, Leiden: Brill.

de Commaille, E. (1905), 'L'Evolution des Sociétés secretes au Tonkin', *La Voie*, 14: 42–50.

de Pouvourville, A. (1896), 'Le Taoïsme et les Sociétés Secrètes Chinoises', *L'Initiation*, 33 (1): 4–34.

de Pouvourville, A. (1905), 'Laotseu', *La Voie*, 12: 481–506.

de Pouvourville, A. (1936) 'Aux Tournants de la Voie [1]', *La Nouvelle Revue Indochinoise*, no 5: 223–26.

Giles, H. A. (1889), *Chuang Tzŭ: Mystic, Moralist, and Social Reformer*, London: Bernard Quaritch.

Girardot, N. J. (2002), *The Victorian Translation of China*, Berkeley: The University of California Press.

Godwin, J., C. Chane and J. P. Deveney (1995), *The Hermetic Brotherhood of Luxor: Initiatic and Historical Documents of an Order of Practical Occultism*, New York: Weiser.

Goossaert, V. (2007), *The Taoists of Peking, 1800-1949: A Social History of Urban Clerics*, Cambridge, MA: Harvard University Press.

Guénon, R. (1932), 'Taoïsme and Confucianisme', *Le Voile d'Isis*, May: 485–508.

Hammer, O. (2004), *Claiming Knowledge: Strategies of Epistemology from Theosophy to the New Age*, Leiden: Brill.

Hanegraaff, W. (2014), *Esotericism in the Academy: Rejected Knowledge in Western Culture*, Cambridge: Cambridge University Press.

Kilcher, A. B., ed. (2010), *Constructing Tradition: Means and Myths of Transmission in Western Esotericism*, Leiden: Brill.

Kirkland, R. (1997), 'The Taoism of the Western Imagination and the Taoism of China: De-colonizing the Exotic Teachings of the East', Paper Presented at the University of Tennessee, 20 October. Available online: http://kirkland.myweb.uga.edu/rk/pdflpubs/pres/TEN 97.pdf (accessed 14 July 2022).

Kirkland, R. (2004), *Taoism the Enduring Tradition*, London: Routledge.

Komjathy, L. (2014), *Daoism: A Guide for the Perplexed*, London: Bloomsbury.

Legge, J. (1891), *The Texts of Taoism*, Oxford: Clarendon Press.

Lévi, É. (1860), *Histoire de la magie*, Paris: Germer Baillière.

Lovecraft, H. P. (1928), 'The Call of Cthulhu', *Weird Tales*, 11 (2): 159–78.

Mundus, A. (1900), 'La Grande Societe Secret Chinoise', *L'Initiation*, 47 (9): 221–49.

Nilsson, J. (2013), 'Defending Paper Gods: Aleister Crowley and the Reception of Daoism in Early Twentieth Century Esotericism', *Correspondences*, 1 (1): 103–27.

Nilsson, J. (2020), 'As a Fire Beneath the Ashes: The Quest for Chinese Wisdom within Occultism, 1850-1949', PhD diss., Centre for Theology and Religious Studies, University of Lund.

Old, W. R. (1892), 'Tao', *Lucifer*, 11 (63): 204–14.

Rasmussen, L. (2016), *C.H.A. Bjerregaard og det indre liv: en dansk mystiker i New York*, Copenhagen: Booktrader.

Saint-Yves d'Alveydre, J. A. ([1884] 1981), *Mission des Juifs*, Paris: Éditions Traditionnelles.

Santucci, J. A. (2008), 'The Notion of Race in Theosophy', *Nova Religio: The Journal of Alternative and Emergent Religions*, 11 (3): 37–63.

Sedgwick, M. (2017), *Western Sufism*, Oxford: Oxford University Press.

Spurgeon Medhurst, C. (1909), 'Chinese Esotericism 1', *The Theosophist* 31 (3): 331–44.

Trompf, G. W. (1998), 'Macrohistory in Blavatsky, Steiner and Guénon', in A. Faivre and W. J. Hanegraaff (eds), *Western Esotericism and the Science of Religion*, 269–96, Leuven: Peeters.

Trompf, G. W. (2008), 'Macrohistory', in W. Hanegraaff (ed.), *Dictionary of Gnosis and Western Esotericism*, 701–16, Leiden: Brill.
von Stuckrad, K. (2005), *Western Esotericism: A Brief History of Secret Knowledge*, London: Equinox.

6

Do what dao wilt

The integration of East Asian concepts and practices into Aleister Crowley's Thelema

Gordan Djurdjevic

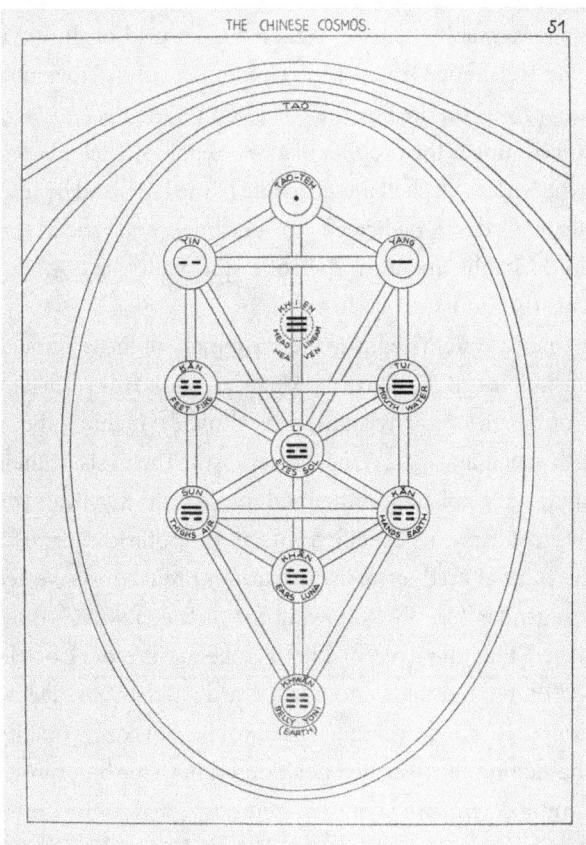

Figure 6.1 'The Chinese Cosmos', by O. Hopfer, in Crowley, *The Book of Thoth: A Short Essay on the Tarot of the Egyptians* (1944), p. 270. © Ordo Templi Orientis /Oskar Hopfer Estate. Used with permission.

Introduction

On 20 November 1945, seventy-year-old British occultist Aleister Crowley (1875–1947) entertained to lunch Enid, Countess of Kenmare (1892–1973), and the wife of the Chinese ambassador, Mrs Wellington Koo (1889–1992), at a guesthouse in the coastal town of Hastings, his last home.[1] Writing the following day to his disciple Karl Germer (1885–1962), Crowley (1945) noted that he 'insisted very strongly' at the lunch that China should be spiritually unified by relying on her traditional philosophy and ethics. He continued: 'I further made the point that, as between the Eastern and Western points of view, my own work in identifying the system of the Tao and of the Yi King with our own of the Qabalah was the one matter of supreme importance' (1945). The significance of Crowley's statement, evaluating the importance of his own work at the sunset of a long and rich career as a practitioner and theoretician of various branches of esotericism, is remarkable.[2] Crowley entered the world of the occult by taking initiation in the Hermetic Order of the Golden Dawn in November 1898.[3] His subsequent career was marked by the reception of *The Book of the Law* in 1904, which announced him as the prophet of a new religion, Thelema, with its central tenet of 'Do what thou wilt shall be the whole of the Law', and by his involvement in two esoteric Orders, dedicated to personal and social promulgation, exploration and establishment of Thelemic spirituality: the A∴A∴ and Ordo Templi Orientis (O.T.O.).[4]

Crowley named a system dedicated to the pursuit of the religious, philosophic and ethical principles of Thelema as Magick. Aside from Thelema, the main constituents of Magick as envisioned by Crowley include the traditions of Western, South Asian and East Asian esotericism. The basis of their correlation was the system of Kabbalah, ingrained in Jewish mystical traditions, but eventually divorced from its specific roots as an esoteric exegesis of the Torah and employed, in its altered form, by the various branches of Western occultism for their own agendas (see the following for further remarks on this subject). Crowley believed that the Tree of Life, a schematic model of classifying the universe based on ten numbers and twenty-two letters of the Hebrew alphabet, could function as a filing cabinet that would not only qualify individual phenomena based on their ascribed position on the Tree but, more importantly, illustrate the mutual sympathy between items assigned to the same place. Thus, he believed he was able to correlate the Tree of Life with what he termed the 'Chinese cosmos', by which he had in mind the concepts of *dao* 道, *de* 德, *yin* 陰, *yang* 陽 and the eight trigrams that form the basis of *Yijing* 易經 (Classic of Changes). This correlation was precisely what Crowley considered 'the one matter of supreme importance'. What follows will investigate the main steps that led him to arrive at this particular juncture.

Early writings on Daoist themes: 'Thien Tao', 'Liber Trigrammaton' and 'The Soul of the Desert'

Crowley travelled through China in 1906, of which journey he wrote appreciatively in his autobiographical *Confessions*.[5] His first published work reflective of East Asian spiritual philosophy was a short satirical essay entitled 'Thien Tao or The Synagogue of Satan', included in his 1907 volume *Konx Om Pax*. Described by its author, who rarely lacked a glorified view of his own compositions, as 'my solution to the main ethical and philosophical problems of humanity with a description of the general method of emancipating oneself from the obsession of one's own ideas' (Crowley 1989: 537), the essay proposes a way of equilibrium as a proper model for restoring political, economic, spiritual and personal well-being in a fictionalized Japan ruled by a *daimyō* 大名. This is achieved by deliberately engaging in the activities that are contrary to one's habitual way of life:

> To the prostitute I prescribe a course of training by which she shall comprehend the holiness of sex. Chastity forms part of that training [...]. To the prude equally I prescribe a course of training by which she shall comprehend the holiness of sex. Unchastity forms part of that training [...]. To the bigot I commend a course of Thomas Henry Huxley; to the infidel a practical study of ceremonial magic. (Crowley 1907: 62)

The whole project is summarily described in a biblical metaphor (a paraphrase of Isa. 11.6): 'Give the lion the heart of the lamb, and the lamb the force of the lion; and they will lie down in peace together' (Crowley 1907: 64). It is noticeable that the method, intentionally or not, resembles the general principle behind Chinese traditional medicine, which attempts to heal the disease by treating the assumed imbalance of the internal energies within the body.

The course of action described earlier is prescribed to the daimyō by a fictionalized and idealized Crowley in his persona of a Daoist adept, the philosopher Kwaw, who 'landed at Nagasaki after an exhilarating swim from the mainland' (Crowley 1907: 58).[6] It is worthwhile to consider the description of his spiritual progress, which indicates Crowley's take on the trajectory of East Asian esoteric endeavours and one facet of their correlation with the kabbalistic Tree of Life (Crowley 1907: 58):

> In the first year he disciplined and conquered his body and its emotions.
> In the next six years he conquered his mind and its thoughts.
> In the next two years he had reduced the Universe to the Yang and the Yin and their permutations in the trigrams of Fo-hi and the hexagrams of King Wu.
> In the last year, he abolished the Yang and the Yin, and became united with the great Tao.

The ten years of practice in the quote correspond to the aspects of the ten *sephiroth* ('numbers') on the Tree: the first year correlates with *Malkuth*, which in the occultist Kabbalah stands for the material plane of existence and physical body; the following six years refer to the aspects of *Ruach*, associated with the various faculties of the mind, broadly conceived; the following two years of practice correspond to the *sephiroth Chokmah* and *Binah* ('Wisdom' and 'Understanding'), which Crowley here correlates with *yang* and *yin* respectively and at other places with *liṅga* and *yoni*,[7] divine father and mother and the related binary concepts; and finally, the tenth year of practice refers to the *sephirah Kether* ('Crown'), where the pertinent spiritual achievement in the terminology of Western mysticism would be a union with God and is here described as a union 'with the great Tao'.[8]

A similar model of spiritual journey is depicted in Crowley's short text 'The Way of the Dao',[9] written in 1907, which describes a series of proposed practices, or rather trials, that involve an ascending initiatory trajectory along the Tree of Life. The practices are so designed that they correspond to the attributes of the respective stations (paths or *sephiroth*) along the Tree. Thus, the first four trials involve facing four aspects of the lowest *sephirah* on the Tree, the *Malkuth*, associated with the material plane and conventionally divided into four segments that correlate with the traditional 'elements' (earth, water, fire and air): the candidate for initiation is facing darkness while fasting for twenty-four hours (corresponding to earth); is bathed, eats and drinks cold food and wine and contemplates the universe as made of water; is exposed to heat and eats and drinks fiery food and wines while contemplating the universe as fire; and is exposed to air, preferably on a mountaintop, while meditating on the universe as composed of air. The practices continue in a similar manner, ending with annihilation, that is, 'crossing of the Abyss',[10] which is one of the two main tasks in the system of the A∴A∴ (the prior one consists in obtaining 'the Knowledge and Conversation of the Holy Guardian Angel'). What is interesting is that there is nothing specifically Daoist in the depiction of any practice, with the important exception of the text's title. The assumption is that the model of the Tree of Life represents an objective illustration of the external (and internal) universe, constituting thus a natural template of the realm that needs to be spiritually mastered, and that progress along the path of achievement is best described as the 'Way of the Dao'.[11]

A deep and overt correspondence between Chinese and Thelemic esotericism is on full display in a short, inspired text called 'Liber Trigrammaton' (Crowley 1983: 43–9). Subtitled as 'The Book of the Trigrams of the Mutations of the Tao with the Yin and the Yang', this is one of the so-called 'Holy Books of Thelema'. Crowley, their avowed scribe, wrote about their genesis (1989: 559): 'I can only say that I was not wholly conscious at the time of what I was writing... The prose of these books ... is wholly different from anything I have written myself.... I cannot doubt that these books are the work of an intelligence independent of my own.' Based on Crowley's diaries, 'Liber Trigrammaton' was received on 14 December 1907 (see Crowley 1983: xix). The text operates with three symbols and their permutations (always in sets of three): the point, symbolizing the *dao* (1), the full, *yang* line (2) and the broken, *yin* line (3). The threefold symbols are accompanied by a short (typically one sentence), poetic and often enigmatic text; the first symbol consists of three dots; the last eight symbols correspond to the trigrams of the *Yijing*. (Since the texts operates with mutual combinations of three symbols, there are twenty-seven resulting trigrams.) 'Liber Trigrammaton' in its terse prose describes, in Crowley's own words (1919: 13), 'the Course of Creation under the Figure of the Interplay of Three Principles'. In the present context, however, the significance of the text itself, its subject matter and its manner of composition, places it also within a long tradition of similarly inspired, received Daoist texts.[12]

Crowley formally introduced elements of East Asian thought in the 'Appendix' to his 1909 textbook of kabbalistic correspondences, *777*.[13] The 'Appendix' lists the eight trigrams and sixty-four hexagrams of the *Yijing* and correlates them to their elemental and planetary analogues as well as parts of the body (in case of the trigrams). Two of the eight trigrams are also correlated with the *sephiroth* on the Tree of Life, while the remaining six are associated with the paths. This arrangement was later modified while preparing a revised edition of *777* around 1925, where all the trigrams are placed on the *sephiroth*, in addition to *yin* and *yang* line, as well as the point which by its lack of dimensions was chosen as symbolically appropriate to represent the roots of both *dao* and *de* and placed on the highest *sephirah*, Kether (see Figure 6.1). The *dao* was also attributed to the so-called 'veil of the negative' that surrounds the complete Tree of Life.[14] It is this final correlation between the Hebrew and Chinese models that Crowley considered his major achievement and contribution to comparative esotericism.

Of interest also is the essay 'The Soul of the Desert', written at Tozeur in Tunisia and originally published in *The Occult Review* in 1914.[15] The argument of the text is rather subtle as some of its main points are only implied by the overt thematic contents. Explicitly, the essay addresses the mental attitude that manifests while facing the naked simplicity of the desert environment. The soul, devoid of the external stimuli, 'realizes itself as itself, as a thing separate from that which is not itself, from God' (Crowley 1998: 53). This is resolved in one of two possible ways: either the ego clings to itself, afraid of its dissolution and is consequently 'slowly torn by the claws of circumstance, disintegrated bitterly, for all its struggles, throughout ages and ages' (Crowley 1998: 54). Alternatively, 'the soul that has understood the blessedness of resignation which grasps the Universe and devours it, which is without hope or fear, without faith or doubt, without hate or love, dissolves itself ineffably into the abounding bliss of God' (Crowley 1998: 54). What Crowley actually addresses here is a description of what he elsewhere designates as 'crossing the Abyss'. The 'Abyss' is occasionally symbolized by a desert (e.g. Crowley 1913: 53). And what connects the essay with Chinese spirituality is the argument that the soul in this environment faces 'the eight genii of the desert', which are 'the eight Elements of Fu-hsi [i.e., Fuxi 伏羲]', idiosyncratically defined as *liṅga*, the Sun, fire and air (all male), and *yoni*, the Moon, water and earth (all female). In other words, 'the eight genii of the desert' are the four classical 'elements', the two main luminaries, and the two generative principles. The further implication is that while the eight constitutive trigrams of *Yijing* comprise the essence of the phenomenal universe, they are simultaneously translatable into archetypal principles that are both nearly universal (the Sun, the Moon, the four 'elements'), or equivalent to specific concepts as found in other cultures – in this case, the Indian Tantra (*liṅga, yoni*).[16] In doing so, Crowley arguably achieved two purposes simultaneously: he not only demonstrated that the 'Chinese esotericism' is compatible with other regional varieties, but equally importantly he established in what manner and to what degree that compatibility pertains.

'Translating' Daoist classics: Crowley's versions of the *Qingjing jing* and the *Daodejing*

Arguably, the most important events related to Crowley's involvement with East Asian religious thought occurred during what he referred to as a 'Great Magical Retirement' on Esopus island, on the Hudson river in the state of New York, in the summer of 1918. During this period, he claimed to have recovered a memory of a series of previous lives,[17] one of which was as Ko Hsüan (i.e. Ge Xuan 葛玄, 164–244), a 'disciple of Lao Tzu', the 'author' of the *Qingjing jing* 清靜經, the 'Classic of Purity' (Crowley 1989: 839).[18] Crowley 'translated' it into English during the retreat, relying on the published version of the famous Victorian-era sinologist James Legge (1815–97) (Legge 1891b: 247–54) and putting the text into a rhyme (Crowley 1939).[19] Even more significantly, at the time Crowley also 'translated' the *Daodejing* 道德經. He describes the circumstances that resulted in this accomplishment in his 'Introduction' to the text, published posthumously (Crowley 1995: 10):

> From 1905 to 1918, the *Tao Te Ching* was my continual study. [. . . Disappointed with Legge's translation] I felt myself impelled to undertake the task of presenting Lao Tzu in language informed by the sympathetic understanding which initiation and spiritual experience had conferred on me. [. . .] I set myself to this work, but I discovered immediately that I was totally incompetent. I therefore appealed to an Adept named Amalantrah, with whom I was at that time in almost daily communion. He came readily to my aid, and exhibited to me a codex of the original, which conveyed to me with absolute certitude the exact significance of the text.

As Hymenaeus Beta (William Breeze), the editor of the 1995 publication of the text, mentions in his 'Foreword', the discarnate adept Amalantrah, who provided Crowley with 'a codex of the original' text of *Daodejing*, belongs to a class of spiritual beings that 'a Taoist would most likely term an "immortal [i.e., *xian* 仙]"' (Crowley 1995: x). Crowley's claim, while obviously fully vulnerable to criticism from the point of view of sinological scholarship, is nevertheless in harmony with numberless examples of similarly received texts, which examples are a staple not only of the Daoist tradition but are virtually universal in 'world religions'. It would be inconsistent to reject Crowley's assertion regarding the perceived source of his inspiration while treating considerately other documents that claim to be a fruit of spiritual experiences. What is involved here are epistemological and ontological issues that transcend the scope of this paper. I will only point out an additional element of interest in Crowley's account. It concerns the Theosophical Society's notion of reading from the 'Akashic Records', understood, as Brandt and Hammer (2012: 122) explain the term, 'in the sense of a comprehensive world memory (and possibly also a repository of future events)'.[20] In the subtitle of the text, Crowley explicitly states that it was 'translated from the code manifested in the *Ākāśa*'. This is a relatively rare example of Crowley's overt adoption of Theosophical nomenclature. He tended to have negative views of the contemporary Society, despite his professed admiration of Madame Blavatsky (1831–91).

Regarding formal differences between Legge's and Crowley's versions of the text, the latter is more succinct and is consequently more readable. Generally speaking, however, Crowley's rendition of the *Daodejing* is not radically different from Legge's. His innovation is to add titles to each of the eighty-one chapters of the text. Understandably, the ideas and, in some instances, even phrasings from *The Book of the Law* occasionally show up in his version. References to the Thelemic world view are, however, more prominent in his comments to the text.[21] To provide an example, the first verse of the Chapter VII is articulated, by Crowley (1995: 22), as: 'Heaven and Earth are mighty in continuance, because their work is delivered from the lust of result.'[22] He comments (1995: 22, n.17): 'See *CCXX* [*The Book of the Law*, I: 44] as to "lust of result". The general idea of the Way of the Tao is that all evil is interference. It is unnatural action which is error. Non-action is commendable only as a corrective of such; to interfere with one's own true Way is Restriction, the word of Sin.' Here, a phrase from *The Book of the Law* was used in the rendition of a verse from the *Daodejing*, while the commentary accomplishes a tour de force of harmonizing the 'Way of the Tao' with Thelema by elucidating precepts of the former through a quotation from the sacred text of the latter (interference with the way of the Dao is explained as 'Restriction', which *The Book of the Law* [I: 41] defines as 'the word of Sin'). The aforementioned remarks apply equally to Crowley's version of *Daodejing* and to his commentaries to its contents: his version tends to suggest a commonality between Daoist and Thelemic world views, which is more explicit in his commentaries to the text, written at a later period.

Working with the *Yijing*: Crowley's interpretation of the eight trigrams

Crowley's involvement with *Yijing* was a complex affair.[23] Fascinated by its merits, he employed it for divinatory purposes for decades, virtually on a daily basis. As Richard Smith (2012: 191) commented, Crowley 'adopted a self-consciously mystical approach to the *Changes* – a harbinger of countercultural enthusiasm for the document that would peak worldwide in the 1960s and 1970s'. Crowley (1997: 253) argued that it is 'in some ways the most perfect hieroglyph ever constructed. It is austere and sublime, yet withal so adaptable to every possible emergency that its figures may be interpreted to suit all classes of questions'. Yet, he was not familiar with either of the two traditional methods of *Yijing* divination: neither with the manipulations of fifty stalks of yarrow, nor with the other, simpler technique, of tossing the three coins. Instead, he devised a method of using six painted wooden sticks, one side representing the *yang* and the other the *yin* line. By laying them down, after shuffling them while focused on the question, and starting with the bottom line stick, he would formulate a hexagram, which was then identified and consulted by reference to the relevant section of *Yijing*. An apparent shortcoming of this method is that it could not as such produce the 'moving' lines. Numerous examples of Crowley's use of the *Yijing* in his diaries confirm that he was treating given hexagrams as a whole, with no references to moving lines, which would otherwise produce an additional hexagram for consideration in the course of divination.

Crowley's source for *Yijing* was Legge's (1891b) translation. As was the case with the *Daodejing* and the *Qingjing jing*, he eventually produced his own version of the text (also published posthumously). In this instance, however, he did not claim mystical inspiration behind his efforts. Again, he simplified the text, making it more succinct, and he put it in a rhyme. There are no overt references to Thelemic doctrine, except in Crowley's rendition of Hexagram thirty-two ('Hang'/'Heng'), where the phrase 'lust of result' reappears in the verse comment on the uppermost line, while in the second of the two verses addressing the whole hexagram (so-called 'judgement' lines), there appears another important quote from *The Book of the Law* (III: 60): 'There is no law beyond Do what thou wilt.'[24]

More original than his rendition of the text of the *Yijing* is Crowley's interpretation of the eight trigrams that serve as the basis for the sixty-four hexagrams of the system and their incorporation into the occultist-kabbalistic model of the Tree of Life. We have seen that the earliest attempts to correlate the two systems of esotericism were published by Crowley as early as 1909 in the appendix to his book *777*. The reader will remember that the trigrams also featured in the 1914 essay 'The Soul of the Desert' (see above). Here Crowley (1998: 52) interprets the trigrams as follows (they are divided into 'Male' and 'Female' subgroups; traditional designations [e.g. Adler 2022: 10; Legge 1891b: 11, 32] are in square brackets):

Male:
- ☰ The *liṅga* (Life) [Heaven]
- ☲ The Sun [Fire; the Sun[25]]
- ☳ Fire [Thunder]
- ☴ Air (Wood) [Wind/Wood]

Female:
- ☷ The *yoni* (Space. The stars.) [Earth]
- ☵ The Moon [Water; the Moon[26]]
- ☱ Water [Lake; Water[27]]
- ☶ Earth [Mountain]

It will be obvious that the main difference introduced by Crowley mostly concerns only the two major trigrams: *qian* 乾 and *kun* 坤. Traditionally, they represent Heaven and Earth: the former consists of the male *yang* lines only, while the latter has all three *yin* lines. Heaven is an active, creative force, while the Earth is its opposite, a supremely receptive and passive entity. Crowley, however, approaches this essential dyad with a 'decidedly sexual interpretation' (Smith 2012: 192) and identifies them with the Hindu Tantric polarity of *liṅga* (phallus) and *yoni* (womb). But despite the apparent incongruency of engaging South Asian religious concepts in order to illustrate Chinese religio-philosophical ideas, the basic import of his interpretation is not fundamentally different from the traditional Chinese views on the subject: in both cases, the binary pair represents the ultimate complements, the interplay of which creates the totality of reality.[28]

In other words, Crowley's arrangement and interpretation of the *Yijing* trigrams emphasizes, first of all, the primary dyad of *yang* and *yin*, 'which correspond exactly to the Lingam and the Yoni. These being clothed about become the popular symbols of Father and Mother' (Crowley 1944: 269). Smith is correct in calling this a 'decidedly sexual interpretation', but the truth of the matter is that while this certainly is an interpretation, it is at the same time hardly a *misinterpretation*.[29]

Conclusions

Aleister Crowley was not a sinologist, nor was he a scholar, his erudition notwithstanding. He was primarily, in his own preferred nomenclature, a practitioner of Magick.[30] As such, he approached Chinese religious traditions from a pragmatic perspective. At the same time, he valued and even praised those traditions as spiritually sublime, and he attempted to correlate their principles with the tenets of Western esotericism. Crowley's admiration for Laozi 老子 is evident from the fact that he included the Chinese sage in the list of seven historical Magi[31] – understood as spiritually enlightened cultural heroes. He argued (Crowley 1991: 69) that 'His Doctrine hath been lost or misinterpreted, and it is most needful to restore it. For this Tao [understood as Laozi's "Word" that encapsulates his doctrine] is the true Nature of Things, being itself a Way or Going, that is, a kinetic and not a static Conception.'[32] Crowley thus drew – here and elsewhere – a parallel between Daoism and Thelema, suggesting that to follow the 'Way of the Tao' is essentially equivalent to following one's true will, the essence of Thelema.³³ In addition, he was continually engaged in the attempt to incorporate elements of 'the Chinese cosmos' onto the Western occultist Tree of Life. As already addressed, he considered his achievement in this regard as one of his main contributions to the comparative esotericism.

Crowley's accomplishment is however seldom acknowledged in the academic literature and when commented upon, it tends to be criticized as an example of his *misunderstandings* of the matter. His Kabbalah was mocked by Gershom Scholem (1897–1982), the major twentieth-century scholar of Jewish mysticism, as 'the highly coloured humbug' (1941: 2). The Jewish scholar was unequivocal and unimpressed: 'No words need to be wasted on the subject of Crowley's "Kabbalistic" writings in his books on what he was pleased to term "Magick," and in his journal, The Equinox' (1941: 349, n.3). Similarly, in their erudite volume *Teaching the I Ching (Book of Changes)*, Geoffrey Redmond and Tze-ki Hon introduce Crowley not only as an 'early devotee of the *Yijing*' (2014: 234) but also ad hominem as an 'occultist, drug addict, and iconoclast, labeled by the media as "the wickedest man in the world"' (2014: 234). While admitting that he was 'ahead of his time in discovering the *Changes* well before the Wilhelm-Baynes version made it a countercultural classic' (2014: 234), the authors opine that although 'Crowley regarded his proposed equivalence of the *Yijing* and the cabala as one of his greatest accomplishments [. . .] similarities between the Chinese and Jewish systems seem far fewer than dissimilarities' (2014: 235).³⁴

It is easy to understand the dismissals of Crowley's take on their respective domains of expertise in the accounts of Scholem, Redmond and Hon. The last thing Scholem wanted to do, while devoting his life-work to legitimizing Kabbalah, was to hitch his wagon to the maligned 'wickedest man in the world' and the self-proclaimed Great Beast. Redmond and Hon similarly wrote in the specific (current) moment in history when the awareness of and the concerns about cultural appropriation are at their highest point, just as the last decades of the twentieth and the first decades of this century were marked by a suspicion of universalist and perennial claims, the emphasis being on the specific, local and individual marks of identity. From such a perspective, where the stress is on the difference (or *différance*), Crowley's assertions about identifying the dao, the *Yijing* and the Kabbalah necessarily appear reductionist, vague and suspicious. And yet, without denying the validity of the aforementioned critical remarks, there is another way of looking at the issue, where Crowley's take on 'the one matter of supreme importance' does make sense and has its own cogency.

The issue is that Crowley was not a proponent of the traditional Jewish Kabbalah. His field of inquiry and interest was what is sometimes referred to as the 'hermetic' or the 'occultist Kabbalah'. And his main goal, as far as Kabbalah was concerned, was on developing a sophisticated method of correlative thinking, where the diverse phenomena could be reduced to their supposed essence reflected in their numerical equivalence. He explains the ultimate purpose of the method to his disciple Charles Stansfeld Jones (1886–1950) as follows (Crowley 1991: 2):

> Do thou study most constantly, my Son, in the Art of the Holy Qabalah. Know that herein the Relations between Numbers, though they be mighty in Power and prodigal of Knowledge, are but lesser Things. For the Work is to reduce all other Conceptions to these of Number, because thus thou wilt lay bare the very Structure of thy Mind, whose rule is Necessity rather than Prejudice. Not until the Universe is thus laid naked before thee canst thou truly anatomize it. The Tendencies of thy Mind lie deeper far than any Thought, for they are the Conditions and the Laws of Thought; and it is these that thou must bring to Naught.

Crowley's efforts in correlating his understanding of the principles of Chinese thought with the Western Qabalah need to be seen and understood within the horizon of intellectual and spiritual programme encapsulated in the quote. Whatever one may think of the claims to truth implied in such endeavour, there is no denying that it not only has its own internal coherence but is also a world view similar to the assumptions present in a variety of esoteric systems, including East Asian, which likewise suggest that the apparently discrete phenomena – physical, mental and spiritual – conform to each other as well as to some deeper metaphysical levels of reality based on their presumed analogical correspondence. Arguably, Crowley is also comparatively less engaged in the acts of appropriation because, unlike those Chinese religionists who considered Buddhism a 'Western' form of Daoism,[35] his point was not to reduce Asian metaphysics to Western, but to suggest that both are reducible to pure number,[36] which he takes to lie at the fundamental structure of the human mind, irrespective of cultural conditionings and local particularizing.[37]

Crowley's intuitions about the meaning of the basic tenets of Daoism, mostly based on his study of *Daodejing*,[38] led him to believe that there was a deep affinity between it and his own Thelema. He understood them both as philosophies that glorify the precept of living in accord with the natural order of things, whether this natural order manifests internally, as one's true will, or externally, as the *dao*.[39] He stressed (Crowley 1954: 153–4) the commonality between the two world views explicitly: '*The Book of the Law* states the doctrine of Tao very succinctly: "Thou hast no right but to do thy will. Do that, and no other shall say nay. For pure will, unassuaged of purpose, delivered from the lust of result, is every way perfect."' This is immediately followed by a quotation from *Daodejing* VII, 2, which is, by juxtaposition, obviously meant as an illustration of the preceding: 'Thus also the sage, seeking not any goal, attaineth all things; he doth not interfere in the affairs of his body, and so that body acteth without friction. It is because he meddleth not with personal aims that these come to pass with simplicity' (Crowley 1954: 154; see also Crowley 1995: 22). He even correlated Nuit and Hadit, the two major divinities from *The Book of the Law*, with the principles from the Chinese classic, as he understood them, when he commented (Crowley 1996: I, 23): 'The theogony of our Law is entirely scientific. Nuit is matter, Hadit is motion, in their full physical sense. They are the *tao* and *te* of Chinese Philosophy; or, to put it very simply, the Noun and Verb in grammar.' And he maintained that an adept in following the path of Thelema is simultaneously acting in accordance with the *dao*.

Crowley was eclectic in his pursuit of Magick, and, if not the pioneer, he was at least a gutsy practitioner of comparative and syncretic esotericism, an area as yet insufficiently explored and deserving of closer study. The driving mechanism at the heart of comparative esotericism lies in the pursuit of analogical or correlative thinking, assumed to be a key to understanding of reality. Richard Smith (2008: 248) reflects on the wide-ranging tradition of commentarial hermeneutics witnessed in a number of religious systems that are based on correlative thinking and points out that they are 'especially prominent at all levels of *Changes* [i.e. *Yijing*] exegesis, but they also appear in a variety of Jewish, Buddhist, Christian, Islamic, and Hindu texts'. He suggests that both the similarities as well as differences between various systems that are the subject of comparative studies that he is advocating for, whether they relate to 'great' or 'lesser' works under scrutiny, allow us 'excellent opportunities for cross-cultural understanding, for as the context broadens, our understanding deepens' (2008: 249). The occultist engagement with aspects of Daoism and the system of *Yijing*, as exemplified by Crowley's efforts discussed earlier, contributes towards this wider understanding by broadening the context to include the aspects of Western esotericism and the new religious movement of Thelema.

Throughout his longer career, Aleister Crowley engaged, often *in situ*, aspects of theory and practice of, among others, Jewish Kabbalah, Hindu Tantra and Yoga,[40] Buddhist metaphysics and meditation,[41] Islamic mysticism[42] and East

Asian spirituality,[43] focused on explorations of the *Daodejing* and divinations with the *Yijing*. A strong case could be made that in no other religious tradition did he find a world view as congruent with his 'Law of Thelema' as in the systems of what he tended to call 'the Chinese Cosmos' and 'the Way of the Tao'.

Notes

1. I am grateful to William Breeze and William E. Heidrick for research assistance and access to unpublished Crowley material.
2. See also a letter to a disciple, written on 19 March 1943 (in Crowley 1954: xi): 'I do not think I am boasting unfairly when I say that my personal researches have been of the greatest value and importance to the study of the subject of Magick and Mysticism in general, especially my integration of the various thought-systems of the world, notably the identification of the system of the Yi King with that of the Qabalah.' On 8 November 1943, Crowley similarly wrote to his disciple Jane Wolfe: 'I've got the Spiral Universe aligned with modern science, and the Qabalah dovetailed not only with Yi King but with Geomancy, and so on. For the first time in my life I'm fully satisfied with the scholarship of it. Everything fits like a glove. Behold me happy!' (Churton 2021: 249–50).
3. The Hermetic Order of the Golden Dawn was the most influential western esoteric and initiatic Order at the turn of the last century. It taught a syncretic form of occultism, with a pronounced emphasis on Egyptian symbolism. The prominent members included, aside from the three founders (Samuel Mathers, Wynn Westcott and William Woodman), Mina Bergson, Florence Farr, Arthur Machen, Arthur Waite and William Butler Yeats. See Howe (1972) and Gilbert (2006). There are more than a dozen biographies of Crowley, so far; the most informative single volume is Kaczynski (2010).
4. In simplified terms, the A∴A∴ may be seen as a 'reformed' Golden Dawn – it concerns individual's ascent towards spiritual self-realization through practice of, primarily, ritual magic and yogic meditation. The O.T.O. has its roots in Freemasonry, from which it differs by admitting women; it is more socially involved than the A∴A∴ and is oriented towards wider promulgation of Thelema. Both are initiatic Orders, still active. On O.T.O., see Pasi (2006).
5. For example, Crowley (1989: 491): 'China has been the most civilized country in the world.'
6. Crowley would later create another fictionalized and idealized self-portrait as an aged detective, Thelemic magician and Daoist sage, Simon Iff. See Crowley (1929 and 2012). Introduced by his young student as 'my friend and master, Mr. Simon Iff', the latter replies, 'I am not really the master. . . . I am only a student of Chinese

Philosophy' (Crowley 1929: 20). Iff describes his philosophy of non-interference in the course of natural unfolding of the events as being in accord with the truth that 'lies at the base of the Taoistic doctrine of non-action; the plan of doing everything by seemingly doing nothing. Yield yourself utterly to the Will of Heaven, and you become the omnipotent instrument of that Will' (Crowley 1929: 26). The attunement of the personal agency to 'the Will of Heaven' is significant in light of Crowley's philosophy of Thelema, based on the principle of living in accordance with one's true will, which is thus implicitly assigned divine, or 'Heavenly', status.

7   The terms *liṅga* and *yoni* literally refer to male and female sexual organs, but acquire significantly deeper metaphysical connotation in especially Hindu Tantric metaphysics, where they symbolize the divine pair Śiva and Śakti, understood as the ontological ground of everything.

8   Crowley's point is not to reduce the *dao* to the Western idea of God; instead, his position is that both the *dao* and God are ultimately local metaphors for what he assumes is best described if reduced to a number – in this case, the number One. (In other contexts, he also tended to assign zero to the *dao*.)

9   Crowley (1980: 466–8).

10 In simplified terms, the 'Abyss' separates the noumenal world, represented by the three highest *sephiroth* on the Tree of Life, from the world of the manifest phenomena. To 'cross the Abyss' implies an annihilation of the ego-bound individuality.

11 The phrase 'the Way of the Dao' or its near equivalents reappears in several of Crowley's writing. In Crowley (1929: 64), Simon Iff (see above, n. 6) contrasts, and implicitly criticizes, the path of action involved in ritual magic with an alternative: 'For my part, I prefer the Way of the Tao, and to do everything by doing nothing.' The same description of 'the Way of the Dao' as doing everything by doing nothing is found in Crowley 1991 (written in 1918): 29 and 57; importantly, this doctrine is clearly distinguished from abstinence to act: 'the Withdrawal from Activity is not the Way of the Tao' (1991: 23); 'Do not think then that by Non-action thou dost follow the Way of the Tao' (1991: 30). Describing a 'Master of the Temple,' (i.e. the person who has 'crossed the Abyss'), he claims that such individual 'is totally indifferent to the Event; so then he acts and reacts with perfect elasticity. This is the Way of the Tao; and that is why you cannot grasp the very idea of that Way – much less follow it! – unless you are a Master of the Temple' (Crowley 1954: 229).

12 For an analysis and interpretation of 'Liber Trigrammaton' from the perspective of a contemporary exponent of Thelema, see Gunther, forthcoming.

13 See 'Appendix I' in Crowley (1909: 46–54).

14 Crowley also identifies the *dao* with the 'kabbalistic zero' (e.g. Crowley 1954: 153). The suggestion is that any positive signification (i.e. any definitive 'number') would in this context be misleading. It is another way of saying that the *dao* cannot be told.

15 Crowley (1914). My references are to a slightly edited version in Crowley (1998).

16 See the following for further remarks concerning this essay.

17 Crowley (1989: 838): 'I refuse to assert any theory of what this really means. . . . I am quite willing to interpret the experience as a dreamlike imagination, a dramatization of certain deeper elements in my character. I may, however, argue on the other side, that my present life is, almost equally, an artistic representation of my nature.'
18 See Crowley (1989: 839). Current scholarship considers the text to be composed by an anonymous author several centuries after Ge Xuan. Crowley's source for the authorship attribution was Legge (1891b: 248).
19 See also Crowley (1995: 101–8). For an alternative translation, see Kohn (2019: 25–9). For a book length treatment, see Wong (1992). For a hagiographic account of Ge Xuan that Crowley claimed he was a reincarnation of, see the depiction penned by his grandnephew Ge Hong 葛洪 (283-343) in Campany (2002: 152–7). Campany translates *xian* 仙, as 'transcendent'.
20 As Brandt and Hammer clarify (2012: 122, n.28), 'Theosophical interpretations of the term as referring to a cosmic memory bank have little if any basis in Indian religious terminology.' Instead, the source of Blavatsky's ideas on the subject is, in the authors' opinion, most likely Éliphas Lévi's concept of the 'astral light'.
21 Hymenaeus Beta (in Crowley 1995: xv) remarks that 'while the main text was written in 1918 and the commentary in 1919, these were revised as late as 1944.'
22 Legge (1891a: 52) translates this as: 'Heaven is long-enduring and earth continues long. The reason why heaven and earth are able to endure and continue thus long is because they do not live of, or for, themselves. This is how they are able to continue and endure.'
23 Literature on the *Yijing* is extensive. For an overview, see Wilhelm (1975) (for Crowley entries see p. 16) and Hacker, Moore and Patsco (2015) (for Crowley entries, see pp. 27–9). For accessible general introductions to the genesis, cultural context and history of interpretations of the text, both in China and abroad, see in particular Smith (2012) and Adler (2022).
24 It would be advantageous to illustrate the difference between Legge's and Crowley's version of the *yi* as it relates to King Wen's comment on the Hexagram 32. Legge (1891b: 125) translates it as: 'Hang indicates successful progress and no error (in what it denotes). But the advantage will come from being firm and correct; and movement in any direction whatever will be advantageous.' Crowley (1971: 32) renders the same passage as: 'By persistence are great empires built. / There is no law beyond Do what thou wilt.' The economy of Crowley's version is noteworthy, irrespective of what one may think of the merits of his interpretation of the text's meaning.
25 Legge (1891b: 11) lists 'the sun' as one of the meanings of this trigram.
26 Legge (1891b:11) includes 'the moon' as one of the several meanings of this trigram.
27 Legge (1891b:11).

28 *Qian* and *kun* are also associated with father and mother, respectively, in the 'family sequence' of trigrams (Adler 2022: 53), making the conceptual range of their meanings close to Crowley's proposal (*liṅga* and *yoni* are also primary symbols of Śiva and Śakti, who are from that point of view identified as father and mother of all beings; in fact, their sexual union produces the whole manifest universe).

29 Recent discoveries of the earlier versions of *The Book of Changes,* such as the one preserved in the Mawangdui silk manuscript, led some scholars to propose that the two trigrams discussed earlier, consisting of 'pure' *yang* and *yin* lines respectively, originally referred to the male and female sexual organs. See Shaughnessy (1996: 17), and Smith (2008: 51).

30 Stoddard Martin's (1989: 7) description of Crowley as 'one of the few educated men of [the twentieth] century to have dared present himself as a "magician"' seems particularly apt in this context.

31 The seven Magi are: Laozi, Gautama (the Buddha), Kṛṣṇa and Dionysus (understood as equivalent in their doctrine and thus counting as one), Tahuti, Moses, Muḥammad and To Mega Therion (i.e. Crowley as a Magus). See Crowley (1991: 69–75), and slightly different interpretation of the list in Crowley (1913: 15).

32 Compare this with Adler's (2022: 20) description: 'The Dao is a dynamic pattern, not a static one like a blueprint.' See also Crowley (1954: 155), 'For now we see why Tao may also be translated 'The Way': for it is the *motion* of the structure we observe. There is no Being apart from Going.' Emphasis in the original.

33 In another visionary text, both Laozi and Fuxi (the legendary creator of the original *Yijing* hexagrams) were included in the list of members of the 'Great White Brotherhood.' See Crowley (1938).

34 Richard Smith was more appreciative of Crowley's efforts, but even he considered that his correlation of Daoist and Kabbalistic principles was 'highly imaginative' (2012: 192). The first scholar to mention Crowley's treatment of *Yijing* was Hellmut Wilhelm (1905–90), who mentions four of his books in his Bibliography. Wilhelm's comments were confined to the summaries of the content and did not engage in the judgements of the same. He thus simply states, with respect to Crowley (1909): 'The book contains a coordination of trigrams and the hexagrams with the data of other mystical traditions' (Wilhelm 1975: 16).

35 Livia Kohn (2019: 121) relates that in the medieval account of Laozi's 'conversion of the barbarians', the sage is reunited with the guardian of the pass, who was instrumental in persuading him to write down the *Daodejing*, and together travel, converting people to Daoism, and reach India: 'In India, moreover, this conversion results in the rise of Buddhism, after its first arrival in early medieval China is understood as a western form of Daoism'. (In this case, the adjective 'western' obviously refers to the simple fact that India lies to the west of China.)

36 Crowley (1989: 465): 'The fundamentals of mathematics are the basis of the Holy Cabbala. It is natural and proper to represent the cosmos, or any part of it,

or any operation of it, or the operation of any part of it, by the symbols of pure mathematics.'

37 On the link between the early modern reception of China and the Kabbalah, see also the chapters by Franz Winter and Julian Strube in this volume.

38 His preference for the foundational text and disregard for the religion based on it is evident when he proclaims (Crowley 1954: 31): 'Taoism has as little to do with the Tao Teh King as the Catholic Church with the Gospel.'

39 For example, he argues (Crowley 1954: 87–8) that 'the will must be identified with the Divine Will, so called. One wants to become like a mighty flowing river, which is not consciously aiming at the sea, and is certainly not yielding to any external influence. It is acting in conformity with the law of its own nature, with the Tao.'.

40 Crowley's involvement with the South Asian traditions of Yoga and Tantra have so far received most scholarly attention: see, in particular, relevant studies by Henrik Bogdan, Keith Cantú, Hugh Urban and the present writer.

41 On Crowley and Buddhism, see Djurdjevic (2019).

42 On Crowley and Islam, see Pasi (2021).

43 On Crowley and East Asian esotericism, see Nilsson (2013).

References

Adler, J. A. (2022), *The Yijing: A Guide*, New York: Oxford University Press.

Brandt, C. and O. Hammer (2012), 'Rudolf Steiner and Theosophy', in O. Hammer and M. Rothstein (eds), *Handbook of the Theosophical Current*, 113–33, Leiden and Boston: Brill.

Campany, R. F. (2002), *To Live as Long as Heaven and Earth: A Translation and Study of Ge Hong's Traditions of Divine Transcendents*, Berkeley, Los Angeles and London: University of California Press.

Churton, T. (2021), *Aleister Crowley in England: The Return of the Great Beast*, Rochester: Inner Traditions.

Crowley, A. (1907), 'Thien Tao or The Synagogue of Satan', in *Konx Om Pax: Essays in Light*, 53–67, London and Felling-on-Tyne: Walter Scott Publishing.

Crowley, A. (1909), *777 vel Prolegomena Symbolica ad Systemam Sceptico-Mysticae Viae Explicandae, Fundamentum Hieroglyphicum Sanctissimorum Scientiae Summae*, London and Felling-on-Tyne: Walter Scott Publishing.

Crowley, A. (1913), *The Book of Lies: Which is also Falsely called Breaks*, London: Wieland.

Crowley, A. (1914), 'The Soul of the Desert', *The Occult Review*, XX (July–December): 18–24.

Crowley, A. (1919), 'A∴A∴ Præmonstrance', *The Equinox*, III (1): 11–17.
Crowley, A. (1929), *Moonchild: A Prologue*, London: Mandrake.
Crowley, A. (1938), *The Heart of the Master*, London: O.T.O.
Crowley, A. (1939), *Khing Kang Khing: The Classic of Purity: First Written Down by me, Ko Yuen in the Episode of the Dynasty of Wu and now made into a Rime by Me Aleister Crowley*, London: O.T.O.
Crowley, A. (1944), *The Book of Thoth: A Short Essay on the Tarot of the Egyptians*, London: O.T.O.
Crowley, A. (1945), Letter to Karl J. Germer, 21 November 1945, O.T.O. Archives.
Crowley, A. (1954), *Magick Without Tears*, edited by. K. J. Germer, Hampton: Thelema Publishing.
Crowley, A. (1971), *Shih Yi: A Critical and Mnemonic Paraphrase of the Yi King by Ko Yuen*, Oceanside: H. Parsons Smith/Monthelema.
Crowley, A. (1980), 'The Way of the Dao', in M. Motta (ed.), *The Chinese Texts of Magick and Mysticism by Aleister Crowley: The Yi Jing, The Dao De Jing, The Jin Gan Jing, and Others Commented, Being Equinox Vol. V, No. 3*, 466–8, Nashville: Thelema Publishing Company.
Crowley, A. (1983), *The Holy Books of Thelema*, York Beach: Samuel Weiser.
Crowley, A. (1989), *The Confessions of Aleister Crowley: An Autohagiography*, edited by J. Symonds and K. Grant, London: Arkana.
Crowley, A. (1991), *Liber Aleph vel CXI: The Book of Wisdom or Folly*, York Beach: Samuel Weiser.
Crowley, A., trans. (1995), *Lao Tzu: Tao Te Ching: Liber CLVII: Translated with an Introduction and Commentary by Ko Hsüan (Aleister Crowley)*, edited by H. Beta, York Beach: Samuel Weiser.
Crowley, A. (1996), *The Law Is for All: The Authorized Popular Commentary on Liber AL vel Legis sub figura CCXX The Book of the Law*, edited by L. Wilkinson and H. Beta, Tempe: New Falcon Publications.
Crowley, A. (1997), *Magick: Liber ABA: Book Four*, 2nd revised edn, edited by H. Beta, San Francisco and Newburyport: Weiser Books.
Crowley, A. (1998), 'The Soul of the Desert', in H. Beta and R. Kaczynski (eds), *The Revival of Magick and Other Essays: Oriflamme 2*, 47–55, Tempe: New Falcon in association with Ordo Templi Orientis.
Crowley, A. (2012), *The Simon Iff Stories and Other Works*, edited by W. Breeze, London: Wordsworth Editions.
Djurdjevic, G. (2019) '"Wishing You a Speedy Termination of Existence": Aleister Crowley's Views on Buddhism and Its Relationship with the Doctrine of Thelema', *Aries: Journal for the Study of Western Esotericism*, 19: 212–30.
Gilbert, R. A. (2006), 'Hermetic Order of the Golden Dawn', in W. J. Hanegraaff (ed.), *Dictionary of Gnosis and Western Esotericism*, 544–50, Leiden and Boston: Brill.
Gunther, J. D. (forthcoming), *Fires Upon the Earth: A Commentary on Liber Trigrammaton*, Murfreesboro: Wennofer House.

Hacker, E. A., S. Moore and L. Patsco, eds (2015), *I Ching: An Annotated Bibliography*, London and New York: Routledge.

Howe, E. (1972), *The Magicians of the Golden Dawn: A Documentary History of a Magical Order 1887–1923*, London: Routledge and Kegan Paul.

Kaczynski, R. (2010), *Perdurabo: The Life of Aleister Crowley*, revised and expanded, Berkeley: North Atlantic Books.

Kohn, L. (2019), *Daode Jing: A Guide*, New York: Oxford University Press.

Legge, J., trans. (1891a), *The Texts of Taoism: Part I*, Oxford: Clarendon Press.

Legge, J., trans. (1891b), *The Texts of Taoism: Part II*, Oxford: Clarendon Press.

Martin, S. (1989), *Orthodox Heresy: The Rise of 'Magic' as Religion and Its Relation to Literature*, New York: Palgrave Macmillan.

Nilsson, J. (2013), 'Defending Paper Gods: Aleister Crowley and the Reception of Daoism in Early Twentieth Century Esotericism', *Correspondences*, 1 (1): 103–27.

Pasi, M. (2006), 'Ordo Templi Orientis', in W. J. Hanegraaff (ed.), *Dictionary of Gnosis and Western Esotericism*, 898–906, Leiden and Boston: Brill.

Pasi, M. (2021), 'Aleister Crowley and Islam', in M. Sedgwick and F. Piraino (eds), *Esoteric Transfers and Constructions: Judaism, Christianity, and Islam*, 151–93, Cham: Springer Nature.

Redmond, G. and T. Hon (2014), *Teaching the I Ching (Book of Changes)*, New York: Oxford University Press.

Scholem, G. (1941), *Major Trends in Jewish Mysticism*, New York: Schocken.

Shaughnessy, E. L. (1996), *I Ching: The Classic of Changes*, New York: Ballantine Books.

Smith, R. J. (2008), *Fathoming the Cosmos and Ordering the World: The Yijing (I Ching or Classic of Changes) and Its Evolution in China*, Charlottesville and London: University of Virginia Press.

Smith, R. J. (2012), *The I Ching: A Biography*, Princeton and Oxford: Princeton University Press.

Wilhelm, H. (1975), *The Book of Changes in the Western Tradition: A Selective Bibliography*, Seattle: University of Washington.

Wong, E., trans. (1992), *Cultivating Stillness: A Taoist Manual for Transforming Body and Mind: With a Commentary by Shui-ch'ing Tzu*, Boston and London: Shambhala.

An exoticism of rationality and social order?

Examining the East–West binary in late nineteenth- and early twentieth-century esoteric representations of China

Johan Nilsson

Introduction

It is not unreasonable to point out that Edward Said (1935–2003) and the early critics of orientalism generally disregarded the role played by esoteric movements in the shaping and popularization of notions about the 'East' in both Europe and globally. Nonetheless, aspects of the Saidian critique have proved to be quite fruitful in the analysis of the discourse about 'Eastern' wisdom produced by Theosophy and other esoteric movements. This is particularly the case with regard to a version of the East–West binary that portrays the perceived resources of 'Eastern' spirituality as the remedy to a perceived 'Western' overreliance on rationality and materialism. This way of conceptualizing the relationship between 'East' and 'West' emerged out of a form of cultural criticism common to many esoteric or occult movements in the post-Enlightenment era. At least from the middle of the nineteenth century most of the influential proponents of such movements became deeply concerned with what they believed to be a danger developing within their own cultures, namely, a perceived loss of religious belief and a slowly expanding materialism (e.g. Blavatsky 1877: 102). Although they were not the only ones expressing such concerns at the time, their version of this criticism of the 'West' had certain original elements. Among the solutions to the problem that existed within the broad and diverse esoteric environment of the period was the notion that cultures in the 'East' had preserved a secret tradition of ultimate truth and ancient wisdom that could be used as an inspiration and impetus for a spiritual revival in the Occident. In recent years, several scholars have explored the ways this binary could be said to express the fundamental assumptions on which esoteric movements, like Theosophy, built their interpretation of 'Eastern' wisdom, especially in connection with India (e.g. King 1999; Baier 2016; Partridge 2020). This specific understanding of esoteric Orientalism described by these scholars, however, faces some difficulties when applied to the fascination with China in the esoteric movements of the same period. Whereas India had been known in Europe as a place of strong religious sensibilities since antiquity, China had been seen as a place of moderate religion by influential proponents of its culture (see below). This chapter explores the extent to which the aforementioned characterization of esoteric Orientalism is applicable to the way late nineteenth- and early twentieth-century esoteric writings portrayed China and Chinese culture.[1] In order to give an account of the most relevant aspects of the intellectual background against which nineteenth century esoteric movements formulated their understanding of Chinese culture, I will briefly examine some of the key actors and periods in the history of the European encounter with China.

The Jesuits

Until the end of the eighteenth century the European understanding of Chinese culture was heavily influenced by the early Catholic missionary activities in East Asia, especially the Jesuit missionaries in China (Gregory 2002: 36–51; Mungello 1999: 36–49; Clarke 2000: 37–40; Jones 2001: 14–27). This was somewhat ironic, for, as John S. Gregory (2002: 36) has pointed out, 'their influence, as measured by the sustained acceptance of their ideas, was greater on Europe than on China'. Indeed, the Jesuits managed to create a lasting interest in Europe for the works of Confucius and other Chinese classics. Furthermore, their interpretation of these works would influence the understanding of China among European intellectuals far into the eighteenth century.

In the 1500s, Catholic missionaries reached China after a long period of minimal contact between Europe and East Asia. They were dominated by the Portuguese and the Jesuit order, although some were Dominicans and Franciscans. Among them were figures like the Italian Jesuit Matteo Ricci (1552–1610), who would later become well-known for his work in establishing a Catholic missionary presence in China and his writings on the country and its culture. Ricci, who was well educated and had a gift for languages, decided that his best chance for a long-time strategy for converting the Chinese to Christianity was to focus on the country's elite – to which he and later Jesuits had some success. Missionaries gained positions within the government bureaucracy and published writings about science and Christianity aimed at an educated Chinese readership. Subsequently, the Jesuits' overriding aim was to find some sort of common ground with Confucianism and, on that basis, attempt to replace what they saw as the degenerate spiritual elements of both Daoism and Buddhism with the far superior spiritual ideals of Christianity (Mungello 1999: 64; Clarke 2000: 38). In practice this meant a parallel strategy of depicting Christianity as valuable to those educated in the Confucian classics and portraying Confucius in a positive light for their Christian audience. As Gregory (2002: 37) remarks, '[the Jesuits] sought to promote a Constantinian conversion, one led from above by the ruling elite, and in order to win over that elite they strove to make themselves not just acceptable but useful to it'.

The second part of the strategy was essentially accomplished by focusing on the Confucian classics as the essence of Chinese culture, while concurrently insisting on the non-religious nature of those works and the tradition that was primarily associated with them. The writings and practices that would later be classified as Buddhist and Daoist were toned down and sometimes attacked as superstitious paganism. Furthermore, the Jesuits were careful to place Confucius and his followers under the category of philosophy. Being a non-religious figure, Confucius could be seen as compatible with Christianity; he was thus subjected to a treatment similar to that of Plato and Aristotle in earlier European history. This strategy rested on the assessment that if the Church forced Chinese converts to condemn Confucius or other aspects of educated culture, it would seriously hurt the missionary endeavour and likely get the Catholics expelled from China. (In fact, this is more or less what happened in the early eighteenth century.) However, this should not obscure the fact that the Jesuits had a genuine respect for Confucianism as well as for many other aspects of Chinese culture.

Confucius as enlightenment philosopher

The Jesuit writings exerted an influence in Europe long after their missionary activities began to be suppressed in China in the 1720s. Perhaps surprisingly, the enlightenment thinkers of the eighteenth century were to a large extent inheritors of the Jesuit understanding of Chinese culture. Even in instances when the ideological context was very different from that of the sixteenth- and seventeenth-century missionary movement, intellectuals during the period defended an understanding of Chinese culture with significant similarities to the one that had been articulated by Ricci and others. J. J. Clarke (2000: 39) gives a succinct account of this development:

> The most important group of people to inherit and propagate this Jesuit-inspired picture were the philosophical thinkers of the seventeenth and eighteenth centuries. They relied largely on Jesuit sources for their information about China, and wove these sources with considerable alacrity and skill into their own radical programme.

One example of this can be found in the mid-eighteenth-century writings of Voltaire (1694–1778). Voltaire was a product of Jesuit education and he was well aware of the order's activities in China. He wrote a number of texts that explicitly discuss Chinese culture and religion, and frequently used China as an example in the philosophical and political debates in which he participated. He wrote a paraphrase of a drama from the thirteenth century, published as *L'Orphelin de la Chine* (The Orphan of China; 1755), which lauds Chinese civilization and portrays the Mongols as violent and barbaric. At roughly the same period, he discussed China in his grand historical study *Essai sur les moeurs et l'esprit des nations* (Essay on the Mores and the Spirit of the Nations; 1756), and later penned *Lettres chinoises, indiennes et tartares* (Chinese, Indian and Tartar Letters; 1776). Voltaire's view of China is largely very favourable and emphasizes Confucianism as the true expression of Chinese culture (App 2010: 32–76). He generally stressed the same benefits of Chinese culture as the Jesuits did, but for different reasons. To him, Confucianism was not laudable because it was compatible with Christianity; rather, in some ways, it was actually preferable. For Voltaire, the Confucian tradition was tolerant, rational and lacked a priestly class. Moreover, its influence had contributed to the well-ordered nature of the Chinese state. In his view, Confucianism focused on moral behaviour and the orderly organization of society under the law. It did, however, recognize the existence of a supreme deity, but only in so far as this deity was knowable through rationality and the observation of nature. The veneration of this deity is without any superstition; it is, in Urs App's terminology, an 'uncluttered monotheism' (App 2010: 33). Voltaire deemed Confucianism a minimalist form of religion free from all the things he disliked in the Catholicism of his native France. It is, in fact, the perfect expression of the kind of Deism he promoted. Finding examples of this in cultures across the globe was a way for Voltaire to counter claims of Christian exceptionalism, while the perceived age of Chinese culture allowed him to subvert biblical chronology.

Some intellectuals active in the eighteenth or the late seventeenth century were more critical of Chinese culture. For example, the renowned historian and political philosopher Charles-Louis de Montesquieu (1689–1755) famously regarded the Chinese state as an example of despotism (Jones 2001: 30–1). Nonetheless, views similar to those of Voltaire were widespread. The French eighteenth-century economic theorist François Quesnay (1694–1774) was influenced by what he understood to be Chinese economic practices. And it is well-known that some years earlier, Gottfried Wilhelm Leibniz (1646–1716) had expressed his admiration for the Chinese social order (Spence 1999: 82–7; Mungello 1999: 138).

From the land of Deism to the home of ancient wisdom

As we have seen, the notion that Chinese culture was rational and well-ordered but not especially characterized by religion or any form of secret spiritual tradition had been influential in Europe for a long period.[2] Nonetheless, a cursory glance at esoteric writers of the late nineteenth and early twentieth centuries show that China was indeed one of the places were representatives of the esoteric movements of the period searched for hidden spiritual wisdom. Esoteric writers were not primarily interested in what they saw as the prosaic morality of Confucius; rather, they took an interest in some of the subjects most earlier Europeans had dismissed as superstition. The shift in focus is apparent for example in an article published in *The Theosophist* (est. 1879), arguably the most prominent Theosophical journal of the time, with the title 'Ancient China & the Elixir of Life' (Hadland Davis 1915: 155–6):

> Long ago in ancient China there were men who dreamed dreams and saw visions as splendid as those of the Yellow Emperor: men who, in a hut on some lonely mountain-side, or in grove or cave, sought to discover the elixir that would confer immortality and the stone that would transmute base metal into gold. In those days there were magicians who spoke of glories more beautiful, more enduring, than the pomp and circumstance of kings. Some, no doubt, were charlatans, but there were a few who had lifted a corner of the veil and caught a glimpse of the Far Beyond. In Cathay alchemy had its original source, and from thence came to Arabia.

Other writers described China as a place where magic was taught. The spiritualist and occultist Emma Hardinge Britten (1823–99) described Laozi 老子 as a '"saint," an ascetic, a wonder worker' and claimed that his followers had as their 'bible' a book 'full of magical rites, invocations of Spirits, wise sayings, and divine revelations' (Hardinge Britten 1884: 293). Many did not hesitate to call Laozi and his followers 'mystics', and by that they meant something positive (e.g. Medhurst 1905). They also took an interest in some rather technical aspects of esoteric knowledge thought to have been preserved in China. Esoteric writers speak of knowledge of animal magnetism in Chinese medicine (Paladin 1879: 30), techniques related to visionary mental states (Hardinge Britten 1884: 293), knowledge of the world of spiritual beings (Blavatsky 1891) and, most prominently, the secrets of divination related to the *Yijing* (Lévi 1860: 409–10; de Pouvourville 1904;[3] Rohmer 1914; Crowley n.d.[4]). Although most of these subjects remained minor preoccupations among occult writers who were more interested in the doctrines of *wuwei* 無為 (non-action), Daoist cosmogony, and, as we shall see, matters related to the social consequences of wisdom (Nilsson 2020: 217–78),[5] they still constitute a real shift in the way Chinese culture was understood and written about in Europe. So, what had changed?

If the European understanding of Chinese culture and religion was comparatively stable for a long period, it would undergo radical changes during the nineteenth century that would make the overall image of China in Europe murkier. This shift had begun already in the eighteenth century but gained force in the 1800s. The changes were in part consequences of shifting intellectual trends in Europe, but it was also a result of European imperialism in East Asia. Both the expanding European colonial holdings in China and the wars fought by European powers like Britain, France and Germany did of course have complex consequences for the way Chinese culture was imagined. Some of these are difficult to trace, but others are quite straightforward. For example, regarding the latter, the opium wars and related conflicts opened China up to an unprecedented volume of missionary activity. The treaties of Nanjing (1842) and Tianjin (1858) – signed after the First and Second Opium Wars, respectively – did not only regulate trade relations and finalize the secession of Hong Kong to Britain, but they also resulted in more liberal rules for the promulgation of Christianity in China (Wong 1998; Reinders 2004). Earlier missions, like that of the Jesuits, had been tightly controlled by the Chinese government and limited with regard to their access to the Chinese citizenry. The nineteenth century, however, allowed entry to a type of missionary that no longer needed to weigh their words and tread carefully when they described Chinese culture. This resulted in a flood of literary works written in European languages that painted Chinese religious life in the darkest colours. Whereas the Jesuits had mostly toned down those aspects of religion in China that could not be described as moral philosophy, metaphysical theory or traditional ceremonies, many of the missionary writers of the nineteenth century emphasized the colourful and complex pantheons and temple cults of everyday Chinese religion. To their European audiences, who often financed the missionary movements, this was generally understood as the worst kind of paganism and idolatry. The missionary literature on China in the nineteenth century, and to some extent academic sinology as well, heralded an important shift away from the understanding of Chinese culture as almost uniquely minimalist in its religious sensibility. The period saw a wave of translations of texts presented as being associated with Daoism, as well as an (often negative) acknowledgment of aspects of Chinese religion, like polytheism (Reinders 2004). For example, the influential sinologist and former missionary James Legge (1815–97) wrote of the 'idolatry' of Daoism and contemporary Chinese religion, and concluded that '[n]o polytheism could be more pronounced, or more grotesque, with hardly a single feature of poetic fancy or aesthetical beauty' (Legge 1880: 170). Nevertheless, the theme of irreligiousness did not completely disappear. It survived in modified form in the background of the nineteenth-century missionary literature, although it was now generally seen as a negative trait of Chinese culture rather than freedom from superstition and excessive religious sentiments.

The portrayals of Chinese culture within late nineteenth- and early twentieth-century esotericism were naturally influenced by this broader cultural shift. One example of this is the change in focus away from Confucianism. Changes like these, however, should not be seen as a mere reaction to external cultural forces. Esoteric writers contributed to some of them and were involved, for example, in creating the growing popular interest in Daoism in Europe and North America during the period. There were also some wider developments within the esoteric discourse of the time that likely contributed to a change in the understanding of Chinese culture within many esoteric movements. Most important among these was probably the interest in alternative historiography within the esoteric environment of the period. Esoteric historiography often took the form of what has been called ancient wisdom narratives, that is, genealogies of wisdom describing how truth, that was once revealed to humanity in the distant past, survived through the centuries and spread over the earth (Trompf 2008; Kilcher 2010; Hanegraaff 2014; Nilsson 2020). Such stories became very widespread among nineteenth-century esoteric movements, likely in part as a reaction to increasing information about non-European religious traditions. Thus the famous and influential occult writer Éliphas Lévi (1810–75) speaks of 'the orthodox tradition' of magic being transmitted from Chaldea to China (Lévi 1860: 151); Theosophists like Alfred Percy Sinnett (1840–1921) and Charles Spurgeon Medhurst (1860–1927) claimed that spiritual teachings from the lost Atlantean civilization survived in Chinese culture (Sinnett 1984: 58; Medhurst 1909); and Joseph Alexandre Saint-Yves d'Alveydre (1842–1909) saw remnants of the superior wisdom of the ancient Empire of Ram[6] in Chinese classical texts and social institutions (Saint-Yves d'Alveydre [1884] 1981: 232). There were many other examples. One of the fundamental consequences of this incorporation of China into these genealogies of wisdom was that China became an inheritor of ancient truths, even if most esoteric writers would have looked for those truths elsewhere. Still, if Chinese culture had received a historical transmission of wisdom, this wisdom could be sought for and found in various expressions of that culture. This way of thinking tended to make very different, and sometimes unexpected, aspects of Chinese culture into possible vehicles of hidden wisdom.

However, although this was clearly a shift in how Chinese culture was understood, it did not, as we shall see, completely expunge all the old conceptions, attitudes and associations that particular culture was connected to, both as a whole and in part.

The esoteric interpretation of China from the perspective of the Orientalist binary

Does the cultural shift that took place in the portrayal of Chinese culture mean that the esoteric understanding of China during the relevant period can be understood as an expression of the Orientalist binary mentioned earlier? In 'Theosophical Orientalism and the Structures of Intercultural Transfer', Karl Baier (2016: 318–24) performs an analysis of Theosophical notions of South Asia influenced by Richard King, Gerd Baumann and the tradition of postcolonial research following Edward Said. Although more developed, it largely coincides with the views of King and Christopher Partridge regarding the East–West binary. Like other forms of Orientalism, Baier argues, Theosophical Orientalism is based upon the distinction between 'East' and 'West'. Although the critical study of Orientalism insists that this divide is a hierarchical one, favouring the 'West', this does not imply that Orientalist thinking associates the 'West' with exclusively positive, and the 'East' with exclusively negative, characteristics. As Baier (2016: 319) writes, 'the Oriental Other was not only denigrated by the Westerners but also functioned as an object of desire, a remnant of the lost golden childhood of mankind'. He goes on to explore some of the areas where the Theosophical form of Orientalism differs from nineteenth-century Orientalism in general. Here, however, I will focus on the binary of 'Western' materialism (or secularism) and 'Eastern' spirituality (or mysticism). Baier (2016: 320) points out that '[a]s in other forms of Orientalism, in Theosophy, we find the stereotype of Western secularism versus Eastern spirituality', and Partridge (2020: 17)) makes the same point:

> Whereas the East tended to be represented as mystical, exotic, and frozen in religious history, its spiritualities and philosophies being more or less unchanged for millennia, and therefore enlightened and barbaric in equal measure, the West was understood to be technologically advanced and materialistic, detached from its spiritual roots.

Despite having the positive traits of rationality and technological development, the 'West' is associated with materialism and atheism, and although it once possessed a version of the universal wisdom, this tradition is in serious decline or has disappeared altogether (Baier 2016: 320). Conversely, the 'East' is hampered by technological and social stagnation but has preserved its tradition of spiritual wisdom to a higher degree than the 'West'. The binary also contains some other oppositions, like 'dynamic' and 'stationary' (or active and passive, as others have termed it). Furthermore, Baier argues that the understanding of the relationship between 'East' and 'West' contained here was of great importance in facilitating 'Western' appropriation or cultural transfers of ideas and practices from South Asia (2016: 315–24). So how does this analysis apply to the esoteric understanding of China? I will argue that it does so to a certain extent but with significant reservations, some of which are likely applicable to this way of characterizing esoteric notions of the 'East' in general. In what follows, I will first give an account of the strengths of the Orientalist binary as applied to conceptualizations of Chinese culture within the esoteric environments of the late nineteenth and early twentieth century. Thereafter, I will present what I regard as some possible objection toward this characterization of esoteric Orientalism in this context.

As we have seen, esoteric writers from the late nineteenth century onward mentioned a number of aspects of Chinese culture which they considered to be expressions of ancient wisdom. This primarily regarded the doctrines of non-action (*wuwei*) and emanationist cosmogony, as well as practices like divination. However, a number of other phenomena, like alchemy, are also mentioned.[7] As I have shown, some of these writers also constructed genealogies that traced the historical transmissions that were understood to have carried this wisdom to China. Thus, so far, the depiction of China fits in well with the characterization of the nature of the 'East' in accounts of Theosophical Orientalism. That is also true regarding the notion of 'Western' materialism and the disenchantment of its culture, especially in relation to science. Although this is not the place for a detailed exploration of this concept within late nineteenth- and early twentieth-century esotericism, it is true that it was a widespread and generally accepted belief (Hanegraaff 2008, 2013: 7–10; Pasi 2006). The question of whether the Chinese version of ancient wisdom was generally understood to be *better* preserved than the 'Western' version of wisdom is significantly more difficult to answer. Most writers who took an interest in China did not explicitly express an opinion one way or the other.[8] Some of these writers were likely more interested in finding parallels to their own beliefs in other cultures in order to argue for the soundness of those beliefs than in finding examples of a purer form of wisdom to appropriate. Such a project was similar to Voltaire's interest in Confucianism.[9] That is, it was not part of a strategy of turning France into a Confucian country, but as a way of arguing for the universality and therefore the naturalness and usefulness of the Deist principles Voltaire himself believed to have detected in Confucianism (App 2010: 33). Nevertheless, there are some examples of representatives of the esoteric environment of the period who probably did see *aspects* of Chinese culture as containing a purer form of wisdom, with Albert de Pouvourville and Aleister Crowley (1875–1947) being among them. At least in some of his works, de Pouvourville did present a vision of Chinese culture that has preserved the original wisdom of humanity particularly well. Thus, the teachings of the *Daodejing* 道德經, the *Yijing* 易經 (Classic of Changes) and some secret societies are seen by him as (or among) the foremost preserved sources of truth in existence (de Pouvourville [1907] 1974; Nilsson 2020: 151–214). Crowley, although not as emphatic, did in some instances present Daoism as the principal expression of esoteric truth.[10] It could be said that both de Pouvourville and Crowley participated in the cultural transfers that brought teachings and practices associated with Chinese culture to Europe and America. This is especially evident in Crowley's engagement with divinatory techniques connected to the *Yijing*, since his version of these techniques spread and to some extent survived within the esoteric and religious tradition of Thelema which he himself created (Nilsson 2020: 211–14). It should be clear by now that the Theosophical Orientalist understanding of India does indeed have some similarities to some aspects of the esoteric understanding of China. Nonetheless, its application also raises some significant challenges.

Some objections

An important argument presented by Richard King (1999) and others with regard to Orientalism is that the construction of the 'East' as spiritual or mystical excludes important aspects of culture. Baier (2016) presents the spirituality and wisdom connected to India as distinct from and mirroring the sciences and rational investigation associated with the 'West'. Likewise, King makes a similar point in one of his main arguments in *Orientalism and Religion*. He maintains that Orientalism has tended to regard the 'East' as mystical and the 'West' as rational. Although the mystical here is not identical to the 'spiritual' referred to by Baier, the concepts have many similarities. King's analysis focuses on the aspects of culture that he argues are being excluded by constructing South Asian cultures as mystical. These include social and public aspects of culture as well as the rational, philosophical or scientific. Perhaps most important, however, is the exclusion of politics from 'Eastern' mysticism and thus from certain ways of understanding the 'East' (King 1999: 98).

This suggested consequence of Orientalism is less easy to apply to the esoteric understanding of China. Although some of the things esoteric writers looked for in Chinese culture could be described as spiritual or mystical, many did not easily fit those categories. For example, the English occultist Hargrave Jennings (1817–90) claimed that universal wisdom expressed itself through Chinese architecture and fashion of dress, and the French esoteric writer Saint-Yves d'Alveydre argued likewise for the imperial examination system and Chinese traditional forms of education (Jennings 1884: 158; Saint-Yves d'Alveydre [1884] 1981).[11] The esoteric tendency to see aspects of the Chinese social system as expressions of ancient wisdom is even more difficult to reconcile with the claim that esoteric Orientalism removes the political from the realm of spiritual truth. On the contrary, it could be argued that an interest in the organization of Chinese society (regardless of how it was constituted and perceived at any specific time) as well as a willingness to appropriate aspects of what could be termed Chinese political theory was a constant of European thinking about China. This was true to some extent for the early missionaries, (at least some of) the Enlightenment intellectuals, the Maoists of the mid-twentieth century, and it was also true for many of the representatives of late nineteenth- and early twentieth-century esotericism. Saint-Yves d'Alveydre took a keen interest in a political ideology he called 'Synarchy' which entailed the ordering of society into three harmoniously cooperating classes. He saw this type of social system as a reconstruction of the utopian order of the ancient Empire of Ram and believed that knowledge about it had been inherited through history by the same masters and secret societies that preserved other forms of esoteric knowledge (Saint-Yves d'Alveydre [1884] 1981: 232). For Saint-Yves d'Alveydre, knowledge about Synarchy was ancient wisdom, and this type of knowledge had been preserved in the Chinese social system (Saint-Yves d'Alveydre [1884] 1981: 187–8). De Pouvourville, on the contrary, saw political action as a traditional function of the Daoist secret societies that he understood as the vehicles of ancient wisdom. He argued that these societies have historically served and protected Chinese diaspora communities and thus performed a social function. They were also deeply involved in revolutionary activities and anti-colonial insurrections like the Boxer rebellion and Liu Yongfu's 劉永福 (1837–1917) fight against French forces in northern Indochina (de Pouvourville [1907] 1974: 106; Davis 2017). It is also likely, although the topic has not been fully explored, that the individualist, or even anarchic, aspects of Crowley's Thelema were in part influenced by the ascetic, individualist and hermitical passages of the *Daodejing* and the *Zhuangzi* 莊子 (e.g. Crowley 1995).[12] Even the writer and librarian C. H. A. Bjerregaard (1845–1922) states that '[i]n China, Mysticism is closely connected with the social-political order' (1912: 35).[13]

Beyond the question of politics, some of the esoteric authors wrote about rationality and sentimentality in a way that poorly conformed with the Orientalist binary. For example, de Pouvourville *emphatically did not* see the kind of teachings and practices he attributed to a Chinese tradition of wisdom as sentimental notions that would balance 'Western' rationality. Such an idea would have horrified him. To him, 'Western' sentimentality was one of the reasons that Europeans could learn something from East Asia in the first place. It is Europe, not China, that would have forsaken rationality (de Pouvourville 1905).

It is also important to remember that many esoteric writers during this period looked for wisdom not in the 'East' but in Christianity as well as in other religious traditions that they perceived as 'Western'. This is true even for many Theosophists – not least in local European contexts.[14] Furthermore, even if we restrict ourselves to those representatives of the esoteric environment who argued that the wisdom of China was in some ways superior, they did not generally argue that esoteric wisdom in Europe had been completely 'spoiled by the domination of exoteric Christianity' (Baier 2016: 320). Even if Crowley was an enthusiastic admirer of Daoism and a fervent critic of Christianity, he was primarily involved with Thelema, which is (in his emic understanding) a product of 'Western' esoteric tradition. In contrast, de Pouvourville was among those who saw 'Gnosticism' as a representative of a surviving wisdom tradition in Europe (de Pouvourville [1907] 1975).

Thus, even if the materialism–spirituality binary reflects some aspects of the esoteric understanding of China fairly well, it has some clear limitations. It tends to exaggerate the purity and uniqueness of Chinese wisdom in the imagination of the esoteric writers of the period. Furthermore, it does not reflect the manner in which esoteric truth was tied up with social organization and political action. (It should, however, be acknowledged that both King and Baier associate the binary with Theosophy rather than esotericism in general, and that seems to better reflect the attitudes of Theosophical writers.)

Hence, what are the possible reasons for the problems in applying the Orientalist binary on esoteric writings about China? One reason may be that some of the earlier European attitudes about Chinese culture, emphasizing its perceived rationality and well-functioning social order, survived in post-Enlightenment esotericism despite the general shift in the portrayal of China that began in the eighteenth and was concluded in the nineteenth century. This survival is sometimes explicit. Especially among French writers, it was comparatively common to refer to pre-nineteenth-century sources, but it may also, at times, be indirect and even unknown to the authors in question. It is also possible that research on esotericism in the late nineteenth and early twentieth centuries as a whole has not fully taken into account the extent to which the esoteric ideas of the period were tied up with politics and utopian social projects. If this is the case, it is possible that King's approach may be more problematic than expected even when applied to the esoteric interest in the 'East' in general.

Concluding remarks

In recent years, several scholars influenced by postcolonialism and the Saidian critical study of Orientalism have suggested that the way in which esoteric movements in the late nineteenth and early twentieth century portrayed India was structured by a binary relationship between an imagined rational and materialistic 'West' and a spiritual 'East'. This characterization may seem ostensibly self-evident, and it is easy to find support for it in esoteric sources from this period. Polemics against the 'materialism' of European culture are common in the esoteric literature of the time, as are also enthusiastic descriptions of the ancient wisdom supposedly preserved in the 'East'. However, when it comes to the esoteric interest in China, the ideas expressed by the Orientalist binary are not necessarily as easily applicable. Historically, European ways of imagining

Chinese culture tended to emphasize its rationality and pragmatism rather than connecting it with religion or superstition.

In the nineteenth century, and parallel to the European colonial expansion in China, a shift in the portrayal of Chinese culture that had begun a century earlier had a broad impact. Part of this shift was a focus on aspects of Chinese religion that did not fit in with the older emphasis on a rational, philosophical and pragmatic Confucianism. This shift was noticeable in the esoteric movements of the late nineteenth century as well. At the same time, the esoteric focus on a universal type of wisdom, inherited from ancient sources and spread throughout the world, tended to depict Chinese culture as the vehicle of the same type of spiritual tradition that could be found in India and elsewhere. Thus, it is true that esoteric portrayals of Chinese culture are more similar to the esoteric depictions of India than the historical European image of China would suggest. Nonetheless, there are some problems with characterizing the esoteric portrayal of China as structured by a binary relationship between 'Eastern' spirituality or mysticism on the one hand and 'Western' materialism on the other. This characterization tends to exaggerate the importance of Chinese wisdom in the imagination of esoteric writers and overstates the way in which these same writers understood the esoteric wisdom of Europe to have been lost. Furthermore, the ancient wisdom discussed by many of the proponents of esoteric teachings during this period did in some cases include phenomena like systems of education, social structures or ideas that could reasonably be called political. This implies that the esoteric interpretation of Chinese culture could be quite broad and include things not typically considered spiritual.

Notes

1 The sources used here are esoteric textual sources mentioning China, published (or in some cases written) during the period 1860–1949. I use the word 'esoteric' following Kocku von Stuckrad (2005: 10), although the movements, texts and individuals mentioned in this chapter would be considered esoteric in most scholarly senses of the word currently accepted.
2 Although there existed earlier examples of esoteric interpretations of China that were often connected to attempts of interpreting the *Yijing*. For example, see Smith (2012). The *Yijing* in fact had a long and interesting history of reception in Europe (von Collani 2007).
3 For de Pouvourville (1861–1939), see the chapter by Davide Marino in this volume.
4 For Crowley, see the chapter by Gordan Djurdjevic in this volume.

5 'Wisdom' is a term often used by some esoteric movements. Here, however, I use it in an etic sense signifying knowledge relevant to the development of humanity and specific individuals in line with the particular ideals of any esoteric movement. Wisdom need not be spiritual or religious.

6 The notion of the Empire of Ram was primarily developed by Antoine Fabre d'Olivet (1767–1825) and was very loosely inspired by the *Ramayana*. In Saint-Yves d'Alveydre's version, the empire is a utopian state guided by the political principles of Synarchy, a political theory emphasizing the harmonious coexistence of different social classes. The Empire of Ram disintegrated around five millennia ago but some of its knowledge has been preserved by wise men and sages throughout history (Saint-Yves d'Alveydre [1884] 1981; Saunier 1981).

7 It should be noted that most of these doctrines and practices had close similarities in other cultures and religious traditions.

8 It is always unadvisable to argue for the absence of a specific claim. However, several of the esoteric writers mentioned in this chapter (including Jennings, Hardinge Britten and Saint-Yves d'Alveydre) bring up China mostly in passing. Others (like Medhurst and Bjerregaard) may have been enthusiastic about China but did not clearly, explicitly and consistently argue that Chinese culture represented a purer and more genuine form of truth than what could be found elsewhere in the world.

9 As an example, note Crowley's interest in divinatory techniques associated with the *Yijing*. Crowley was fond of these techniques and used them for decades. He did not, however, argue that they should replace divination by Tarot cards. A book about the Tarot, *The Book of Thoth*, was one of the last things he wrote before his death. When Crowley mentioned the *Yijing* in *The Book of Thoth* his position is clearly that the two divinatory systems shed light on each other, not that one should be abandoned for the other (Crowley 2002).

10 This is especially clear in the essay 'The Three Schools of Magic', reproduced in *Magick Without Tears*. The text is attributed to Crowley's friend, the journalist Gérard Aumont, but it is uncertain to what extent Crowley was involved with its composition or its content. It had been published at least one time before, in 1928, by Thelema Verlag in Leipzig. It should be noted that even if Aumont was the sole author of the text, Crowley saw it as representative of his own ideas, thus its reproduction in *Magick Without Tears* (Crowley [1954] 1994: 64–90).

11 One should remember that theories of education were a major interest of many esoteric movements and writers during this period, with Katherine Tingley (1847–1929) and Rudolf Steiner (1861–1925) being two prominent examples.

12 Although the question needs to be systematically explored, some provisional arguments could be made for this thesis. For example, Crowley's commentaries to his own paraphrase of the *Daodejing*, which proport to reveal the true meaning of the text, show that he identified some of the fundamental concepts of Thelema

in some of the passages of the *Daodejing*. One example would be a concept of individualist ethics where what is virtuous varies, depending on the nature of each person, a concept that had political consequences for Crowley. We know that at least part of these commentaries was written in 1919. During or slightly after this period, Crowley also wrote a large part of the commentaries (the so-called New Comment) to his own sacred text, *The Book of the Law*. This suggests that Crowley was in an important phase of developing the philosophies of Thelema while he was also interpreting the *Daodejing*. Nevertheless, the case should not be overstated. There would have probably been enough building blocks for Thelema even if Crowley never encountered any Chinese texts (Crowley 1995; Bogdan 2012). For a discussion of European and American interpretations of Daoism as individualist or revolutionary, see Clarke (2000: 103–11).

13 For Bjerregaard, see the related chapter by Johan Nilsson in this volume.
14 For example, Swedish Theosophical journals from the period, like the Adyar related *Teosofisk Tidskrift* (Theosophical Journal) and Point Loma-associated *Theosophia*, published many texts about Christian esotericism, and seldom (if ever) argued that the 'Western' tradition of wisdom needed to be supplanted by 'Eastern' teachings.

References

App, U. (2010), *The Birth of Orientalism*, Philadelphia: University of Pennsylvania Press.

Baier, K. (2016), 'Theosophical Orientalism and the Structures of Intercultural Transfer: Annotations on the Appropriation of the *cakras* in Early Theosophy', in J. Chajes and B. Huss (eds), *Theosophical Appropriations: Esotericism, Kabbalah, and the Transformation of Traditions*, 309–52, Beer Sheva: Ben-Gurion University Press.

Bjerregaard, C. H. A. (1912), *The Inner Life and the Tao-Teh-King*, New York: The Theosophical Publishing Co.

Blavatsky, H. P. (1877), *Isis Unveiled: A Master-Key to the Mysteries of Ancient and Modern Science and Theology*, vol. 1, New York: J. W. Button.

Blavatsky, H. P. (1891), 'Chinese Spirits', *Lucifer*, 9 (51): 182–7.

Bogdan, H. (2012), 'Envisioning the Birth of a New Aeon', in H. Bogdan and M. P. Starr (eds), *Aleister Crowley and Western Esotericism*, 89–106, Oxford: Oxford University Press.

Clarke, J. J. (2000), *The Tao of the West*, London: Routledge.

Crowley, A. (n.d.), *Shih Yi*, unpublished typescript in the Yorke collection (NS 111). [The Yorke Collection contains the books and papers of Gerald Yorke (1901–1983), a writer, journalist and associate of Aleister Crowley. Yorke was the owner of a large number of manuscripts related to Crowley, including a number of his diaries, letters and unpublished manuscripts. The collection is currently housed at the Warburg Institute at the University of London.]

Crowley, A. ([1954] 1994), *Magick Without Tears*, Tempe: New Falcon Publications.
Crowley, A. (1995), *Tao Te Ching*, York Beach: Samuel Weiser.
Crowley, A. (2002), *The Book of Thoth*, Stamford: U.S. Games Systems.
Davis, B. C. (2017), *Imperial Bandits: Outlaws and Rebels in the China-Vietnam Borderlands*, Seattle: University of Washington Press.
de Pouvourville, A. (1904), 'Les Instruments de la Divination', *La Voie*, 6: 555–66.
de Pouvourville, A. (1905), 'Laotseu', *La Voie*, 12: 481–506.
de Pouvourville, A. ([1907] 1974), *La Voie Rationnelle*, Paris: Éditions Traditionnelles.
de Pouvourville, A. and L. Champrenaud ([1907] 1975), *Les enseignements secrets de la Gnose*, Paris: Robert Dumas.
Gregory, J. S. (2002), *The West and China since 1500*, New York: Palgrave.
Hadland Davis, F. (1915), 'Ancient China & the Elixir of Life', *The Theosophist*, 31 (1): 155–65.
Hanegraaff, W. J. (2008), 'Occult/Occultism', in W. J. Hanegraaff (ed.), *Dictionary of Gnosis and Western Esotericism*, 884–9, Leiden: Brill.
Hanegraaff, W. J. (2013), *Western Esotericism: A Guide for the Perplexed*, New York: Bloomsbury.
Hanegraaff, W. J. (2014), *Esotericism in the Academy: Rejected Knowledge in Western Culture*, Cambridge: Cambridge University Press.
Hardinge Britten, E. (1884), *Nineteenth Century Miracles: Spirits and Their Work in Every Country of the Earth, A Complete Historical Compendium of the Great Movement known as Modern Spiritualism*, New York: Lovell & Co.
Jennings, H. (1884), *Phallicism: Celestial and Terrestrial, Heathen and Christian*, London: George Redway.
Jones, D. M. (2001), *The Image of China in Western Social and Political Thought*, Chippenham: Palgrave.
Kilcher, A. B., ed. (2010), *Constructing Tradition: Means and Myths of Transmission in Western Esotericism*, Leiden: Brill.
King, R. (1999), *Orientalism and Religion: Postcolonial Theory, India and the "Mystic East"*, London: Routledge.
Legge, J. (1880), *The Religions of China*, London: Hodder and Stoughton.
Lévi, É. (1860), *Histoire de la magie*, Paris: Germer Baillière.
Medhurst, C. S. (1905), *Tao the King*, Chicago: Theosophical Book Concern.
Medhurst, C. S. (1909), 'Chinese Esotericism 1', *The Theosophist*, 31 (3): 331–44.
Mungello, D. E. (1999), *The Great Encounter, 1500–1800*, Lanham: Rowman & Littlefield.
Nilsson, J. (2020), 'As a Fire Beneath the Ashes: The Quest for Chinese Wisdom within Occultism, 1850–1949', PhD diss., University of Lund.
Paladin, A. (1879), 'Magnetism in Ancient China', *The Theosophist*, 1 (1): 30.
Partridge, C. (2020), 'Adventures in "Wisdom-Land"', in T. Rudbøg and E. Reenberg (eds), *Imagining the East*, 15–36, Oxford: Oxford University Press.
Pasi, M. (2006), 'Occultism', in K. von Stuckrad (ed.), *The Brill Dictionary of Religion*, 1364–68, Leiden: Brill.

Reinders, E. (2004), *Borrowed Gods and Foreign Bodies: Christian Missionaries Imagine Chinese Religion*, Berkeley: University of California Press.

Rohmer, S. (1914), 'The Occult East', *The Occult Review*, 19 (5): 258–67.

Saint-Yves d'Alveydre, J. A. ([1884] 1981), *Mission des Juifs*, Paris: Éditions Traditionnelles.

Saunier, J. (1981), *Saint-Yves d'Alveydre, ou une synarchie sans enigma*, Paris: Dervy-Livres.

Sinnett, A. P (1984), *Esoteric Buddhism*, London: Trübner & Co.

Smith, R. J. (2012), *The I Ching: A Biography*, Princeton: Princeton University Press.

Spence, J. (1999), *The Chan's Great Continent*, New York: Norton.

Trompf, G. W. (2008), 'Macrohistory', in W. J. Hanegraaff (ed.), *Dictionary of Gnosis and Western Esotericism*, 701–16, Leiden: Brill.

von Collani, C. (2007), 'The First Encounter of the West with the *Yijing*', *Monumenta Serica*, 55 (1): 227–387.

von Stuckrad, K. (2005), *Western Esotericism: A Brief History of Secret Knowledge*, London: Equinox.

Wong, J. Y. (1998), *Deadly Dreams: Opium, Imperialism, and the Arrow War (1856–1860) in China*, Cambridge: Cambridge University Press.

8

The archetypal Dao
A look at C. G. Jung's reception of Chinese thought

Karl Baier

Introduction: The slow arrival of China within the 'Jung and the East' discourse

Among the various types of literature on the famous Swiss psychiatrist, psychologist and psychotherapist Carl Gustav Jung (1875–1961), there is a genre one could call 'Jung and the East'. In the relevant texts, the category 'the East' is hardly ever defined or even critically discussed. Interestingly, until the end of the twentieth century, Jung's 'East' is often more or less identified with South Asian sources, with Jung's commentaries on Buddhist texts of Tibetan and Japanese origin and on Daoist writings being neglected if not entirely disregarded. The best example is Harold Coward's seminal study *Jung and Eastern Thought* (Coward 1985). As Sonu Shamdasani stated in his *Jung's Journey to the East* – an introduction to Jung's lectures on Kundalini Yoga – Coward's book 'remains the most useful overall study of Jung and Indian thought, upon which it focuses' (Shamdasani 1996: xliii). The fact that Coward's focus reduces the 'East' more or less to South Asia does not seem to be a serious problem.

The paradigmatic status of South Asian traditions for Jung's understanding of 'Eastern' religion is suggested, *inter alia*, by his use of the Sanskrit term 'yoga'. For him, it is a general category for all 'Eastern' religious practices and especially for meditation methods, including their theoretical justification and descriptions of their effects (Coward 1985: 3).[1] He was particularly interested in comparing 'Eastern' yoga with his 'Western' psychotherapy and the experiences he made with his patients. This contributes to the impression that South Asian concepts dominated his understanding of Eastern thought *in toto*.

Additionally, the South Asian bias one can find in interpretations of Jung's relation to 'the East' is supported by the sheer quantity of texts that Jung produced referring to Sanskrit sources and to India in general (see the bibliography in Borelli 1985). Thus, with a superficial glance at the matter, and guided by older secondary literature, one could readily conclude that Jung's intellectual journeys to 'the Orient', like his real travels, ended on the Indian subcontinent and did not continue further East.

It was not until the 1990s that more attention was given to Jung's relationship to Daoism, and again Coward played a leading role in this development. The turn started with John Clarke's inclusion of a chapter on Daoism in his monograph on *Jung and Eastern Thought* (Clarke 1994: 80–103). In 1996, Coward contributed to the debate with a surprising article on Jung's reception of Daoist concepts (Coward 1996), where he revised central claims of Clarke's study and asserted hitherto underestimated Daoist influences on the Swiss psychologist, in particular with regard to his notion of the Self and his theory of synchronicity. At the beginning of the twenty-first century, the significance of Daoism for Jung, as highlighted by Clarke and Coward, found its way into the seminal *Encyclopedia of Psychology and Religion* (Schlamm 2009).

Independent from the domain of psychology, research into the modern reception history of Chinese traditions outside China has flourished since the second decade of the twentieth century. To date this highly interesting field is dominated by the Chinese classics and their interpretations by Western sinologists and philosophers. Jung is addressed occasionally, mainly because of his collaboration with Richard Wilhelm (1873–1920), the most famous German sinologist of the first half of the twentieth century (e.g. Walf 2005: 281–2). The impact of Jung's reference to Chinese thought for a broad global audience, and especially in the counter culture of the 1960s and early 1970s, with psychologized New Age religion and today's holistic milieu as its offspring, has thus far not been mapped.

Situating Jung within modern psychology and religion

Jung was one of the leading figures in the formative phase of modern psychology and psychotherapy (Shamdasani 2003). Besides his contributions to psychology in general he became a pioneer in the field of the psychology of religion (e.g. Wulf 1997). What makes his case intricate is that he was not only a psychotherapist and psychologist studying the psychological dimensions of religion, but through his writings also acted as a player within the religious field. That alone would not be a problem if he would not have mixed the two roles in a questionable but nonetheless extremely influential way. His way of thinking has many roots. Looking at the historical conditions of his works reveals a fertile rhizome from which they emerged.

Jung belonged to those European intellectuals who had been socialized in a nineteenth-century Protestant-Christian culture with which they could no longer identify as young adults due to biographical reasons and the profound cultural, social and political changes of the long nineteenth century, with the First World War being its disastrous climax. Like many other members of his generation, he did not completely abandon religion. The search for sources of a post-Christian religiosity plays an important role in his life and work. He considered a psychology based on data from psychotherapeutic treatments as the possible birthplace of future religion. Furthermore, he was also influenced by texts, symbols and myths from different religious traditions made available by translations, comparative religious studies and the modern historiography of religions. He participated to a certain extent in the widespread fascination with 'Eastern' religions among the European and American educated classes, which promised to offer alternatives to the outdated forms of Christianity.

Jung reports that even in his childhood he had dreams and experiences that alienated him from his religious environment. In his student years, he intentionally sought alternatives to the conventional Protestant faith represented by his father who was an Evangelical Reformed pastor. He did not have to look far. His interest in the spiritualist movement, which was very popular at the time, found support in the maternal line of his kinship, which had a spiritualist branch. Between 1895 and 1899, Jung attended and organized séances in which his cousin, Helene Preiswerk (1881–1911), acted as medium through which different spirits spoke. In the oldest known lectures of Jung, which he gave at meetings of the student fraternity Zofingia between 1896 and 1899, he advocates a philosophical spiritualism based on empirical research (Jung 1983). As warrantors for this project he refers to outstanding spiritualists like the physicist Friedrich Zöllner (1834–82), the philosopher Carl du Prel (1839–99) and the chemist and physicist William Crookes (1832–1919), who in 1897 became elected president of the Society for Psychical Research.[2]

In *Memories, Dreams, Reflections* (Jung 1995: 120) he mentions in passing that during this time he also read representatives of German Romantic mesmerism (perhaps mediated through his reading of du Prel, who builds on them), namely, Carl August Eschenmayer (1768–1852), Johann Karl Passavant (1790–1857) and Justinus Kerner (1786–1862).[3] It is difficult to estimate how influential Romantic mesmerism on Jung actually was, as he hardly refers to it explicitly besides this unique reference. It seems that for him Kerner's *Die Seherin von Prevorst* (The Seeress of Prevorst; 1829) was the most important work in this regard.[4] Jung read it in 1897 when he was regularly attending séances and gave it as a birthday present to his somnambule cousin who subsequently called herself a reincarnation of Friederike Hauffe (1801–29), the seeress of Prevorst. As late as 1933–4, he treated Kerner's book at length in his lectures on the history of modern psychology at the ETH Zürich as an instructive study of what happens in cases of extreme introversion (Jung 2019a). At least at that time his attitude towards Kerner and Romantic mesmerism was anything but uncritical. He stated (Jung 2019a: 39):

> Justinus Kerner's *The Seeress of Prevorst* is not a case history in a modern sense, but as it were a dubious account of one of the peculiar and romantic lives that were quite common at the time. Kerner belonged to the school of Romantics. He was not a scientist, and his book contains a series of more or less naïve observations and interpretations. So please do not think that I subscribe to anything and everything that my deceased colleague Dr. Kerner tells us in his book.

In later years, Jung repeatedly conceded the proximity of his psychology to German Romanticism, especially the theory of the unconscious formulated by Carl Gustav Carus (1789–1869) in his late Romantic *Psyche. Entwicklungsgeschichte der Seele* (Psyche: Developmental History of the Soul; 1846).[5] Moreover, he underlined that the scientific-rationalistic line of his thought would be as important as his roots in Romanticism (von Stuckrad 2022: 81). The combination of both, that is, influences from Romanticism and a more rationalistic approach, can be found in representatives of what was called 'scientific occultism' or 'psychical research', to which the aforementioned theoreticians and researchers of spiritualism contributed in a contested way, as well as in representatives of the psychology of the unconscious (diverse hypnotherapists, Flournoy, Freud, etc.) (Ellenberger 1994).

Spiritualism influenced his religious quest and at the same time opened the door to a promising field of psychological research that was just emerging (Charet 1993). After his study of medicine in Basel, Jung started to work at the 'Burghölzli', the Psychiatric University Clinic of Zürich. His chief, the famous psychiatrist Eugen Bleuler (1857–1939), who was also interested in spiritualism and attended séances, supervised his doctoral thesis on *Die Psychologie und*

Pathologie sogenannter occulter Phänomene (The Psychology and Pathology of so-called Occult Phenomena) based on notes taken at the séances Jung had organized. It was published in 1902 by the spiritualist press of Oswald Mutze (Jung 1902). Jung's thesis is a good example of how psychology and psychiatry around 1900 were intertwined with psychical research and the seemingly paranormal phenomena produced by somnambules and spiritualist mediums (Treitel 2004: 29–30). His concept of 'synchronicity' that is also highly relevant for his reception of Chinese thought (see below), and on which he worked until his late years, shows that he remained involved in this kind of research.[6] He was also in contact with Joseph B. Rhine (1895–1980) and followed the statistical method of the American parapsychologist in his empirical astrology study. Apart from this work, Jung was too little involved in the field to be called a full-fledged parapsychologist. He remained a psychologist in favour of psychical research, who insisted on the scientific examination of each individual case and considered psychological explanations as very useful but not completely sufficient. Jung believed that there was enough empirical evidence for most paranormal phenomena to consider their existence proven (Main 2004: 71). This applied to apparitions of the deceased as well as materialization and dematerialization phenomena, poltergeist apparitions, precognitions and prophetic as well as telepathic dreams.

I suggest that his attitude towards religious topics throughout his later life followed the basic trajectory of those scientists and occultists around 1900 who pursued psychology and psychical research as scientific disciplines in which religion and empirical science could be reconciled in one way or the other. The settings of his experiments which should provide the data for this synthesis switched from the séance room and the laboratory of empirical psychology to the intimate spaces of his meditative self-experimentation and of the psychotherapeutic encounter with his patients.

Jung's thesis nonetheless manifests a change of thought that was to shape his entire work. Spiritualistic mediums as revelators of metaphysical truths receded into the background as Jung pursued a more psychological approach. The model for this were the works of several psychologists engaged in psychical research, and especially the Geneva-based Théodore Flournoy (1854–1920), whose study of the medium Hélène Smith (real name: Catherine Élise Müller; 1861–1929) *Des Indes à la plànete Mars* (1900) had become a bestseller.

> What was novel about Flournoy's study was that it approached her [Helene Smith's] case purely from the psychological angle, as a means of illuminating

the study of subliminal consciousness. A critical shift had taken place through the work of Flournoy, Frederik Myers, and William James. They argued that regardless of whether the alleged spiritualist experiences were valid, such experiences enabled far-reaching insight into the constitution of the subliminal, and hence into human psychology as a whole. (Shamdasani 2009: 8)

The spirits encountered by mediums retain to some extent their status of objective realities, but they cease to be inhabitants of the Otherworld and become instead 'objective psychic phenomena' (Jung 1995: 120). The framework for this interpretation is a theory of the unconscious that assumes a creativity of the psyche independent of ego-consciousness. In the case of splits in consciousness, unconscious personalities are formed that take on the features of independent actors. Jung could easily extend this approach beyond the spiritualist context to an 'intrapsychic model of religion' (Aziz 1990: 9–51) that, not least through his influence, also gained ground in transpersonal psychology and alternative religious currents of the second half of the twentieth century.[7] As Hanegraaff (1996: 252) observes with reference to transpersonal psychology,

[t]he angelic and demonic realms [. . .] are identified as realms of the human unconscious, and this collective unconscious is in turn identified with an objective transpersonal realm [. . .]. This is how the 'gods' that seemed to have been banned from heaven reappear [. . .] from the depths of the human psyche.

In Jung's case, the relocation of the divine and demonic within an extended psyche was not merely a theoretical move. The psychologized religious world that puts personal experience at the centre is connected with transformative (therapeutical) practices that help cope with emotional problems and improve the relationship with oneself and the world one lives in.

The initial success he had with his merger of personal religious interests and academic research was crucial for his further career: in his later professional life as founder of an influential form of psychology and psychotherapy, he continued adhering to the programme of translating both his own religious explorations and experiences as well as those of his patients into psychological theory. For the interpretation of dreams and visions he did not ignore the contribution of psychoanalysis, but also drew on material provided by the historiography of religions, including the study of myths.

During the First World War and in the years that followed, Jung went through a midlife crisis and immersed himself into his subconscious by means of a meditation practice that he developed at that time and later called 'active imagination' (Baier 2009: 623–47; Baier forthcoming). Struggling to articulate his own myth, he drew on a similarity between his thoughts and ancient gnostic authors (Segal 1992). At the end of the 1920s, inspired by a Daoist treatise that he commented on for Richard Wilhelm (see the following), the study of European alchemy took the place of processing the productions of his own unconscious in his famous *Red Book* (Jung 2009), which remained a fragment. Via his research on alchemy, Jung deeply immersed in early modern Paracelsism and Hermeticism. From the 1920s, he further broadened his knowledge of religions by conversations with scholars of different traditions, among them specialists of Asian religions like the Indologists Jakob Wilhelm Hauer (1881–1962) and Heinrich Zimmer (1890–1943), but above all the Protestant theologian and sinologist Richard Wilhelm.

With the help of these sources, Jung attempted to extract from his own biographical experience and from the material provided by his patients a type of inner logic of personal development or, as he called it, the 'individuation process'. In this process independent psychic factors called 'archetypes' interact (in the form of mental images and sometimes even through manifestations in the material world) with the conscious personality like characters in a stage play.[8] The drama of individuation ultimately leads to symbolic manifestations of the archetype of the Self which indicate the emerging unity and wholeness of the psyche and the union of its opposites, especially the balance between consciousness and the unconscious. The following quote from Jung's *The Relationship between the Ego and the Unconscious* (1928) illustrates his concept of the Self. In his typical way, Jung switches back and forth between two poles: (1) a spatial choreography of his drama psychological theory in which the separate areas of the conscious ego and the unconscious are finally reconciled by the Self as the emerging center of the whole space, and (2) the appropriation of elements from various religious traditions, in this case Christianity and Daoism (Jung 1972b: 221–2):

> If we picture the conscious mind, with the ego as its centre, as being opposed to the unconscious, and if we now add to our mental picture the process of assimilating the unconscious, we can think of this assimilation as a kind of approximation of conscious and unconscious, where the centre of the total personality no longer coincides with the ego, but with a point midway between the conscious and the unconscious. This would be the point of new equilibrium, a new centering of the total personality, a virtual centre which, on account of its focal position between conscious and unconscious, ensures for the personality a new and more solid foundation. [. . .] I could say the same thing in the words of St. Paul: 'Yet not

I live, but Christ liveth in me.' Or I might invoke Lao-tzu and appropriate his concept of Tao, the Middle Way and creative centre of all things. In all these the same thing is meant. Speaking as a psychologist with a scientific conscience, I must say at once that these things are psychic factors of undeniable power; they are not inventions of an idle mind but definite psychic events obeying definite laws and having their legitimate causes and effects, which can be found among the most widely differing peoples and races today, as thousands of years ago.

According to Jung, a huge part of the human psyche – the so-called collective unconscious – contains patterns and laws (e.g. the archetype of the self and the rule of unification of opposites on the path of individuation), which are independent from specific individual, cultural and historical contexts but interact with the given circumstances so that culture-depending images and concepts of the archetypes and travelogues for the path to individuation emerge. Thus, the powerful impact of these transcultural dimensions of the soul is responsible for the formation of diverse myths, religious symbols, and world views around the globe. One could call this a historically relativized perennialist theory of religion with a psychological twist. Jung's concept of the self and the whole process of individuation that results with the emergence of symbols of this archetype have an obvious religious connotation as he himself, for example, identifies Jesus Christ and the Dao as images of the Self in the aforementioned quote and elsewhere. The process of finding one's personal identity becomes the stage where numinous powers manifest.

Psychologization in this sense does not mean that religion is reduced to the realm of mere subjective human wishes, images and thoughts. On the contrary, Jung tries to show that religiously charged 'numinous' intra-psychical symbols and figures are real powers that transcend the insights and desires of the (conscious as well as unconscious) individual psyche and decisively influence the life of everyone. He argues that they have to be respected if the process of becoming oneself is to succeed. His theories and psychotherapeutic practice contributed to the creation of sociocultural spaces in which religious dreams and visions were accepted and could flourish without being dominated by the distinct views of certain faith communities or dismissed as infantile.

It was this approach that made Jung one of the mentors of the emerging unchurched religiosity of the twentieth century.[9] His influence on the New Age movement and the contemporary holistic milieu is well known (Hammer 2006). Important New Age authors like Fritjof Capra (b. 1939) and Marilyn Ferguson (1938–2008) referred to him (Gruber 2000: 240–1). He also became a crucial figure for twentieth-century astrology and modern interpretations of the Tarot. Jung's thoughts were and still are present within the Wicca movement (Hanegraaff 1996: 90) and modern magic (Luhrmann 1991: 280–2). With regard to the reception of Chinese sources in these areas, so far Jung has been mainly mentioned because of his preface to the English edition of Wilhelm's translation of the *Yijing* 易經 (Classic of Changes) (see, e.g., Redmond 2021). Only recently, in a study on the psychologization of Eastern religions, which extensively considers alternative religious contexts, did Elliot Cohen devote a section of the chapter on 'The Dao of Psychologisation' to Jung's understanding of Daoism (Cohen 2022: 61–4).

Jung's reception of Daoism before his encounter with Richard Wilhelm

As far as we know, Jung only began studying Chinese sources after the publication of *Wandlungen und Symbole der Libido* (literally, Transformations and Symbols of the Libido, whereas the title of the English version in Collected Works 5 is 'Symbols of Transformation') in 1912. In this study he already incorporated many materials from the history of religions, including translations from the Vedas, but China was not mentioned. In Jung's left behind library there is a copy of Alexander Ular's (1876–1919) translation of the *Daodejing* 道德經 in the German edition from 1912. He must have been reading in it because one passage is marked (Shamdasani 2012: 138). No further details are known. The first references to Chinese sources can be found in his *Psychologische Typen* (Psychological Types) published in 1921. As the foreword to this work is dated "Spring 1920," he apparently finished writing it already in early 1920.

A subchapter to the chapter "Die Bedeutung des vereinigenden Symbols" (The Significance of the Uniting Symbol) deals with "Das vereinigende Symbol in der chinesischen Philosophie" (The Uniting Symbol in Chinese Philosophy) (Jung 1971: 214–21). In it, Jung focuses on discussing the concept of *dao* in the *Daodejing*. His textual basis is the third section of the first volume of Paul Deussen's (1845–1919) *Allgemeine Geschichte der Philosophie* (A General History of Philosophy; 1908) that contains an appendix on Chinese and Japanese philosophy ('Einiges über die Philosophie der Chinesen und Japaner'; Deussen 1908: 673–715). Deussen presents basic concepts of the *Daodejing* using the translation of Viktor von Strauss (Deussen 1908: 692–704). Jung takes his Laozi quotations from there.

The psychologist treats the *Daodejing* in the context of a comparison of different uniting symbols within three kinds of religion: primitive, Eastern and

Western. The discussion of his understanding of 'primitive' religion is beyond the scope of this chapter. With the term 'Western religions' he refers to the Christian denominations and Judaism. Brahmanism, Buddhism and Daoism comprise 'Eastern religions'. Jung's orientalism, evident in his East/West opposition, is discussed in more detail later. He focuses on demonstrating that uniting symbols play a central role in both Western and Eastern religions. However, both have developed a different type.

As can be seen from the *Red Book*, the reconciliation of opposites was at that time neither a purely theoretical question for Jung nor a problem he faced mainly through his patients. It was central topic of his own crisis (Shamdasani 2009: 58–9). He was personally involved in finding a way to cope with inner contradictions and experienced the power of uniting symbols during his visionary self-experimentation.

According to Jung, uniting symbols represent an attitude that reconciles conflicting psychic tendencies through an irrational unification of opposites and thus banish the danger of a split of the psyche. The flow of libido, or life force, that is always directed towards the vital optimum 'withdraws from the opposing extremes and seeks a middle path which must naturally be irrational and unconscious, just because the opposites are rational and conscious' (Jung 1971: 194). The emergence of the middle path finally unites the contradictions. It is experienced as redemption from the conflict of opposite aspirations and as the creation of a new potential, a new manifestation of life (Jung 1971: 199, 193). The unconscious integration process enters consciousness in the form of uniting symbols. Jung describes the difference between Western and Eastern uniting symbols as follows (Jung 1960: 207, my translation; the English translation in Jung 1971: 194 is misleading):

> For our Western forms of religion, which are more primitive in terms of insight, the new possibility of life appears as a God or Savior who, out of love or paternal care, but out of his own decision, cancels the split when and how it suits him for reasons that are hidden from us. The infantility of this view is striking. The East has recognized this process for millennia, and has therefore established a doctrine of salvation which places the path of redemption within the realm of human intention.

Jung criticizes that Judaism and Christianity believe in God as an authoritarian father-figure who redeems people through acts of his arbitrariness without them understanding the reasons or being able to contribute anything themselves. The rejection of this infantile image of God is combined with a criticism of the heteronomous morality that according to Jung, is connected with this form of religion. 'We are still so uneducated that we actually need laws from without, and a task-master or Father above, to show us what is good and the right thing to do' (Jung 1971: 213). Against this view, Jung argues that mature morality is based on freedom. But to gain this freedom and overcome heteronomy requires more than the simple abolishment of external laws and values, and giving in to one's immediate urges and desires (Jung 1971: 213, original emphasis):

> *There is no morality without freedom.* When the barbarian lets loose the beast within him, that is not freedom but bondage. Barbarism must first be vanquished before freedom can be won. This happens, in principle, when the basic root and driving force of morality are felt by the individual as constituents of his own nature and not as external restrictions.

Jung then outlines a vitalistic morality that invokes the natural flow of the life force and identifies it with the 'middle way' of Eastern religions. Autonomy does not mean to surrender to every desire one has; rather, it is to listen to one's own nature in the form of the laws of the movement of libido (Jung 1971: 212–13):

> Morality is not a misconception invented by some vaunting Moses on Sinai but something inherent in the laws of life and fashioned like a house or ship or any other cultural instrument. The natural flow of libido, this same middle path, means complete obedience to the fundamental laws of human nature, and there can be no higher moral principle than harmony with natural laws that guide the libido in the direction of life's optimum. [...] The optimum can be reached only through obedience to the tidal laws of the libido, by which systole alternates with diastole – laws which bring pleasure and the necessary limitations of pleasure, and also set us those individual life tasks without whose accomplishment the vital optimum can never be attained.

Jung understands the *dao* as a typical Eastern uniting symbol. He sees a kinship with Vedic thought but also with the philosophy of Henri Bergson (1859–1941). At the time Jung was influenced by the French philosopher whose thought helped him to reinterpret the Freudian concept of libido (for the reception of Bergson by psychoanalysts and especially Jung, see Shamdasani 2003: 227–30). What he would later call the process of individuation is already conceived here as a deliverance from the tension of conflicting opposites that manifests itself as a renewal of the flux of life. Like *brahman*, according to Jung, *dao* not only denotes the ultimate union of opposites, but also stands for the creative process that leads to this unity (Jung 1960: 230, my translation):

> The realization of Tao [. . .] has the same redeeming and uplifting effect as the realization of Brahman: one becomes unified with Tao, with the infinite 'creative duration' [Bergson's *dureé créatrice*], to appropriately add this newest philosophical term to its older relatives, for Tao is also the course of time.

Dao is divided into *yin* and *yang*, the fundamental pair of opposites, which, as universal principles, connect the human microcosm with heaven and earth. 'Yang signifies warmth, light, maleness; yin is cold, darkness, femaleness. Yang is also heaven, yin earth. From the yang force arises shen, the celestial portion of the human soul, and from yin force comes kuei, the earthly part. As a microcosm, man is a reconciler of the opposites' (Jung 1971: 216–17).

Jung understands the *dao* as an 'irrational union of opposites' and identifies it with 'the creative process' (Jung 1971: 215), again with allusions to Bergson. Both the process thought and the emphasis on creativity, as well as the use of the term 'irrational' – which often appears in this early interpretation of Daoism and in the rest of *Psychological Types* – point to Bergson's influence. In line with Bergson's critique of intellectualism, Jung defends the significance of the irrational as a realm of experience that is not against reason but outside its reach (see Jung 1971: 454; Shamdasani 2003: 229).

From the irrationality of the *dao* it follows that it cannot be attained through will-driven action (Jung 1971: 217, original emphasis):[10]

> This lends particular significance to another specifically Chinese concept, *wu wei*. *Wu wei* means 'not-doing' (which is not to be confused with 'doing nothing'). Our rationalistic 'doing,' which is the greatness as well as the evil of our time, does not lead to *tao*.

In a manner typical of the period after the First World War, Jung combines the reception of Chinese 'not-doing' with a critique of the rationalism and activism of Western culture as it was widespread in the Lebensreform and youth movement and the Keyserling circle. He does not go into detail here about what this concept means and what therapeutic significance it could have. A little later, however, he became acquainted with a Chinese method of recognizing the direction of the flow of time without using one's own will: the *Yijing*.

It is an open question why Jung does not yet refer to the *Yijing* in *Psychological Types*. Deussen's appendix to the *Allgemeine Geschichte der Philosophie*, Jung's major source with regard to Chinese thought, contains an introduction to this divination text, which the psychologist very likely read. Jung may also have been pointed to the *Yijing* by his patient, lover and collaborator Toni Wolff (1888–1953), whose father was a sinologist (Main 2004: 77). Obviously, however, his interest in the text was not aroused by Deussen or Wolff. In the summer of 1919 he held a seminar in London at the medical practice of his friend, the neurologist and psychiatrist Maurice Nicoll.[11] On 3 June 1919, he wrote from London to his wife that he had become acquainted with the magic of the *Yijing* and would try to get a copy of it.[12] The fact that Jung speaks of having been made familiar with the magic of the *Yijing* suggests that he was not only referred to the book, but also had practical experience with the oracle in London. As far as we know today, this was the beginning of his decades-long preoccupation with the book.[13]

Most likely during the summer holidays of the following year, Jung himself began to practice the divination method described in the book. His interest in divination techniques was not new. As can be seen from a letter to Sigmund Freud (1856–1939) from 1911, he was already engaged at that time in making horoscopes of his patients and checking whether they could be used for diagnosis. He wrote to Freud that his experiments with astrology had amazing results, which he assumed would certainly seem incredible to the Viennese psychoanalyst (Jung 1972a: 45).

In the case of the Chinese oracle, Jung again claims the role of the observing researcher who was not convinced from the outset that it would produce some sort of insights (Jung 1995: 407):

> One summer in Bollingen I resolved to make an all-out attack on the riddle of this book. Instead of traditional stalks of yarrow required by the classical method, I cut myself a bunch of reeds. I would sit for hours on the ground beneath the hundred-year-old pear tree, the I Ching beside me, practicing the technique by referring the resultant oracles to one another in an interplay of questions and answers.

According to Jung, this procedure led to 'remarkable results' in the sense of the emergence of meaningful connections between the oracle's messages and his own thoughts, connections which he was not able to explain: 'During the whole of those summer holidays I was preoccupied with the question: are the I Ching's answers meaningful or not? If they are, how does the connection between the psychic and the physical sequence of events come about?' (Jung 1995: 407). In later years, he would have continued his experiments with the *Yijing* with some of his patients and again came to the result 'that a significant number of answers did indeed hit the mark' (Jung 1995: 407).

The ground was well prepared for the encounter with the rising star of German sinology, whose work, like Jung's, was not limited to the confines of a particular scientific discipline and connected sociocultural reform efforts with his scholarly expertise.

Magic in the air: Jung's relationship with Richard Wilhelm

> It was a tremendous experience for me to hear through him, in clear language, things I had dimly divined in the confusion of our European unconscious. Indeed, I feel myself so very much enriched by him that it seems to me as if I had received more from him than from any other man. (Jung 1966: 62)

In summer 1920, the Lutheran missionary, educator, translator and connoisseur of Chinese culture Richard Wilhelm left the seaport Qingdao 青岛 where he had lived since 1899 because the German colony to which Qingdao belonged was handed over to Japan (Wippermann 2020). He went back to his homeland and prepared his final settlement there by establishing new contacts and building on old ones. These included his acquaintance with the philosopher Hermann Count Keyserling. Keyserling traveled to China in 1912 shortly after the Xinhai 辛亥 Revolution and visited Qingdao to meet Wilhelm. The meeting of the two was instigated by Keyserling's diplomat friend Gerhart von Mutius.[14] In his 1919 bestseller *Reisetagebuch eines Philosophen* (Travel Diary of a Philosopher; English translation: Keyserling 1925), the Count notes that in Qingdao Wilhelm introduced him to representatives of the (disempowered) political and cultural elite who had gathered there because of the revolution and interpreted between him and his Chinese interlocutors (Keyserling 1925: 39).[15]

The *Reisetagebuch* had a major impact on the popularity of Daoism in 1920s Germany. Using Wilhelm's translation of the *Daodejing* Keyserling defended 'Daoist wisdom' against accusations of being a kind of 'unfruitful quietism'. It would indeed fail in the conscious, volitional shaping of life, the Count conceded, but then continued (Keyserling 1925: 47, translation slightly altered):

> It cannot be denied, however, that the works of the Taoist classics contain, perhaps, the profoundest sayings of wisdom which we possess, the profoundest precisely from the angle of our ideal, the ideal of creative autonomy. How is this possible? It is possible, because the Tao, 'Meaning' (as Richard Wilhelm translated it so admirably) – is expressed more perfectly so far in the creativity of nature than in the freest realization of freedom; so that a life which reflects the workings of nature cannot but lead to perfection.

When the *Reisetagebuch* was published, Wilhelm was no longer unknown in the German-speaking world. Together with Martin Buber's (1878–1965) *Die Reden und Gleichnisse des Tschuang-Tse* (The Discourses and Parables of Tschuang-Tse; 1910), his translations *Laotse: Tao Te King. Das Buch des Alten vom SINN und LEBEN* (Laotse: Tao Te King. The Book of the Old one about MEANING and LIFE; 1911) and *Dschuang Dsi – Das wahre Buch vom südlichen Blütenland* (Dschuang Dsi – The True Book of the Southern Blossom Land; 1912) caused a 'Dao fever' that particularly infected the postwar alternative cultures of the German Lebensreform and youth movement (Pohl 1999: 29–30; Grasmück 2004: 25–8).

When Wilhelm arrived in Germany, Keyserling was just preparing the foundation of the so-called 'School of Wisdom', which eventually took place at an inaugural conference in November 1920 in Darmstadt. Keyserling's School became an elitist center for adult education and a meeting point of renowned intellectuals. Its fame in the Weimar Republic was based on its conferences, where scholars from various fields lectured.[16] The activities of the School of Wisdom were designed to contribute to the spiritual and cultural renewal of postwar Germany and the European civilization in general (Gahlings 1996: 120–59). A lecture of Keyserling held at the inaugural conference on *Indische und Chinesische Weisheit* (Indian and Chinese Wisdom) made clear that one of the main aims of the School of Wisdom was the study of Asian thought and the development of a concept of wisdom that integrates European, Indian and Chinese traditions.

Despite the pluralist outlook of the conferences, Keyserling pursued a kind of perennialism that was connected with a criticism of the materialism and rationalism of the modern world and of modern democracy as the rule of mediocrity. The concert of voices from different religions, philosophies and sciences should, through the contrast of diverse historical manifestations, lead to a realization of the timeless basic truths that shape the course of history but are in danger of being forgotten in the modern times.

In a letter to Wilhelm he wrote that the purpose of the School of Wisdom would be 'to let the eternal basic tones, which underlie all spatio-temporal melodic formation of a religious, social and philosophical kind, resound as such – we take nothing from any special form, add something to each'.[17] The Chinese would have been the first to recognize these basic tones and at the same time were able to take account of the changing historical situations (Letter to Wilhelm, 29 August 1921) – obviously a reference to the *Yijing*, which thus becomes, at least in this letter, the historical model for Keyserling's own philosophical approach and for the kind of insights his conferences aimed at.

It was only after the inaugural conference that Keyserling heard about Wilhelm's return to Germany and it was him who took the initiative to contact Wilhelm. In a letter dated 8 February 1921, he invited him via Wilhelm's publisher

Eugen Diederichs (1867–1930) to speak at the first official conference of the School of Wisdom in May.[18] Wilhelm received this letter belatedly on February 26. He replied immediately telling Keyserling that he had given a talk in Beijing on the relationship between Chinese and European philosophy just before he left for Germany. Therein, he would have called for 'European philosophy to depart from its purely theoretical nature and offer wisdom of life'.[19] He would have seen it as a confirmation of his thoughts that immediately after his talk, he had received the news that Keyserling had founded a School of Wisdom. It would therefore go without saying that he would have been very delighted to lecture there.[20] Finally, Wilhelm not only gave two lectures at the May conference, but also participated as a speaker in the second conference, again with two talks. In between, he visited the School of Wisdom's famous Tagore week that took place between 10 and 14 June 1921. Through these activities, he became a formative figure in the early days of Keyserling's School. The Count's network was useful for his career in Germany but his proximity to the School of Wisdom also provoked criticism (Wippermann 2020: 61, 73, 75–6).[21]

Decades later Jung recounts that he got to know Wilhelm at a meeting of the School of Wisdom but only vaguely dates this to the early 1920s (Jung 1995: 407). It would be possible that Jung attended at least one of the early Darmstadt conferences and met Wilhelm there. But it is more likely that his memory is mistaken in this respect as no other source mentions such a visit. His first attested participation in Keyserling's School of Wisdom took place in April 1927. Additionally, Wilhelm gave a talk about the *Yijing* at the Psychological Club in Zurich as early as 15 December 1921 – and not in 1923, as Jung mistakenly claims in *Memories, Dreams, Reflections* (Stein 2005: 211). As far as we know today, the first verifiable encounter of the two took place on this occasion.

At the Psychology Club, Wilhelm did not only talk about the *Yijing* but also demonstrated how to make it work as an oracle. Jung tells us: 'At his first lecture at the Psychological Club in Zurich, Wilhelm, at my request, demonstrated the use of the I Ching and at the same time made a prognosis which, in less than two years, was fulfilled to the letter and with the utmost clarity.' Wilhelm would have confirmed what he already knew of the *Yijing* in the conversations that took place at their first meeting and would also have taught him many new things (Jung 1969b: 590). Both were practitioners, convinced of the oracle's divinatory power. Additionally, it was used as a therapeutic device by Jung and Jungian therapists (Smith 2012: 198).

Soon after this meeting, the connection between the two was interrupted or at least significantly impeded, as in January 1922 Wilhelm went back to China to work as scientific advisor at the German Embassy in Beijing and as a lecturer at Beijing University.[22] In 1924 he returned to Germany where he finally received a professorship in Chinese history and philosophy at the University of Frankfurt and founded the China-Institute there which he directed until his death.

In the same year, the translation and commentary of the *Yijing*, on which he had been working with his Chinese teacher Lao Naixuan 勞乃宣 (1843–1921) since 1913, was published as *I Ging. Buch der Wandlungen* (I Ching: Book of Changes). Jung was very impressed by this work. He thought it surpassed by far previous translations and suggested to his American collaborator and translator Cary F. Baynes (1883–1977) to translate it into English.[23] Baynes started her translation in 1929. After Wilhelm's death in 1930, her work progressed slowly (McGuire 1989: 19). It was not until 1950 that it was published with a foreword by Jung as volume XIX of the Bollingen Series, named after the Bollingen Tower, Jung's country home in Bollingen (Wilhelm 1997). The *I Ching or Book of Changes* became a bestseller and until today is the most popular English version of the *Yijng*. Jung's preface affirmed the importance of the *Yijing* as a source of wisdom and offered an explanation for the functioning of the divination technique associated with the book combined with a criticism of Western rationalism. It thus supported the spread of the *Yijing* in the counterculture of the 1960s and 1970s (Redmond 2021). Given the success of the book, Jung's foreword most likely became the most read text that he ever published (Karcher 1999: 296).

Jung not only learned from the sinologist. In fact, some of Wilhelm's commentaries on the *Yijing* point to Jung's incipient influence on him, particularly those that refer to the powers of the unconscious, such as in his introduction (Wilhelm 1997: liv):

> The only thing about all this that seems strange to our modern sense is the method of learning the nature of a situation through the manipulation of yarrow stalks. This procedure was regarded as mysterious, however, simply in the sense that the manipulation of the yarrow stalks makes it possible for the unconscious in man to become active. All individuals are not equally fitted to consult the oracle. It requires a clear and tranquil mind, receptive to the cosmic influences hidden in the humble divining stalks.

Later in the text he explains that, according to the *Yijing*, the unconscious not only receives influences but, in a very concentrated state of mind, mysterious currents of force emanate from it to go beyond the individual and affect the unconscious of other people and even the realm of physical cosmic phenomena (Wilhelm 1997: 360).

Lu Zhao deserves credit for pointing out the role of the unconscious in Wilhelm's interpretation of the Yijing (Zhao 2021: 160–5). Probably because of the aforementioned misleading statements by Jung regarding the history of his relationship with Wilhelm, he supposes that Jung only became interested in Wilhelm's scholarship through his reading of *I Ging. Buch der Wandlungen* in 1924, and that they began to strongly influence each other from the latter's trip to Zurich in 1926. As a result, Zhao assumes that Wilhelm's concept of the unconscious in *I Ging* owes nothing to the Swiss psychiatrist but it is drawn from nineteenth-century theories from Friedrich Schelling (1775–1854) up to Eduard von Hartmann. In light of Wilhelm's *Yijing*-focused visit to Zurich in 1921, I find it more plausible that through Jung's influence Wilhelm conceived the unconscious as key factor for the assumed divinatory power of the *Yijing*. They apparently developed their understanding of the unconscious as an explanatory principle for paranormal forces and occurrences in dialogue with each other and through theoretical and practical engagement with the Chinese text (or, in Jung's case, its translations).

The fact that Jung first mentions the term 'synchronicity' in his 1930 obituary of Wilhelm is significant (Jung 1966: 56). Jung developed this concept – not exclusively, but to a large extent – in dialogue with Wilhelm and in the context of their practice of the *Yijing*. I will return to this later.

Without any doubt, the relationship between the two intensified during the second half of the 1920s. Wilhelm again lectured at the Psychology Club, now on *Chinesische Jogapraxis* [sic] (Chinese Yoga Practice) and *Chinesische Seelenlehre* (Chinese Doctrine of the Soul) in May 1926, and on *Einige Probleme der buddhistischen Meditation* (Some Problems of Buddhist Meditation) in January 1929 (Stein 2005). In April 1927, Jung and Wilhelm lectured at the seventh annual conference of the School of Wisdom.

One year later, Wilhelm sent his translation of the Chinese alchemical treatise *Taiyi jinhua zongzhi* 太乙金華宗旨 (translatable as The Great Unity's Principle of the Golden Fluorescence/Flower)[24] to Jung with the request to write a commentary that would be published along with the translation. Jung agreed and the volume appeared in 1929 with the title *Das Geheimnis der Goldenen Blüte. Ein chinesisches Lebensbuch* (The Secret of the Golden Flower: A Chinese Book of Life) – later in this chapter, I will go into the content of Jung's commentary in more detail; here I focus on the biographical circumstances.

The arrival of Wilhelm's manuscript was accompanied by a strange coincidence that caught Jung's attention. He was just painting an image that he felt had a Chinese atmosphere. It showed a symmetrically structured fortified city with a golden castle in the middle. Later he wrote a legend beneath his painting, in which he hints at the similarity between the symbolism of the Chinese text and his creation. 'When I painted this image, which showed the golden well-fortified castle, Richard Wilhelm sent me from Frankfurt the Chinese, thousand-year-old text of the golden castle, the embryo of the immortal body' (Jung 2009: 422, n307).

The reading of Wilhelm's manuscript of the *Golden Flower* had a profound impact on Jung's work that underwent a difficult phase at the time. In the preface to the second edition of the *Golden Flower* he writes that he had so far searched in vain for examples from cultural and religious history that were comparable to the results of what he calls his 'investigating the processes of the collective unconscious' – that is, of his visions and active imaginations in which he had been intensively immersed since 1913 (Jung 1968: 3).[25] The insights he had obtained from his self-experimentation and also from the psychotherapies he conducted were far from the categories and methods of recognized forms of psychology. He felt that his research results were in a state of limbo unless he was able to prove that this personal material transcends the realm of private fantasies and enters into the sphere of universal human ('collective') relevance testified by historical sources.

Thus far he had found the greatest similarities in late antique gnostic systems. But Jung was not satisfied with this 'strange and confused literature' for various reasons. He found the gnostic scriptures to consist more of systematic speculations than references to direct experience. Moreover, most of what we know about Gnosticism were accounts of its Christian critics. He would also have missed key points of his own experience in it: 'The text that Wilhelm sent me helped me out of this difficulty. It contained exactly those items I had long sought for in vain among the Gnostics. Thus, the text afforded me a welcome opportunity to publish, at least in provisional form, some of the essential results of my investigations' (Jung 1968: 4). From then onward he regarded alchemy to be the link 'between Gnosis and the processes of the collective unconscious that can be observed in modern man' (Jung 1968: 4). Wilhelm, for his part, was thrilled by Jung's commentary. Thenceforth, Jung considered him a close ally and they became friends.

At least one of the aims of the work on the *Red Book* was to create a document that would compensate for the lack of historical writings that would testify the significance of the visionary process he was going through. It is therefore understandable that the *Golden Flower* eventually led him to stop working on it. 'The beginning of the end came in 1928, when Wilhelm sent me the text of the "Golden Flower", an alchemical treatise. There the contents of this book [the *Red Book*] found their way into actuality [*Wirklichkeit*, in the sense of historical reality, KB] and I could no longer continue working on it' (Jung 2009: 555). Furthermore, his interest in alchemy as symbolic expression of a psychological and spiritual transformation process deepened significantly through the Chinese text.[26] Subsequently, he started to collect old alchemical texts and the study of European alchemy became a focus of his research for more than twenty years.

The commentary to the *Golden Flower* is the most important of Jung's texts that emerged from the collaboration with Wilhelm. At its beginning Jung argues that from the perspective of prevailing Western intellectualism and overvaluation of conscious will, Eastern ideas and values, including Chinese philosophy, seem to have no practical relevance and are at best perceived as curiosities (Jung 1968: 10). Modern psychology, however, would offer a way to understand and appreciate 'Eastern wisdom' (Jung 1968: 11). He then tries to substantiate this claim by interpreting basic notions and certain elements of the practice described in the *Golden Flower*.

The subsequent commentary deserves a closer examination. I can only address one point here, however, which is suitable for linking to the section on Jung's early reception of Daoism and at the same time building a bridge to topics yet to be dealt with in the present chapter.

Jung reports on a line of development which he had observed in certain patients and which, in his opinion, corresponds to a path known in the East for a long time (Jung 1968: 13–19). These would be people with a highly developed but one-sided consciousness and strong will who are harassed by contents rising from the unconscious, which rebel against their conscious attitude and cannot be assimilated. Both for him as a therapist and for those patients, the basic problem presented itself as unsolvable if one did not want to act violently to one or the other side of the patient's being. This is the situation already described in the chapter on the uniting symbol in *Symbols of Transformation* discussed earlier and with which Jung himself had to cope during his crisis. Some patients would have failed. Often, however, they would not have solved the unsolvable problem, of course, but would have, as Jung says, 'outgrown it' (Jung 1968: 14–15; in the German original text Jung speaks of *überwachsen*). They would have reached a higher level of personal growth from which the insurmountable aporia lost its urgency. In light of *Symbols of Transformation*, one can say that they have thus found the kind of solution that is represented by unifying symbols.

Jung tells us that he noticed a commonality in the fates of these patients. The salutary new thing that approached them from the 'dark field of possibilities' never came only from outside or only from within (Jung 1968: 15; the English translation is misleading, so I stayed closer to the German original): 'If it came from outside, it became a profound inner experience; if it came from inside, it became an outer happening. In no case was it conjured into existence intentionally or by conscious willing, but rather seemed to be borne along on the stream of time' (Jung 1968: 16). Jung alludes here to the topic of synchronicity and its time-theoretical justification, to which a separate section is devoted below, because they are of utmost importance for Jung's approach to Chinese thought.

Jung asks what these people would have done to bring about the redemptive progress, and states (Jung 1968: 17, original emphasis):

> As far as I could see they did nothing (*wu wei*) but let things happen. As Master Lü-tsu teaches in our text, the light circulates according to its own law if one does not give up one's occupation. The art of letting things happen, action through non-action, letting go of oneself as taught by Meister Eckhart, became for me the key to open the way. *We must be able to let things happen in the psyche.*

In the following passages, which I cannot go into further analysis here, he discusses the difficulty of letting go with reference to his method of active imagination. Compared with *Symbols of Transformation* where he commented on *wuwei* 無為 for the first time and rather vaguely, he is now relating it to his therapeutical and meditation experiences. His reception is still to some extent in line with the Lebensreform movement and related forms of cultural criticism. There, alongside the Daoist *wuwei*, Meister Eckhart's *Gelassenheit* was an important point of reference for a critique of the will-driven activism of modern Western civilization (Largier 1991).

In April 1929, he managed to have Wilhelm invited to a psychotherapy congress at Nauheim and enthusiastically wrote about this to him: 'This is historic! Think about what this means if medical practitioners, who reach the ordinary people directly in their most vulnerable areas, become inoculated with Chinese philosophy! [. . .] This hits the bull's eye. Medicine is powerfully converting itself to the psychic, and here the East must enter!' (Jung 1973: 63; quoted after Stein's translation of the original German letter in Stein 2005: 215).

After Wilhelm had sent him a reply in which he agreed to speak at the congress, Jung replied: 'Dear Friend, It is lovely to hear the word "friend" from you. Fate seems to have assigned us the role of being two pillars that support the weight of the bridge between East and West' (Jung 1973: 66; quoted after Stein's translation of the original German letter in Stein 2005: 216).

Wilhelm's lecture at Nauheim eventually did not take place, as he died in March 1930, only fifty-seven years old. It fits the relationship of the two that Jung foresaw Wilhelm's death in a vision:

> A few weeks before his death, when I had no news from him for a considerable time, I was awakened, just as I was on the point of falling asleep, by a vision. At my bed stood a Chinese in a dark blue gown, hands crossed in the sleeves. He bowed long before me, as if he wished to give me a message. I knew what it signified. (Jung 1995: 410)

Wilhelm died of tropical sprue, a chronic disease he contracted while in China and which was diagnosed late. Jung interpreted the deadly disease of his friend as psycho-somatic expression of a deep inner conflict that Wilhelm could not properly cope with. The psychologist had the impression that Wilhelm was totally absorbed by Chinese thought when he returned to Germany. 'The Oriental point of view and ancient Chinese culture had penetrated him through and through' (Jung 1995: 409). But there he was exposed to the pressure of the European spirit, and his older Christian convictions came more and more to the fore.

> I saw it was a reassimilation to the West, and felt that as a result of it, Wilhelm must come into conflict with himself. Since it was, so I thought, a passive assimilation, that is to say, a succumbing to the influence of environment, there was the danger of a relatively unconscious conflict, a clash between his Western and Eastern psyche. [...] If such a process takes place without a strong, conscious attempt to come to terms with it, the unconscious conflict can seriously affect the physical state of health. (Jung 1995: 409–10)

Jung warned him and, according to the psychologist, Wilhelm agreed to a certain degree to his analysis, but was not really able to deal with this problem.

From this interpretation of Wilhelm's early death it is clear that Jung understood bridge-building between East and West to be not only a demanding but also a dangerous undertaking. It puts the mental health and sometimes even the lives of those involved at risk. He was not thinking of political or socially motivated physical attacks, but on cognitive and emotional dissonances that can arise through intercultural processes – the latter Jung conceptualizes against the backdrop of slightly psychologized Orientalist East/West stereotypes, discussed in the next section. As a psychologist, he could easily connect to the Orientalist view because it was already based on the assumption of different emotional and cognitive attitudes, which were held responsible for social and religious differences.

Jung's orientalism

The orientalist juxtaposition of 'the East' and 'the West' functioned, on the one hand, as an ideology to justify colonialism by emphasizing the superiority of the West. On the other hand, it could be used to put the Western mindset into perspective as historically conditioned and launch a self-critique of Western culture and a related reform agenda. As Gert Baumann pointed out, the usual Orientalist scheme combines a negative mirroring of West and East with its positive reversal: 'What is good in us is (still) bad in them, but what got twisted in us (still) remains straight in them' (Baumann 2006: 18–21). This pattern can also be found in Jung's reflections on Eastern and Western psychology (Jung 1976b: 654–5):

> Knowledge of Eastern psychology provides the indispensable basis for a critique of Western psychology, as indeed for any objective understanding of it. And in view of the truly lamentable psychic situation of the West, the importance of a deeper understanding of our Western prejudices can hardly be overestimated.

For Jung, East and West not only denote different ways of thinking that can cross-fertilize each other. They are spheres that compete with each other on different levels. In this fight Jung takes a stance and supports the claim of Western supremacy. Western knowledge in the form of Jungian psychology would be able to elevate the insights of Eastern wisdom to a scientific level and thus develop a superior Western response to the challenge of the spirit of the East. In his commentary to the *Golden Flower*, he (1968: 43) writes:

> The East came to its knowledge of inner things in childlike ignorance of the external world. We, on the other hand, shall explore the psyche and its depths supported by an immense knowledge of history and science. [...] We are already building up a psychology, a science that gives us the key to the very things that the East discovered – and discovered only through abnormal psychic states.

Given the scope of this chapter, I cannot go into detail; I will only give a rough overview of the way in which Jung constructs the stereotypes of East and West (Table 8.1).

He conceives cultures as independent plantlike entities that develop, stagnate and finally decline according to their inner laws. China (and the same could be said of India) is an ancient culture 'which grew logically and organically from the deepest instincts, and which, for us, is forever inaccessible and impossible to imitate' (Jung 1968: 8). This also applies to the history of religion that Jung

Table 8.1 Jung's Orientalist East/West Polarity

	West	East
Direction of Libido	Extraversion	Introversion
Relationship between consciousness and the unconscious	Dissociation; exclusion of unconscious contents under the rule of the ego	Connectedness and compensation; ego in danger of being overwhelmed by the unconscious
Prevailing world view	Materialism (outer world as true reality)	Idealism (soul as true reality)
Dominant form of knowledge	Analytical differentiation Science Technological know-how One-sided intellectualism	Perception of the totality and paradox polarity of all life; wisdom articulated in parables and images Immature intellect and lack of knowledge of the outer world
Dominant category of thought	Causality	Synchronicity
Typical religious practice	Extraverted prayer and worship directed to 'God in the Heights'	Yoga: methodological introversion through meditative practices of self-development directed to 'God in the depths of the soul'

understands in an evolutionistic manner reminiscent of Edward Burnett Tylor (1832–1917) (Jung 1973: 39, letter to Oskar H. A. Schmitz from 26 May 1923):

> Those [Eastern] people have gone through an uninterrupted development from the primitive state of natural polydemonism to polytheism at its most splendid, and beyond that to a religion of ideas within which the originally magical practices could evolve into a method of self-improvement. These antecedents do not apply to us.

According to Jung, the dissociation between consciousness and the unconscious, and therefore the rupture within religious evolution which distinguishes the Western from the Eastern psyche, started long ago when Christianity was forcibly grafted onto the European pagan and particularly the Germanic psyche. It has been reinforced by Protestantism and the modern culture of rational knowledge and will. In the light of this history, to take up Eastern practices and superficially adopt Eastern ideas would only mean further strengthening the cramped Western mindset. Nothing should be forced on the unconscious: 'On the contrary everything has to be done to help the unconscious to reach the conscious mind and to free it from its rigidity' (Jung 1969a: 537). The task for the Western mind would be to give the suppressed primitive sides, including archaic religiosity, the chance to develop. To this end, he considers his active imagination, which stimulates the unconscious, to be the appropriate form of meditation for Westerners.

As might be expected, Jung also firmly rejects experimentation with the exercises of inner alchemy as described in the *Golden Flower*: 'There could be no greater mistake than for a Westerner to take up the practice of Chinese yoga, for that would merely strengthen his will and consciousness against the unconscious and bring about the very effect to be avoided. The neurosis would then simply be intensified' (Jung 1968: 14). As we will see in the next section, he makes only one significant exception to this attitude towards Asian practices, namely, the use of the *Yijing* as an oracle and book of wisdom.

The *Yijing* as synchronicity-based science

'Synchronicity' is one of Jung's most contested ideas. His various attempts to define the term are only partially consistent with each other.[27] 'The only definitions he offers that are not at odds with one or other of his examples are such basic ones as "meaningful coincidence" and "acausal connection"' (Main 2004: 47). In the literal sense, 'synchronicity' means the simultaneity of events. In some of his examples, Jung indeed describes events whose coincidental and (more or less) simultaneous occurrence makes astonishing sense to those involved. But in other cases, this element is missing. In 1951, he distinguished three kinds of synchronicity:

(1) Correspondences perceived as somehow meaningful between a psychic state or content and a simultaneous external event within the perceptual field of the respective person; (2) Coincidences between a psychic state (dream, fantasy, intuition) and a more or less simultaneous external event that takes place outside the perceptual field; (3) Precognitions of future events (Jung 1972c: 526).

Moreover, Jung uses the term to denote a universal connecting principle that underlies the individual synchronistic events. At this level, synchronicity is identical with the meaningful order of the world that encompasses the psychic life and the outer world and relates them to each other. In his view, this ordering principle does not contradict but complete the causal connectedness of phenomena. He is aware of the difference between the empirical-descriptive and the theoretical use of the term and tries to link them. Synchronicity, he says, 'is not a philosophical view but an empirical concept which postulates an intellectually necessary principle' (Jung 1972c: 512). It is not clear from the text what Jung means by an empirical concept 'postulating' a necessary principle.

Presumably, he thought that the empirically ascertainable synchronicities would inevitably lead to the assumption of synchronicity as universal principle.

His earliest recorded reflections on synchronicity were delivered in seminars on dream analysis, which he held weekly at the Zurich Psychology Club for a select small circle of licensed or trainee psychotherapists from November 1928 until the end of June 1930. His contribution to the seminar of 28 November 1928, shows that Jung's orientalism and the *Yijing* were involved in his conceptualization of synchronicity from the outset. In that seminar Jung introduces it under the title 'synchronism' in the following way (Jung 1984: 44):

> The East bases much of its science on this irregularity and considers coincidences the reliable basis of the world rather than causality. Synchronism is the prejudice of the East; causality is the modern prejudice of the West. The more we busy ourselves with dreams the more we shall see such coincidences–chances. Remember that the oldest Chinese scientific ['scientific' is missing in the German version of the Seminar] book is about the possible chances of life.

In a later meeting of this seminar, he refers to astrology and at this occasion formulates the main features of his time-theoretical approach to synchronicity. He explains meaningful relative simultaneities with the assumption that time phases have a certain quality, and events that take place around the same time participate in this quality (Jung 1984; Main 2004: 51–3). It fits with his reflections on time as fundamental reality in *Psychological Types* in which, as shown earlier, he connects the psychoanalytical concept of libido with Bergson's philosophy.

In his obituary of Wilhelm, published in 1930, he uses the term 'synchronistic' publicly for the first time. He praises the translation of the *Yijing* as Wilhelm's greatest achievement and regrets that the book has been misunderstood, among both sinologists and modern Chinese, as a 'collection of absurd magical spells'. In fact, it would embody 'the living spirit of Chinese civilization' like no other work (Jung 1966: 54–5). In this context, Jung recounts that a few years ago, the president of the British Anthropological Society asked him why such an intelligent people as the Chinese had not produced science. He replied that the Chinese did have a science, the standard work of which was the *Yijing*. However, the principle of Chinese science would be fundamentally different from its Western counterpart. Following on from this anecdote, he again contrasts causality and synchronicity as typical forms of Western and Eastern thought: 'The science of the *I Ching* is based not on the causality principle but on one which – hitherto unnamed because not familiar to us – I have tentatively called the *synchronistic* principle'

(Jung 1966: 56, original emphasis). He affirms the explanation of synchronicity developed in the dream analysis seminar (Jung 1966: 56):

> It seems as though time, far from being an abstraction, is a concrete continuum which possesses qualities or basic conditions capable of manifesting themselves simultaneous in different places by means of an acausal parallelism, such as we find, for instance, in the simultaneous occurrence of identical thoughts, symbols, or psychic states. Another example, pointed out by Wilhelm would be the coincidence of Chinese and European periods of style, which cannot have been causally connected to one another.

Accordingly, he claims that the hexagrams of the *Yijing* make the hidden qualities of specific moments in time legible (Jung 1966: 57). He outlines parallels between Western astrology (especially the birth horoscope) and the Chinese oracle. Both would be based on synchronicity, but compared with the European 'twilight of astrological speculation' (Jung 1966: 57), Jung considers the *Yijing* to be a higher developed scientific form of knowledge based on this principle.

Years later, he still advocates the theory of qualitative time in his preface to the English edition of Wilhelm's *I Ging*, published in 1950. The meaningful simultaneity of physical and psychic events emerges time and again 'because they are all exponents of one and the same momentary situation. The situation is assumed to represent a legible or understandable picture' (Jung 1969b: 593). He might have taken from Richard Wilhelm the view that hexagrams indicate time in the sense of the quality of a particular situation, which opens up certain possibilities for future developments. The sinologist writes (Wilhelm 1997: 359):

> The situation represented by the hexagram as a whole is called the time. This term comprises several entirely different meanings, according to the character of the various hexagrams. [. . .] In all cases the time of the hexagram is determinative for the meaning of the situation as a whole, on the basis of which the individual lines receive their meaning.

However, as Main pointed out, Jung distanced himself from his time-theory in the course of the 1950s: 'He came to consider that synchronistic events were not expressions of the already existing quality of a moment of time but created and were constitutive of that quality' (Main 2004: 77).[28] Jung replaced the concept of qualitative time by his theory of the 'psychoid' character of the unconscious, and in particular the archetypes as psychoid factors, which he first elaborated in his essay *On the Nature of the Psyche* (1947/1954) (see Main 2004: 25–6, 51). He used the term 'psychoid' to refer to an inaccessible dimension of the collective unconscious that connects the psyche and the physical world. Insofar as they are 'psychoid', archetypes are no longer only capable of manifesting themselves in the form of inner images and the emotions and attitudes attached to them, but they also constellate outer events that have a meaning corresponding to the inner processes. Thus, in his new theory of synchronicity, the archetypes function as the origin of the quality of a particular time that coordinates mental states and physical events in a meaningful way. Moreover, in the psychoid world, the usual boundaries of time and space are relativized or even abolished, and contact with it makes precognition and other paranormal powers possible (Main 2004: 25–6, 38, 51). Furthermore, Jung postulates that the psychoid unconscious contains an extra-spatial and extra-temporal cognition that he calls 'absolute knowledge' (Jung 1972c: 481, 489, 493, 498, 506).

In the chapter 'Forerunners of the Idea of Synchronicity' of his seminal essay *Synchronicity: An Acausal Connecting Principle* (1952), Jung treats Daoism along with premodern European concepts. This time he takes his quotes of Daoist sources and also parts of his interpretation from Wilhelm's *Chinesische Lebensweisheit* (Chinese Wisdom; 1922) and his translation of the *Zhuangzi* 莊子, *Das wahre Buch vom südlichen Blütenland* (The True Book of the Southern Flower Land; 1912).[29]

He underlines the importance of the *dao* as 'one of the oldest and most central ideas' that 'pervades the whole philosophical thought of China' (Jung 1972c: 486). Thirty years after *Psychological Types*, Jung sketches a new perspective on this topic. He interprets *dao* not primarily as a symbol of the irrational unification of psychological opposites, or as an image of the self as in *The Relation between the Ego and the Unconscious* (1928), nor as the abolition of the separation of consciousness and life in a meditative inner alchemy, as in his commentary to *The Golden Flower*. Rather, he now more or less identifies it with his concepts of the psychoid archetypal unconscious and synchronicity.

Whereas in his commentary to the *Golden Flower* Jung only cited Wilhelm's translation of *dao* as 'meaning' (*Sinn*) alongside others, he now calls it a 'brilliant' interpretation and endorses it (Jung 1972c: 486). This move allows him to build a bridge to synchronicity. Immediately before his reflections on the *dao*, he describes synchronicity as the connection of the terms of a coincidental simultaneity by a shared meaning. Extrasensory perception experiments and other observations would lead to the conclusion 'that besides the connection between cause and effect there is another factor in nature which expresses itself in the arrangement of events and appears to us as meaning' (Jung 1972c: 485). *Dao* would be described as formless, empty and being 'nothing', because 'it does not appear within the world of the senses, but is only its organizer' (Jung 1972c: 487).

In the context of a longer passage consisting more or less of quotations from the *Zhuangzi* that deal with the state of mind necessary to realize the *dao*, Jung says: 'If you have insight, says Chuang-tzu, "you use your inner eye, your inner ear, to pierce to the heart of things, and you have no need of intellectual knowledge."' He comments on this saying by relating it to his concept of the psychoid unconscious: 'This is obviously an allusion to the absolute knowledge of the unconscious, and the presence in the microcosm of macrocosmic events' (Jung 1972c: 489).

Like the concept of synchronicity, Jung first shared his equation of synchronicity and *dao* in the small circle of a seminar at the Zurich Psychological Club; this time in a seminar on the topic of visions given from 1930 to 1934.

On 6 May 1931, he introduced it by telling the story of the rainmaker of Jiaozhou 膠州, a story that was originally told by Richard Wilhelm. Jung obviously appreciated it very much as he often retold it, especially to Jungian therapists. He refers to it in his seminar on Friedrich Nietzsche's (1844–1900) *Zarathustra* and includes it in a footnote of his later major work *Mysterium Coniunctionis*.[30] As the many mentions in internet sources show, it is still popular in the contemporary Jungian community. As is often the case with good stories, several versions are in circulation. This is the one from the 1931 seminar (Jung 2019b: 333):

> There was a great drought where Wilhelm lived; for months there had not been a drop of rain and the situation became catastrophic. The Catholics made processions, the Protestants made prayers, and the Chinese burned joss sticks and shot off guns to frighten away the demons of the drought, but with no result. Finally, the Chinese said: We will fetch the rain maker. And from another province, a dried up old man appeared. The only thing he asked for was a quiet little house somewhere, and there he locked himself in for three days. On the fourth day clouds gathered and there was a great snowstorm at the time of the year when no snow was expected, an unusual amount, and the town was so full of rumors about the wonderful rain maker that Wilhelm went to ask the man how he did it. In true European fashion he said: 'They call you the rain maker, will you tell me how you made the snow?' And the little Chinaman said: 'I did not make the snow, I am not responsible.' 'But what have you done these three days?' 'Oh, I can explain that. I come from another country where things are in order. Here they are out of order, they are not as they should be by the ordnance of heaven. Therefore, the whole country is

not in Tao, and I am also not in the natural order of things because I am in a disordered country. So, I had to wait three days until I was back in Tao, and then naturally the rain came."

In this story, conventional Catholic and Protestant practices as well as Chinese rituals of banning demons are portrayed as being useless. Real help only comes from a Daoist 'rainmaker'. The narrative focuses on the non-causal interweaving of the disorder or order of current external events and the condition of the involved human beings.[31] Once more with a side blow on the Western fixation on causal relationships, Jung (2019b: 333) comments:

> That is how the East thinks – without causality. He simply got back into Tao. You see, when the atmosphere in this room is wrong, I restore here a little bit of Tao and it spreads like a quick-growing tree, with branches extending everywhere. Tao is in the room and nothing wrong can happen. This is the idea of what I call synchronicity. We think according to the Western assumption of causality, that one thing brings about another thing. But that is in itself a magic idea; we give magic value to causes, we think one thing inevitably gives rise to another.

The oracle practice of the *Yijing* is the great exception to Jung's attitude towards the East. He considers its divinatory power to be 'an Archimedean point' from which to unhinge the hegemonial Western mind (Jung 1966: 55). Wilhelm's translation would have inoculated the West with the 'living germ of the Chinese spirit' (Jung 1966: 55). The consequences with regard to the East–West relationships are far reaching. 'We are no longer reduced to being admiring or critical observers, but we find ourselves partaking of the spirit of the East to the extent that we succeed in experiencing the living power of the I Ching' (Jung 1966: 55).

Jung thus breaks through the border between East and West, which he otherwise regards as impermeable. The possibility of a positive, enriching entanglement of cultures becomes apparent at least in this example. As far as I can see, there are three reasons for this:

(1) he appreciates the *Yijing* as a scientific approach to synchronicity, which, unlike Western mantic practices such as astrology, is on par with European science, even if it is built on a different principle; (2) he is convinced that Wilhelm's congenial translation successfully transferred the work into a European language, thus making it part of Western culture; (3) the oracle practice as such is not dominated by mind and will, but overrides mind control through chance operations.

All three reasons taken together banish the danger that *Yijing* practice only reinforces the alienation of the European mind. The unconscious is admitted and addressed through Wilhelm's language in a way that is adequate for Europeans –

not least because the intellectual elaboration of the Chinese oracle is on par with European science, so that no cognitive regression is associated with its practice.

Conclusion

The question of whether Jung's thinking was changed by the Chinese sources he studied or if he was merely citing them as examples and confirmation of his own ideas is not easy to answer. As outlined above, Chinese sources significantly influenced two themes of his thought: his understanding of alchemy as a process of personal transformation and his concept of synchronicity as a scientific principle. The Chinese material does not introduce something completely new into his writings. Claims such as that Jung's discovery of the self should be regarded as a result of his study of Daoism (Coward 1996: 484) have not yet been convincingly demonstrated on the basis of the texts. It is possible that the meaning of 'letting things happen', which Jung knew from his therapeutic experience and his practice of active imagination, was brought to the point for the first time by the principle of *wuwei*.

But even in cases where Jung quotes Chinese sources more extensively to illustrate his own ideas, the text is colored in a certain way by the quotations. The readers receive the Chinese concepts in light of Jung's thinking, but also vice versa – which puts him in a somewhat different light. So, the Jungification of the *dao* is to some extent also a daofication of Jung.

His interest in Asian religious literature and philosophy was manifold. This is also evident from his dealings with Chinese sources. He obviously wanted to confirm his own theories and their universal validity by referring to Daoism and the *Yijing*. Jung also used the reference to Chinese material to verify his psychological, cultural and religious criticism of the 'West' in the mirror of 'the other'. Thus, it strengthened his psychological and cultural reform agenda. Furthermore, Jung's study of Oriental sources was part of a programme to develop a comparative psychology and theory of religion that was intellectually superior to the Eastern traditions. Occasionally, a kind of intellectual colonialism surfaces. This is not precluded by the fact that he saw himself as a bridge builder between East and West, developing keys to understanding Chinese thought. Indeed, his writings contributed to the growth of interest in Daoism and the *Yijing* in Europe and the Americas. Last but not least, Jung was deeply impressed by Wilhelm's version of the *Yijing*. He let himself be influenced by its advices and motivated his students and patients to use it in the same way. Jung was convinced that not only his and their lives could be enlightened by this 'germ of the Chinese spirit'. As was shown earlier, he even expected that the *Yijing* would give decisive impetus to the necessary transformation of Western culture.

Notes

1 Among Jung's acquaintances interested in Eastern wisdom, Hermann Keyserling (1880–1946) had already used yoga as a comparative category and spoke of Daoist yoga before Jung (Keyserling 1925: 111).
2 Additionally, during this period of his life Jung studied the work of the natural scientist, Protestant theologian and visionary Emanuel Swedenborg (1688-1772) (cf. Jung 1995: 120), who articulated his Enlightenment theology and philosophy in the form of visions of the afterlife that became as popular as they were controversial (Stengel 2011). In the nineteenth century, Swedenborg was an important source of modern spiritualism.
3 According to Wouter Hanegraaff (2012: 284), Jung also possessed a copy of Joseph Ennemoser's (1787–1854) *Geschichte der Magie* ('The History of Magic; 1844), but we do not know when and to what extent he studied it.
4 For the importance of Kerner's book for Jung, see Gruber 2000: 219–33; Shamdasani 2012: 31–4.
5 The second author that is often mentioned by Jung with regard to influences of Romanticism is Eduard von Hartmann (1842–1906), who was a bridgebuilder between late Romanticism and the *fin de siècle* currents of psychology, neo-Romanticism and occultism.
6 For a discussion of the relationship between Jung's concept of synchronicity and parapsychological theories, see Palmer (2008).
7 As already pointed out by Aziz and as will be shown later in this chapter, the intrapsychic model of religion was later relativized by Jung through his theory of synchronicity (see Aziz 1990: 167–217).
8 The dramatic nature of his psychology owes much to the practice of active imagination, in which one enters into dialogue with imagined figures.
9 The answer to the question of whether Jung can be called an esotericist depends, of course, on which concept of esotericism one uses and how strictly it is applied. Most of the characteristics of the esoteric form of thought that Antoine Faivre elaborated (correspondences, living nature, importance of imagination and mediations between a seen and an unseen world, transmutation, etc.) can be found in Jung (Main 2010). He was also influenced by writings from the imaginary canon of esoteric literature often assumed in esoteric research. Faivre's attempt at a definition of esoteric thought, however, is highly controversial in esotericism research, and

Hanegraaff surely simplifies a complex matter when he claims that 'Jung himself [...] was essentially an esotericist' whose thinking can be traced back in an unbroken line to Romantic philosophy of nature or even Renaissance esotericism (Hanegraaff 1996: 395; see also 2012: 281–95 now stressing the influence of Romantic mesmerism on Jung). In line with Roderick Main (2010: 172–3), I would argue that the roots and offspring of Jung's thinking are too diverse for that.

10 By 'will' here he obviously understands the rational appetite (Latin: *appetitus rationalis*), that is, a concept that has played a dominant role in European philosophy since Aristotle.

11 Nicoll met Jung in 1912. The fact that he became a follower of Georges I. Gurdijeff (1866–1949) in 1921 is a good example of the close connection of the Jung circle with the alternative-religious milieu of its time.

12 A complete German translation did not exist at that time. The standard English version of the *Yijing* was James Legge's (1815–1897) *The Yi King* published in 1882 as volume 16 of Friedrich Max Müller's (1823–1900) seminal series *Sacred Books of the East*. A complete set of this series is part of the Jung library (Shamdasani 2012: 61). Either Müller's series was not yet in Jung's possession when he wrote this letter, or he was simply not aware that there was already a copy of Legge's translation in his library.

13 I would like to thank Dr. Thomas Fischer from the Foundation of the Works of C. G. Jung for informing me of Jung's mention of the *Yijing* in this previously unpublished letter to his wife. I am also grateful for the exchange with Dr. Fischer about Jung's participation in School of Wisdom events.

14 See the Letter of Gerhart von Mutius to Richard Wilhelm, September 18, 1911, at: http://tudigit.ulb.tu-darmstadt.de/show/Keys-191/0348/.

15 For more details about the relationship of Keyserling and Wilhelm, see Hon (2022).

16 The programmes of the conferences and the content of the publications of the School of Wisdom are treated in Gahlings (1996: 115–83).

17 Letter to Wilhelm, 29 August 1921: 'daß die Schule der Weisheit den Sinn hat, die ewigen Grundtöne, die aller raum-zeitlichen Melodiebildung religiöser, sozialer u. philosophischer Art zu Grunde liegen, *als solche* erklingen zu lassen – wir nehmen keiner Sondergestaltung etwas, geben jeder etwas hinzu' (original emphasis), at: http://tudigit.ulb.tu-darmstadt.de/show/Keys-191/0361/. For his understanding of different cultures as temporal expressions of the absolute reality, see also Keyserling (1925: 364). Keyserling introduced the idea of eternal basic tones of life and their historical manifestations in his *Reisetagebuch* (Keyserling 1925: 119).

18 Cf. letter from Keyserling to Wilhelm, 8 February 1921, at: http://tudigit.ulb.tu-darmstadt.de/show/Keys-191/0357/.

19 'Dabei stellte ich die Forderung auf, dass die Europäische Philosophie von ihrer rein theoretischen Art abkommen und Lebensweisheit bieten müsse.' At: http://tudigit.ulb.tu-darmstadt.de/show/Keys-191/0566/.

20 With regard to the date of the founding of the School, Wilhelm obviously was misinformed or, when writing his letter, he remembered wrongly.
21 Towards the end of the 1920s Wilhelm distanced himself from Keyserling and his School and criticized the superficial enthusiasm for Chinese Wisdom of the postwar era (Wippermann 2020: 221–2).
22 Perhaps Jung wrote letters to Wilhelm during these two years, which have not been published in *C. G. Jung Letters 1906-1950. Vol. 1-3*. These volumes contain only a selection of Jung's letters to Wilhelm from the late 1920s. Earlier letters as well as some of Jung's later ones, and, needless to say, Wilhelm's contributions to this correspondence have not yet been published. Murray Stein (2005) analyses the late correspondence of the two, including all of the extant letters from this period, which are kept in the library of the ETH Zurich.
23 In his foreword to the *I Ching* he explicitly criticizes Legge for not succeeding in making the work 'accessible to Western minds' (Jung 1969b: 589).
24 The text of the *Taiyi jinhua zongzhi* that Wilhelm used was published in 1775 but actually dates from the seventeenth century. It belongs to the so-called Daoist inner alchemy (*neidan*) that deals with the visualization of alchemical processes within the practitioner's body. The *Taiyi jinhua zongzhi* is influenced by Confucian and Buddhist thought. Jung did not know that it is a product of spiritwriting (cf. Mori 2002), but given his interest and interpretation of spiritualism he would have certainly appreciated its origin.
25 Here Jung exaggerates a bit. As mentioned earlier, in Chapter 5 of his *Psychological Types* he had already discussed the resolution of opposites, one of the eminent topics of the *Red Book*, via commenting on historical analogies from Brahmanism, Daoism, Meister Eckhart and examples from poetry. In his commentary on the *Golden Flower*, Jung introduced two other central themes of his visionary explorations, the mandala and the circumambulation of the center, by using analogies from the Chinese text.
26 Jung's reception of alchemy dates from around 1910 (Shamdasani 2009: 86). His first rather Freudian approach to the topic in *Wandlungen und Symbole der Libido* (Symbols of Transformation) was criticized by Herbert Silberer (1882–1923). Jung's later interpretations further developed the theories of Silberer and Flournoy.
27 For a detailed analysis of the problems connected with the concept of synchronicity, see Main (2004: 36–62); Aziz (1990: 51–91).
28 Main here summarizes the basic arguments against the concept of qualitative time that Jung developed in a letter to André Barbault (1921–2019) from 26 May 1954 (see Jung 1976a: 175–7; here p. 176).
29 He also makes sweeping references to two other sources on Chinese thought that would prove its holistic or synchronistic orientation: Marcel Granet's (1884–1940) famous *La pensée chinoise* (1934) and Lily Abegg's (1901–74) *Ostasien denkt anders* (1949), the latter being the work of a Swiss journalist and author influenced by Jung

to which the psychologist had contributed a foreword (see Jung 1976b). Probably influenced by Granet, Jung underlines the orientation of Chinese thought towards wholeness in this essay. It suits his Orientalistic cliché that juxtaposes the analytic West and the synthetic, holistic East.

30   In the Nietzsche seminar he says: 'I always think of the story of the rainmaker of Kiau Tschou. If that fellow had not gone into Tao it would not have rained, yet there is no causality; the two things simply belong together, the order is established when the order is established. He had to experience the order in that chaos, in that disharmony of heaven and earth; and if he had not experienced the harmony, it would not have been' (Jung 1998: 204). In *Mysterium Coniunctionis*, he quotes the story literally from the privately multigraphed notes of the seminar on visions (Jung 1970: 419–20, n. 211).

31   In the seminar of 29 November 1933, he affirms that he believes in the way of the rainmaker and connects it with an anti-political statement: 'I do not believe in magic made by man, magic as made by Germany or in Great Britain or in America; it does not work. But I firmly believe in the natural magic of facts. I believe in the rain maker of Kiao Tchou – that one should do the right thing to oneself and by oneself, and wait until the rain falls' (Jung 2019b: 1204).

References

Aziz, R. (1990), *C. G. Jung's Psychology of Religion and Synchronicity*, Albany: State University of New York Press.

Baier, K. (2009), *Meditation und Moderne*, 2 vols, Würzburg: Königshausen und Neumann.

Baier, K. (forthcoming), 'Intentionality and Non-Intentionality in Jung's Active Imagination', in J. Schlieter, S. Perez and B. van Rijn (eds), *Intentional Transformative Experiences*, Berlin: De Gruyter.

Bair, D. (2005), *C. G. Jung. Eine Biographie*, München: Albrecht Knaus Verlag.

Baumann, G. (2006), 'Grammars of Identity/Alterity. A structural Approach', in G. Baumann and A. Gingrich (eds), *Grammars of Identity/Alterity: A Structural Approach*, 18–50, New York: Berghahn Books.

Borelli, J. (1985), 'Jung and Eastern Religious Traditions: An Annotated Bibliography', in H. Coward, *Jung and Eastern Thought*, 191–212, Albany: State University of New York Press.

Charet, F. X. (1993), *Spiritualism and the Foundations of C. G. Jung's Psychology*, Albany: State University of New York Press.

Clarke, J. J. (1994), *Jung and Eastern Thought: A Dialogue with the Orient*, London: Routledge.

Cohen, E. (2022), *The Psychologisation of Eastern Spiritual Traditions: Colonisation, Translation and Commodification*, London: Routledge.

Coward, H. (1985), *Jung and Eastern Thought*, Albany: State University of New York Press.
Coward, H. (1996), 'Taoism and Jung: Synchronicity and the Self', *Philosophy East and West*, 46 (4): 477–95.
Deussen, P. (1908), *Allgemeine Geschichte der Philosophie mit besonderer Berücksichtigung der Religionen. Erster Band, Dritte Abteilung: Die nachvedische Philosophie der Inder nebst einem Anhang über die Philosophie der Chinesen und Japaner*, Leipzig: F. A. Brockhaus.
Ellenberger, H. F. (1994), *The Discovery of the Unconscious: The History and Evolution of Dynamic Psychiatry*, London: Fontana Press.
Gahlings, U. (1996), *Hermann Graf Keyserling. Ein Lebensbild*, Darmstadt: Justus von Liebig Verlag.
Grasmück, O. (2004), *Geschichte und Aktualität der Daoismusrezeption im deutschsprachigen Raum*, Münster: LIT Verlag.
Gruber, B. (2000), *Die Seherin von Prevorst. Romantischer Okkultismus als Religion, Wissenschaft und Literatur*, Paderborn: Ferdinand Schöningh.
Hammer, O. (2006), 'Jungism', in W. J. Hanegraaff (ed.), *Dictionary of Gnosis and Western Esotericism*, 653–5, Leiden: Brill.
Hanegraaff, W. J. (1996), *New Age Religion and Western Culture: Esotericism in the Mirror of Secular Thought*, Albany: State University of New York Press.
Hanegraaff, W. J. (2012), *Esotericism and the Academy: Rejected Knowledge in Western Culture*, Cambridge: Cambridge University Press.
Hon, T. (2022), 'The Making of a Book of Wisdom: Hermann Keyserling and Richard Wilhelm's *I Ging*', in L. T. Chan and Z. Cai (eds), *History Retold: Premodern Chinese Texts in Western Translation*, 183–203, Leiden: Brill.
Jung, C. G. (1902), *Die Psychologie und Pathologie sogenannter occulter Phänomene. Eine psychiatrische Studie*, Leipzig: Oswald Mutze.
Jung, C. G. (1953–83), *The Collected Works of C. G. Jung* [cited henceforth as *CW* 1–21], 21 vols, edited by Sir H. Read, M. Fordham and G. Adler, translated by R. F. C. Hull, Princeton: Princeton University Press.
Jung, C. G. (1960), *Psychologische Typen*, Zürich and Stuttgart: Rascher Verlag.
Jung, C. G. (1966), 'Richard Wilhelm: In Memoriam' [1930], in *CW* 15, 53–62.
Jung, C. G. (1968), 'Commentary on "The Secret of the Golden Flower"' [1929], in *CW* 13, 1–40.
Jung, C. G. (1969a), 'Yoga and the West', in *CW* 11, 2nd edn, 529–38.
Jung, C. G. (1969b), 'Foreword to the I Ching' [1950], in *CW* 11, 2nd edn, 589–609.
Jung, C. G. (1970), *Mysterium Coniunctionis: An Inquiry into the Separation and Synthesis of Psychic Opposites*, 2nd edn, in *CW* 14.
Jung, C. G. (1971), 'Psychological Types' [1921], in *CW* 6.
Jung, C. G. (1972a), *Briefe in drei Bänden. Erster Band: 1906–1945*, Olten and Freiburg im Breisgau: Olten.
Jung, C. G. (1972b), 'The Relation between the Ego and the Unconscious' [1928], in *CW* 7, 123–245.

Jung, C. G. (1972c), 'Synchronicity: An Acausal Connecting Principle' [1951], in *CW* 8, 2nd edn, 417–519.
Jung, C. G. (1973), *Letters. Vol. I: 1906–1950*, Princeton: Princeton University Press.
Jung, C. G. (1976a), *Letters. Vol. II: 1951–1963*, Princeton: Princeton University Press.
Jung, C. G. (1976b), 'Foreword to Abegg, "Ostasien denkt anders"' [1950], in *CW* 18, 654f.
Jung, C. G. (1983), *The Zofingia Lectures*, Princeton: Princeton University Press.
Jung, C. G. (1984), *Dream Analysis: Notes of the Seminar given in 1928–1930*, edited by W. McGuire, London: Routledge & Kegan Paul.
Jung, C. G. (1995), *Memories, Dreams, Reflections* [1962], recorded and edited by A. Jaffé, London: Fontana Press.
Jung, C. G. (1998), *Jung's Seminar on Nietzsche's Zarathustra*, edited by and abridged by J. L. Jarrett, Princeton: Princeton University Press.
Jung, C. G. (2009), *The Red Book. Liber Novus. A Reader's Edition*, New York: W. W. Norton & Company.
Jung, C. G. (2019a), *History of Modern Psychology: Lectures delivered at ETH Zurich*, vol. 1 (1933–1934), Princeton: Princeton University Press.
Jung, C. G. (2019b), *Visions: Notes of the Seminar given in 1930–1934 by C. G. Jung*, New York: Routledge.
Karcher, S. (1999), 'Jung, the Tao, and the Classic of Change', *Journal of Religion and Health*, 38 (4): 287–304.
Keyserling, H. (1925), *The Travel Diary of a Philosopher*, vol. 2, New York: Harcourt, Brace & Company.
Largier, N. (1991), 'Mystik und Tat. Zur populär-publizistischen Eckhart-Rezeption zwischen 1900 und 1940', in I. von Burg et al. (eds), *Mittelalter-Rezeption IV: Medien, Politik, Ideologie, Ökonomie*, 27–49, Göppingen: Kümmerle Verlag.
Luhrmann, T. M. (1991), *Persuasions of the Witchcraft: Ritual Magic in Contemporary England*, Cambridge, MA: Harvard University Press.
Main, R. (2004), *The Rupture of Time: Synchronicity and Jung's Critique of Modern Western Culture*, Hove: Brunner-Routledge.
Main, R. (2010), 'Jung as a Modern Esotericist', in G. Heuer (ed.), *Sacral Revolutions: Reflecting on the Work of Andrew Samuels–Cutting Edges in Psychoanalysis and Jungian Analysis*, 167–75, London: Routledge.
McGuire, W. (1989), *Bollingen: An Adventure in Collecting the Past*, Princeton: Princeton University Press.
Mori, Y. (2002), 'Identity and Lineage: The *Taiyi jinhua zongzhi* and the Spirit-writing Cult to Patriarch Lü in Qing China', in L. Kohn and H. D. Roth (eds), *Daoist Identity: History, Lineage, and Ritual*, 165–84, Honolulu: University of Hawai'i Press.
Palmer, J. (2008), 'Synchronicity and Psi: How Are They Related?', in L. Storm (ed.), *Synchronicity: Multiple Perspectives on Meaningful Coincidence*, 153–74, Pari: Pari Publishing.
Pohl, K.-H. (1999), 'Spielzeug des Zeitgeistes. Zwischen Anverwandlung und Verwurstung – Kritische Bestandsaufnahme der Daoismus-Rezeption im Westen', in

J. Thesing and T. Awe (eds), *Dao in China und im Westen. Impulse für die moderne Gesellschaft aus der chinesischen Philosophie*, 167–75, Bonn: Bouvier Verlag.

Redmond, G. (2021), 'The Yijing in Early Postwar Counterculture in the West', in B. W. Ng (ed.), *The Making of the Global Yijing in the Modern World: Cross-cultural and Interpretations and Interactions*, 197–221, Singapore: Springer Nature Singapore.

Schlamm, L. (2009), 'Jung, Carl Gustav, and Eastern Religions', in D. A. Leeming, K. Madden and S. Marlan (eds), *Encyclopedia of Psychology and Religion*, 956–9, New York: Springer.

Segal, R. A., ed. (1992), *The Gnostic Jung*, London: Routledge.

Shamdasani, S. (1996), 'Introduction: Jung's Journey to the East', in C. G. Jung, *The Psychology of Kundalini Yoga: Notes of the Seminar given in 1932 by C. G. Jung*, edited by S. Shamdasani, xvi–xlvi, Princeton: Princeton University Press.

Shamdasani, S. (2003), *Jung and the Making of Modern Psychology: The Dream of a Science*, Cambridge: Cambridge University Press.

Shamdasani, S. (2009), 'Liber Novus: The Red Book of C. G. Jung', in C. G. Jung, *The Red Book. Liber Novus. A Reader's Edition*, edited and with an Introduction by S. Shamdasani, New York: W. W. Norton & Company.

Shamdasani, S. (2012), *C. G. Jung: A Biography in Books*, New York: W. W. Norton & Company.

Smith, R. J. (2012), *The I Ging: A Biography*, Princeton: Princeton University Press.

Stein, M. (2005), 'Some Reflections on the Influence of Chinese Thought on Jung and His Psychological Theory', *Journal of Analytical Psychology*, 50: 209–22.

Stengel, F. (2011), *Aufklärung bis zum Himmel. Emanuel Swedenborg im Kontext der Theologie und Philosophie des 18. Jahrhunderts*, Tübingen: Mohr Siebeck.

Treitel, C. (2004), *A Science for the Soul: Occultism and the Genesis of the German Modern*, Baltimore: The Johns Hopkins University Press.

von Stuckrad, K. (2022), *A Cultural History of the Soul: Europe and North America from 1870 to the Present*, New York: Columbia University Press.

Walf, K. (2005), 'Fascination and Misunderstanding: The Ambivalent Western Reception of Daoism', *Monumenta Serica*, 53: 273–86.

Wilhelm, R. (1997), *I Ching, or, Book of Changes* [1950], translated by C. F. Barnes, Princeton: Princeton University Press.

Wippermann, D. (2020), *Richard Wilhelm: Der Sinologe und seine Kulturmission in China und Frankfurt*, Frankfurt: Societas Verlag.

Wulf, D. H. (1997), *Psychology of Religion: Classic and Contemporary*, 2nd edn, New York: John Wiley & Sons.

Zhao, L. (2021), 'Richard Wilhelm's Book of Changes and the Science of the Mind in the Early Twentieth Century', in B. W. Ng (ed.), *The Making of the Global Yijing in the Modern World: Cross-cultural and Interpretations and Interactions*, 155–71, Singapore: Springer Nature Singapore.

Be water my friend
Esotericism, martial arts and entangled histories
Tao Thykier Makeeff

Introduction

Since the late 1960s, what is commonly thought as 'Asian' martial arts have increasingly become paired with esoteric religious practices and have thrived in the wider New Age milieu (Bowman 2021: 130). Most well-known are arts commonly considered Japanese and Chinese, which many practitioners and laymen think of as methods or even expressions of religions, such as Zen Buddhism and Daoism, or more sectarian practices, such as *neidan* 內丹 (alchemical cultivation). It is common to portray this process of reception as one-directional, going from east to west, and there is a tendency to portray the perceived Asian origins as expressions of a particular kind of wisdom and secret knowledge which is lacking in the 'West', and whose absence represents a fundamental difference between 'East' and 'West' that is manifested in the perceived deficiencies in 'Westerners', which can be ameliorated by practising 'eastern' martial arts. However, as I will show, the origins and content of some of the arts, as they have been taught in the twentieth and twenty-first centuries, are complex and the product of multi-directional reception, individual creativity, and entangled histories. Furthermore, the very notion of 'East' and 'West' and, more specifically, the idea of distinctly Chinese or Japanese martial arts are examples of imprecise terminology, masking the fact that an adjective ('Chinese') is often used to describe such diverse origins as pre-dynastic, dynastic, Republican and PRC-China, as well as practices and people with origins in Hong Kong, Taiwan, members of the Sinophone diaspora and their descendants, and other even more complex cases.

In this chapter I engage critically with the process of historical reception and the challenge of binary categories and notions of mono- and bidirectionality between 'East' and 'West'. I begin by outlining key recent discussions about terminology, theory and method in both the study of esotericism and Asian Studies. Through a close reading of Bruce Lee's use of esotericism, I then offer an example of why juxtaposed terminology and simplification often misrepresent the process of reception and demonstrate the high degree of complexity of the amalgamation of esotericism and martial arts. Finally, I show how this amalgamation is a continuing process in esoteric martial arts milieus, by providing examples from a contemporary context.

Esotericism and entangled histories

The notion of 'Asia' and the implicit juxtaposition of 'East' and 'West' has been the subject of some debate in recent years in the scholarly study of esotericism. In 2013, Kennet Granholm criticized the term 'Western esotericism', noting that '[i]n an academic discipline that purports to study something "Western", the meaning of this term could be assumed to be given significant treatment' (Granholm 2013: 18). However, at the time, Granholm observed that, '[f]or the most part the meaning of the term remains implicit' (Granholm 2013: 18). He pointed to '[m]ulti-culturalism and pluralism, along with the "shrinking of the world" in globalization' as factors that were increasingly legitimizing previously '"deviant" religious alternatives' and proposed that the 'popularization of the esoteric, then, creates more diversity in the milieu, which in turn complicates distinctions between "Western" and non-Western' (Granholm 2013: 31). As I have also discussed earlier, Granholm stressed that notions of borders, distinctions and homogenous cultures are 'largely imaginary' (Granholm 2013: 31–2):

> While the use of the term 'the West' in a general way is acceptable, it needs to be kept in mind that actual borders and distinctions are largely imaginary. A view of the West, as well as Europe, must take into notion that it is in fact a conscious project, not an expression of 'natural' identity or culture [. . .]. We do not really need the notion of a 'Pan-European tradition' to motivate solid historical research. By focusing on more specific localities, we are better able to pay attention to the complex interrelations and historical transformations that have occurred and continue to occur in the esoteric milieu.

A few years later, Kocku von Stuckrad argued that 'problematizing dichotomies and juxtapositions is an intrinsic aspect of the study of esotericism; hence it is counterproductive to use the term Western to demarcate the field' (von Stuckrad 2016: 174). To offer an alternative, he suggested the notion of 'entangled histories' as a way of understanding the interconnectedness of culture across the globe. To the question of whether the 'study of esotericism should be dismantled', he answered that the answer is 'both yes and no' (von Stuckrad 2016: 179). He clarified this by suggesting that (von Stuckrad 2016: 179):

> Scholars should stop thinking of esotericism as a field with a clear definition and demarcation or as a tradition that can be retrieved from history. They should also stop fashioning themselves as dissident scholars who represent the oppressed and the marginalized. However, they should not stop researching the themes that constitute this area of research.

Von Stuckrad suggests that Western esotericism 'should be seen as a heuristic concept, a helpful term in establishing a critical perspective on the narratives of European identity' (von Stuckrad 2016: 180). He notes that 'the term has become more and more problematic, to the point of being counterproductive and restabilizing the very narrative it has claimed to overcome' and that it is 'time to leave the term behind and to apply a vocabulary that is more apt to analyze the place of the phenomena under study in their various cultural settings' (von Stuckrad 2016: 180).

The critical discussion about terms like the 'West' or the 'East' is carrying on, most recently, in a 2021 interview with Egil Asprem and Julian Strube in the ESSWE Newsletter.[1] Therein, Asprem clearly expressed his concern 'that terms like "Western esotericism," but also "the West," should not be taken as second-order categories that we as scholars use to classify various materials from the past or present, but rather as historical objects of study that we should analyse and explain'. Asprem describes how '[t]his project runs diametrically opposite to various attempts at revising what we mean by the West' (Sugden 2021: 4):

> Wouter Hanegraaff suggests 'writing better narratives' about the West, for example, and a similar idea has been suggested by Matt Melvin-Koushki who says we must 'expand' the West to include the Middle East, North Africa, Central Asia and so on. In both those approaches, 'the West' becomes something that the scholar should actively negotiate, refine, and in the end continue to use for delimiting their field of study. Our suggestion is quite different: we are not interested in intentionally influencing broader socio-political discourses on what the West is or ought to be, but rather to take the historical actors who've constructed and negotiated this term as part of our source material.[2]

Parallel with this critical debate over terminology among scholars of the study of esotericism, a similar approach was introduced in the field of Cultural Studies with the notion of 'Asia as Method', instigated by the 2010 publication of the influential book *Asia as Method: Toward Deimperialization* by Kuan-Hsing Chen, a Taiwanese Professor of Cultural Studies. He proposed a new combination of methods that included both local, transborder, regional and even intercontinental studies as an alternative to narrowly focused area studies, the restricted focus on individual countries, or the more overarching but potentially more unnuanced approach of regional studies. Instead, he proposed a practice oriented towards 'decolonization, deimperialization, and de-cold war' that began 'with multiplying the sources of our readings to include those produced in other parts of Asia' (Chen 2010: 255). Like the points made by Granholm, Strube, Asprem and von Stuckrad, Chen identified the old juxtaposition of 'East' and 'West' as a simplification and stressed that 'elements of the West have become internal to base-entities in Asia, and hence there is no desire to stress our distinctiveness' (Chen 2010: 255). Chen's project represents an agenda of rethinking (and re-practicing) the notion of the 'East' which includes expanding the 'Northeast Asia–centric imagination to include other parts of Asia, with the hope that our worldview will include heterogeneous horizons'. In addition, he argues that a focus limited to intellectual thought 'in the unfolding of modernity' is a myopic and limiting one and that 'intellectual thought is only one of many historical practices, and the analysis of base-entities will have to operate on different levels of abstraction and in different domains' (Chen 2010: 255). Chen does not mention physical training or martial arts as some of these practices, but his final point is yet both relevant and useful regarding my own line of inquiry in this chapter.

Bodies, images of them, or, in a more general sense, technologies of the body, have played and continued to play a crucial role in the entangled history of the dissemination, reception, amalgamation and reinvention of a culture perceived as 'Asian', to a degree which I propose is comparable to that of texts or information mediated otherwise through language. Obviously, bodies and words are interconnected phenomena and so are their receptions. After all words are produced by brains, mouths and hands. As Sean McCloud points out regarding the dangers of a strictly intellectualist approach to religion, '[t]he process of ordering the messiness of what scholars and practitioners describe as religion by narrowing it down to being primarily a belief system conceals more than it reveals' (McCloud 2020: 21). In the context of martial arts and esotericism, Per Faxneld (2016, 2021) has illustrated this in his discussion of how Ueshiba Morihei 植芝盛平 (1883–1969), the inventor of the martial art Aikidō 合気道 was in part inspired by the Swedish esotericist and mystic Emanuel Swedenborg (1688–1772), something Faxneld also refers to as 'a case of cultural entanglement' (Faxneld 2021: 228). Here we see the entangled history of reception in all its complexity. A Swedish body produced words in various locations in Europe that became physical books, which were in turn translated to Japanese and became ideas in a Japanese man's mind. In turn, these ideas were combined with his previous knowledge – some of which came from his involvement with the new religious movement Ōmoto 大本 and some from several mystic experiences that included hallucinations – and his physical martial arts training to produce an amalgamated approach to moving as well as an intellectual approach to movement and to what it means to have a body and to be alive. In turn, Ueshiba taught his invention to thousands of students from Japan and abroad, and it eventually spread to become a global phenomenon. It changed radically already during his lifetime and was subsequently changed by every individual who learned it. Did Swedenborg's influence mean that Aikidō somehow came home when it began being taught in Sweden? And since Aikidō is now being practiced globally, does it make sense to refer to it exclusively as a 'Japanese' art? I offer no answers to these specific questions in this chapter – and in fact I doubt that these are even questions that can be answered in any simple or meaningful way. More importantly, I believe that the point is to understand the vast complexity that historical entanglement entails, and that simple questions that attempt to elicit a yes or no response, or rigid binary juxtapositions such as 'East' and 'West', are expressions of a longing for simplicity and order where there is none, masking the inherent chaotic nature of culture.

In the following, I discuss a particular human body that perhaps more than any other illustrates the entanglement and complexity of this kind of multi-directional reception. A sweat glistening 'Asian' body that became an icon to millions and sparked a veritable global martial arts fever in the 1960s which echoes to this day; someone who inspired many of the martial arts teachers who have influenced the field and continue to do so: Lee Jun-fan 李振藩 (Li Zhenfan), or as he is better known in the non-Sinophone world, Bruce Lee (1940–73).

Enter the dragon

Bruce Lee was born on 27 November 1940, at the San Francisco Chinese Hospital. He grew up in Hong Kong which was a British colony at the time and later moved back to the United States. It should be stressed from the outset that although he is often considered a 'Chinese' martial artist, this is a gross simplification if not just plain wrong. Even calling him Sinophone would ignore the fact that English was the only official language of Hong Kong from 1883 to 1974, and that he grew up speaking several languages. He was the product of entangled histories, as were his martial art and his text production.

In the past five decades Lee has inspired a myriad of martial arts practitioners to pursue the quest of discovering their own personal way of fighting. As Paul Bowman points out 'it was arguably Bruce Lee films that predominantly inspired and precipitated the rapid explosion and continued growth of participation in martial arts in the "West" since the 1970s' (Bowman 2010: 136). But Lee also inspired many to learn the more elusive art of *fighting without fighting*, which refers to the art of being and of creatively expressing their personality through movement or otherwise. In this sense, Lee is as much a psychological, philosophical and religious role model as he is as role model for people who just want to learn how to take others down.

It could be argued that Lee was almost considered a kind of martial arts messiah by some or that he presented himself – deliberately or not – as one. There are clear soteriological aspects to his project and the practices he has inspired, and the personal cult around his persona and his death places him somewhere between messiah and martyr.[3] Lee presented himself as not only a mediator of Chinese or Hong Kongese martial arts and philosophy, but also as an innovator, as someone who knew the traditional ways but saw their inherent rigidity and wanted to install a new approach, cleansed of the clutter of the old.[4] However, his new approach still rested heavily on key elements of the traditional. This approach was perhaps best summed up by Lee in the maxim found on the inside cover of his posthumously published 1975 book *Tao of Jeet Kune Do*: 'This book is dedicated to the free, creative martial artist: Research your own experience; absorb what is useful, reject what is useless and add what is essentially your own' (Lee 1975: inside cover). Some of the people who recognize Lee as an inspiration in their existential pursuits have used him to validate or understand religious practices that include often eclectic calibrations of religions such as Daoism, Christianity, Islam and even Ásatrú. These types of eclectic receptions of Lee often imply that his words express a deeper truth which is also found in the religion with which the reverence for Lee is combined, as expressions of the same perennial philosophy, or as being analogous to the core values of their religion of choice. In a recent column entitled 'Bruce Lee and the Tao of Ásatrú' on the Contemporary Pagan website *The Wild Hunt*, the scholar-practitioner Karl E. H. Seigfried (b. 1973) discussed his own personal reception of Lee and its consequences for his religious identity and understanding of Old Norse source material (Seigfried 2021):

> For someone who spends so much time engaging with Old Norse mythology and poetry, it's fascinating to read Lee's discussions of the 'kung fu man' focusing chi that evoke comparisons to the Old Norse megin that swells up within Thor when he is in need of great strength. When Lee discusses the meaning of the word tao as way, principle, law, beginning, pattern, and truth, it is reminiscent of siðr, the Old Norse word that can mean custom, habit, manner, conduct, moral life, religion, faith, rite, ceremonial, and more.

Seigfried notes that he does not think that 'such cross-cultural echoes are evidence of some Indo-European relation from the deeps of time'. Rather, he states that he is 'agreeing with Lee that communication across cultural boundaries – which are, by definition, human constructs – can be deeply meaningful and lead us to relate to each other at a higher level'. Curiously, as I will discuss in the following, Lee's cross-cultural echoes were in fact somehow influenced by an 'Indo-European' (in a non-Dumézilian sense of the word) or, perhaps more precisely, an Anglo-Indian relation. Lee was heavily inspired by two people in particular, an Indian man with strong ties to a global religious movement with a partially Anglo-European foundation, and an Englishman living in the United States who was one of the most influential mediators of Chinese, Japanese and Indian religion and philosophy in the Anglophone world at the time: Jiddu Krishnamurti (1895–1986) and Alan Watts (1915–73).

The rise of the Human Potential Movement in the 1960s,[5] combined with a growing interest in what, for lack of a better word, could be called 'Asian' spirituality, provided a fertile ground for the germination and growth of martial arts and their adaptation and absorption into new religious contexts. As Elijah Siegler (2012: 277) notes, '[t]he development of modern Western Daoist groups can be traced to the 1965 changes in the immigration laws of the United States and Canada, which brought more Chinese to North America'. According to Siegler, this growth meant that from the mid-1970s onwards 'Chinese culture – from martial arts to eating with chopsticks – no longer seemed so exotic as it did in the 1940s through early 1970s' (2012: 277). During this period, he adds, the search for spirituality among young North Americans, which 'led them to embrace teachers and practices from Asia', coincided with the presence of Chinese immigrants who 'were experienced in various Chinese religio-physical techniques and eager to teach these skills to willing Americans' (2012: 278). Interestingly, Siegler points to Taijiquan 太极拳 or other martial arts as some of the common gateway practices into Daoist practice in the United States. As early as the first half of the 1960s, Chinese and Hong Kongese immigrant martial artists had already settled in the United States. Most notably perhaps, the Taijiquan teacher T. T. Liang (1900–2002) arrived in the United States from mainland China via Taipei in 1962, and his teacher Zheng Manqing 鄭曼青 (1902–75), who became one of the most influential Chinese martial arts teachers outside the Sinophone world in the twentieth century, arrived in 1964 and began teaching in Manhattan shortly thereafter. Bruce Lee had arrived in San Francisco in 1959, where he started teaching martial arts soon after arriving and appeared in the popular TV-series *The Green Hornet* as Cato in 1966.[6]

The 1970s saw a growing interest in as well as the publication of several important books on Taijiquan. The latter were aimed at a readership of spiritual seekers and presented martial arts as religious and often occult practices that offered a way of accessing secrets of the cosmos and human existence, often described as 'enlightenment' or 'unity with the Dao'. In 1970, Gia-Fu Feng and Jerome Kirk published the influential book *Tai Chi, a Way of Centering and I ching: A Book of Oracle Imagery*, which combined how-to manuals for both Taijiquan and *Yijing* divination – and perhaps more importantly, implied to its readers that martial arts and divination were interconnected *ritual* practices. Shortly after, the artist, musician, dancer and Taijiquan teacher Chungliang 'Al' Huang (Huang Zhongliang 黃忠良; b. 1937) published two works, *Embrace Tiger, Return to Mountain: The Essence of T'ai Chi* (1973) and *Tao: The Watercourse Way* (1975) – the former with a foreword by Watts, the latter written in collaboration with him. During this time, Watts had also befriended Bruce Lee, and the martial arts studies scholar Paul Bowman has suggested that Lee in many ways relied on Watts' translation of 'Oriental ideas', which he in turn reformulated to suit a martial arts-oriented type of reader (Bowman 2010: 193):

> Comparing Lee to Alan Watts like this implies that – just like Watts – Lee translated 'Oriental ideas' into English. However, surely it is significant that many of Lee's 'Oriental ideas' were actually appropriated directly from the writings of Alan Watts himself. Thus, this comparison with Watts seems both lopsided and a little harsh on Watts. For, Lee did not simply translate from Eastern to Western terms, but rather 'translated' many of Watts' ideas into discourse about martial arts topics.

Watts had a huge influence on Bruce Lee. The fact that the latter recycled the former's already translated and often paraphrased versions of historical Japanese and Chinese texts demonstrates the complexity of reception, particularly because

Lee's readers and viewers most likely interpreted his role as that of a 'Chinese' cultural translator who enabled them to access otherwise inaccessible foreign knowledge and made the cryptic relatable. In this light, it could be said that Lee exoticized his own persona. What is perhaps even more interesting is that some of the philosophical content he implicitly presented as 'Chinese' wisdom through his exoticized cultural translator/persona were taken almost directly from Krishnamurti.

Lee apparently began reading Krishnamurti in 1971 when he was recovering from a back injury, and their mutual interest in the importance of varying forms of mental clarity, emancipation from psychological and social conditioning, and selflessness seems to have led Lee to translate Krishnamurti into martial arts lingo as he had done with Watts. It is important to note that much of Lee's use of other authors is found in texts which were compiled and published after his death in the volume *Tao of Jeet Kune Do* (1975). In some instances, Lee uses entire sentences from Krishnamurti with only a few words altered. A short 1986 article by Robert Colet in the martial arts magazine *Inside Kung Fu* clearly outlines the extent of Lee's reliance on Krishnamurti by providing a two-page parallel text with eighteen quotes from each author, demonstrating their clear likeness, which in some instances is bordering plagiarism. To name one example, Lee takes Krishnamurti's sentence '*We* are those books, *we* are those ideas, so heavily are we conditioned by them' and turns it into 'We are those kata, we are those classical blocks and thrusts, so heavily are we conditioned by them' (Colet 1986: 74). Like his use of Watts and Krishnamurti, Lee also relied heavily on texts by many others, including the boxers Edwin Haislet and Jack Dempsey (1895–1983), the fencers Roger Crosnier and Julio Martinez Castello (1882–1973), as well as D. T. Suzuki (1870–1966) and Eric Hoffer (1902–83).

Lee's philosophy, whether in writing, on the silver screen, or when he was teaching in person, consisted of many components, some of which already had a long history of reception and entanglement and some of which were his own. Whereas he did owe much to other contemporary authors, such as Watts and Krishnamurti, he also paraphrased Classical Chinese source texts in ways that appear to have been his own invention (at least partially). One of his most famous philosophical quotes is the water analogy, which he originally presented to the public in 1971 as a line spoken by his character 'Li Tsung' in the TV-series *Longstreet* (1971–2):

> Empty your mind, be formless. Shapeless, like water. If you put water into a cup, it becomes the cup. You put water into a bottle and it becomes the bottle. You

put it in a teapot it becomes the teapot. Now, water can flow or it can crash. Be water my friend.[7]

A 1965 screen test for the role of 'Cato' in *The Green Hornet* (1966–7) shows Lee being asked to explain the analogy of water, which he proceeds to do in a somewhat less poetic manner than he would later do in *Longstreet*. It seems likely that he found at least partial inspiration for this philosophical maxim – that would later become almost synonymous with his persona – in the *Daodejing*, which features similar imagery, particularly in Verses Eight and Seventy-Eight. Lee's innovative approach to martial arts as a method of self-liberation and creative expression was eclectic and playful, and it is perhaps not surprising that a key feature in the reception of Bruce Lee during both his lifetime and posthumously is characterized by a lack of distinction between his on-screen and off-screen personas. In the movie *Enter the Dragon* (1973), the protagonist, played by Lee, explains: 'My style? You can call it the art of fighting without fighting.' Considering his widespread use of the work of others, both as a martial artist and an author, as well as the fact that his perhaps most influential book was compiled from his personal notes and published after his death, it could be argued that he was also a master of the art of writing without writing. Lee's idea of fighting without fighting carries several connotations. It hints at the analogy of water, that is, that fighting is about not going against the opponent but of finding the path of least resistance, an idea in Lee's approach to fighting which is reminiscent of the Daoist notion of 'non-action' (*wuwei* 無為). However, it also implies that fighting is not only about fighting, but about discovering or constructing one's identity and expressing it creatively. This dual focus on martial prowess and personal discovery and expression also seems to characterize much of the later reception of Bruce Lee in the martial arts milieu. He sparked a veritable boom in the interest in martial arts but he also set following generations on the course of using martial arts for esoteric and spiritual purposes.

Hermetic Taijiquan

The popularity of pairing esotericism and martial arts that was proliferated in the 1970s through the writings of authors such as Watts, Lee, Huang, Feng and many others, and which thrived in and cross-pollinated with influential social phenomena – such as the Human Potential Movement and the Hippie movement –

continued in the 1980s and 1990s. There was a considerable production of esoteric martial arts literature, some of which catered to a purist readership that was primarily interested in Oriental spirituality – albeit often in a highly eclectic form that blended terminology and concepts from premodern Japan and China) – as well as a rising interest in comparing, contrasting or combining esoteric content from Europe with 'Asian' philosophy, religion and martial arts. Brian and Esther Crowley's *Moving with the Wind: Magick and Healing in the Martial Arts* (1994) is a good example of this approach to martial arts esotericism. The authors describe martial arts as 'a bridge between East and West', and state that (Crowley and Crowley 1994: 6–7):

> those people involved in Western magickal systems (ceremonial, Wiccan, shamanistic, etc.), if they can be made more aware of the true essence of martial arts forms, might become more inclined to incorporate certain martial arts type exercises in their own routines – simply because of their deep connection with age-old proven systems of mind body discipline and energy control that are in any event, also part of the essential magical traditions of the east.

The book combines Zen Buddhism and Daoist meditation and alchemy with references to Freemasonry, Kabbalah and Anthroposophy, presents a jolly blend of practices and anecdotes from martial arts such as Aikidō, Ninjutsu 忍術 and Taijiquan, and incidentally refers to Bruce Lee as one of the most influential people in martial arts since Bodhidharma. Another genre introduced in this period is the esoteric martial arts (auto-)biography, with Alex Kozma's *Esoteric Warriors* (1999) being a good illustration. It presents nine interviews and biographies of martial arts teachers who represent the role of cultural translator and has a distinct focus on themes such as spirit possession and the transformation and mastery of *qi* 氣. Kozma's book was very influential on the eve of the millennium and arrived at a time when the internet had begun to influence the dissemination of martial arts information but had still not transformed such discourses yet. The book and Kozma's role in martial arts circles (although he was not the only one) also heralded a new tendency in the esoteric martial arts milieu, that of the content provider, the entrepreneur who catered to a growing interest in identity formation and connected isolated individuals and communities in transnational networks of information and practice. Due to the rapid growth of the internet, online information networks interested in martial esotericism gained momentum, first through discussion boards and later with the increasing popularity of video streaming sites, such as YouTube, Daily Motion and Vimeo, as well as social media. Presently, the internet abounds with teachers and content providers that offer various blends of esotericism[8] and martial arts, some of whom are simply enthusiasts or dedicated practitioners without financial ambitions, whereas others are clearly skilled businesspeople.

Recently, a particular combination of martial arts and esotericism seems to be conquering the market in the esoteric martial arts milieu, namely, hermetic Taijiquan.[9] Combinations of hermeticism and martial arts, particularly Taijiquan, are currently being taught internationally by a variety of teachers and, in some cases, professionally marketed. Although none of them refer to what they teach as hermetic Taijiquan – and in some instances have somewhat downplayed their background in hermeticism – I chose to refer to this eclectic style as such for the purposes of the present chapter. Often, hermetic Taijiquan also contains considerable elements from (particularly Thai) Buddhism as well as inspiration from other religious sources. But since the two most important teachers of this type of esoteric martial arts, Adam Mizner and Damo Mitchell, were instructed by Mark Rasmus, who taught them Franz Bardon's (1909–58) hermetic system, Hermeticism is the common esoteric denominator despite their respective individual interests in Buddhism and Daoism. An overwhelming focus on the role of discourse on *qi* in their practices is another important feature they share. While echoing medieval Chinese *neidan*, this focus on knowledge and understanding of *qi*, its accumulation, cultivation and transformation seems to be inspired largely by the more modern Qigong 氣功 fever of the 1980s (Palmer 2007). It is also worth noting that they have all resided in Thailand for extensive periods of time.

Mark Rasmus is an Australian teacher of martial arts, Qigong and esotericism. He started training in Wing Chun 詠春, a martial art popularized by Bruce Lee in the 1970s during the height of the kung fu craze. After opening a martial arts school in Brisbane, Rasmus transitioned to Taijiquan in the mid-1980s. He is a student of William Cook-Edwards (1938–2001) in the Hermetic tradition of Franz Bardon, and in 2020 published his co-authored book (with Jake Senn) *Back Door Into Hermetics: A Guide to Becoming Initiated into the Mysteries*. He has combined this with other practices, including tarot reading, Kabbalah and clairvoyance.[10] Thereafter, he relocated to Chiang Mai, Thailand, and has incorporated a hermetic interpretation of Thai Buddhism into his practice and teaching.[11] Rasmus's approach to martial arts and Qigong is permeated by references to *qi*, which he discusses in terms that echo the seven principles of the 1908 neo-Hermetic text *The Kybalion: A Study of the Hermetic Philosophy of Ancient Egypt and Greece* (Three Initiates 1908) by William Walker Atkinson (1862–1932) – a text which is central to New Age interpretations of Hermeticism.

Rasmus is highly influential in the international esoteric Taijiquan milieu and has a notable presence online with a prolific production of videos and online seminars. However, his student Adam Mizner has taken esoteric martial arts entrepreneurship to new heights in recent years.

Mizner learned Hermetics under Rasmus and has trained with him for years.[12] In 2004 he founded the martial arts organization Heaven Man Earth Taiji International, through which he teaches an esoteric and eclectic interpretation of Zheng Manqing's Yang-style Taijiquan in the tradition of Huang Sheng Shyan and Yang Shao Hou. The organization has grown rapidly since 2004, spreading from Australia (his native country) and Thailand (where he resided for several years) to many other countries worldwide. His entry into the European martial arts scene was facilitated by an invitation by the Taijiquan teacher Alan Skirving to teach a seminar in Glasgow. This led to an interview with Mizner conducted by the famous Taijiquan teacher Ronnie Robinson (1953–2016), which was published in November 2014 on the influential Taijiquan website *Taiji Forum*.[13] In 2016 Mizner was invited to teach at the 16th International Push Hands Meeting in Hannover, an annual gathering of Taijiquan teachers and students, which in turn led to a considerable consolidation of Mizner's influence on the European Taijiquan scene.[14] Mizner describes his teaching as being 'derived from his experience with traditional meditation methods of Daoist, Hermetic and Buddhist traditions'.[15] Since 2008, the Buddhist aspect of his approach was further strengthened when he became a disciple of Ajahn Jumnien (b. 1936) and began teaching his material internationally.[16] With his growing popularity, Mizner has increasingly emphasized his role as spiritual leader, and it is worth noting that Rasmus, one of his former teachers, endorses him as being the most skilled martial artist he has ever met while also stressing that his 'balance of softness and power lays testament to his spiritual essence and skill'.[17]

Damo Mitchell is another of Rasmus's students that also endorses Mizner.[18] Mitchell started his martial arts career running a school in Cardiff, UK, and went on to form the global organization Lotus Nei Gong International, with branches in Europe, Indonesia and the United States. Mitchell is an accredited teacher of Hermeticism under Rasmus and describes it as 'a useful complement to Daoism'.[19] Mitchell's affinity for Daoism is a distinguishing element of his approach. Whereas Rasmus and Mizner emphasize Buddhist elements as part of their martial Hermeticism, Mitchell –although also a student of Thai Buddhism – seems to focus more on Daoism (particularly *neidan*) paired with Traditional Chinese Medicine. Rasmus, Mizner and Mitchell are very successful teachers with a global presence and thriving businesses. In addition, they all three function as teachers of both martial arts and religion, as well as cultural translators of the two. Their success is partially due to their exposure through the website and YouTube channel 'The Martial Man' of the massively influential martial arts entrepreneur Kieren Krygier, who organizes annual events called 'The Martial Camp' in Chiang Mai.[20] Through his online presence and events, Krygier promotes a large group of teachers who focus on the energetic and esoteric aspects of martial arts but who claim to be able to demonstrate their esoteric competencies, energetic mastery and spiritual essence (to borrow Rasmus's wording) by manipulating the bodies of others in the contact exercises known as push hands and sticking hands. Recently, this strategy of using mock combat to validate esoteric, energetic and spiritual superiority was taken to new heights by Mizner when he participated in the documentary film *The Power of Chi* (2022), in which he, in staged interactions, manipulates the bodies of professional athletes, including a Brazilian Jiu Jitsu black belt, and explains it as the result of his mastery of *qi*. The movie features a voice over by actor Morgan Freeman (b. 1937), and one can wonder if the choice of an actor who has previously hosted the documentary *The Story of God* (2005) and even played God in the movie *Bruce Almighty* (2003) was a deliberate attempt to confer legitimacy on Mizner's claims of spiritual, martial and energetic mastery.

Discussion

As I have demonstrated, the relationship between esotericism and martial arts is complex and cannot be reduced to a one-way reception from 'East' to 'West', or even a mere cultural meeting between 'East' and 'West'. Rather, I suggest, these binary concepts are almost useless in understanding the complexity of what von Stuckrad refers to as 'entangled histories'. I agree with Granholm, Strube, Asprem and von Stuckrad that reducing the continuing amalgamation process of cultural elements to juxtapositions only solidifies a problematic tendency to imply ownership of culture through reducing its history to geographical or historical periods, or by implying ownership of geographical regions and history through the control of cultural narratives in scholarship. Building on Chen (2010: 255), I have approached the amalgamation of esoteric practices and martial arts through a combined focus of local, transborder, regional and intercontinental aspects, as well as a multiplicity of sources to produce what Chen has called 'heterogeneous horizons'. From Bruce Lee's creative and personal combinations of elements from Krishnamurti, Watts, the *Daodejing*, and many other sources to the amalgamation of Hermeticism – which has a history spanning from Greco-Egyptian antiquity and via Islamic and Renaissance Italian receptions to a complex modern and postmodern European *nachleben* – martial arts esotericism is both a global and a globalized phenomenon. Separating its conceptual elements and tracking their origins may appear tempting but carries the risk of reductionism. One might, for example, try to interpret Adam Mizner's use of references to the Heaven Man Earth triad[21] as being solely inspired by Classical Chinese philosophy and cosmology, but the inspiration could just as well come from the Hermetic notion of cosmological correspondence, as exemplified in the maxim 'As above, so below'.[22] Similarly, Lee's ideas about complementarity, non-resistance and the analogy of water may well have been partly inspired by the *Daodejing*, but I suspect that they became further consolidated as part of his teachings as they resonated with his broader world view, which was heavily influenced by Krishnamurti, among others. This tendency to combine elements that are perceived as expressions of the same fundamental truths is itself a key Hermetic tenet, the *philosophia perennis*,[23] which enjoys widespread popularity in the broader esoteric and New Age milieus, as well as in many martial arts circles where Lee, Rasmus, Mizner and Mitchell developed their teachings and practices – and to whom these seem to appeal the most.

In his ethnographic study of Taijiquan, Frank (2006: 27) notes how discourses around concepts such as *qi* function as sensual-historical markers that 'evoke a *sense* of Chineseness by appealing to the imagination as well as the intellect'. In the methods of Rasmus, Mizner and Mitchell, *qi* is granted a central place and seems to be emphasized as a factor that bestows on their activities and personas legitimacy and an air of authentic Chineseness. Although they are open about their eclectic backgrounds, both Mizner and Mitchell still present their martial arts method as somehow pristine, original, authentic and distinctly 'Chinese'. More than the other two, Mizner also seems to present himself in an almost guru-like manner, with aspects of Orientalized mannerisms in his intonation, body language and appearance in film and online. In this light, it is interesting that some of the key components of the methods of these teachers have very eclectic origins. Regarding *qi*, common themes include speaking about it as something which has qualities such as rhythm, polarity, frequency and gendered aspects, and most importantly, as something which can be mastered through mentalism and must be cultivated or transformed as part of a developmental process. All these qualities echo principles from *The Kybalion*, but many of them also have Sinophone counterparts. Considering their apparent subscription to the idea of perennial philosophy, this case of multiple origins most likely poses no problem to

Rasmus, Mizner and Mitchell, for whom it may only validate the idea that 'eastern' and 'western' esoteric terminology are expressions of the same truth. For the scholar of reception, on the contrary, it demonstrates the messiness of entangled histories and the difficult – if not futile – task of sorting out exactly which cultural components originate whence. In the case of *qi*, the complexity is only enhanced by the fact that the modern notion of *qi* transformation (*qihua* 氣化) was only introduced in 1949 by Huang Yueting 黃月庭, a Communist Party cadre. Huang in turn borrowed this concept from Tang Zonghai 唐宗海 (1851–1908), the late Qing dynasty founder of the School of Converging Chinese and Western Medicine (*Zhongxiyi huitong xuepai* 中西醫匯通學派), who was directly inspired by a recently imported type of technology in China: the steam engine (Lei 2012).

Conclusion

Can we separate or simplify phenomena such as Bruce Lee – the US-born, multilingual British colony-dweller turned global movie star philosopher – who was inspired by other equally globalized eclectics, such as Rasmus, Mizner and Mitchell – the Anglophone, Thai-Buddhist-inspired, Hermetic martial arts *qi*-masters – who are unknowingly and indirectly influenced by the legacy of technology from British industrialism, into binarily framed or historically linear examples of reception between 'East' and 'West'? I would argue that this is not only impossible, but also an inherently bad idea. Bruce Lee, the widely popular notion of *qi* transformation, and the many amalgamations of Taijiquan and esotericism are all examples of the vast multiplicity of directions in the process of reception and complex transnational and historical entanglement between parts of the globe (and of our conceptualizing minds) that many – out of habit, practicality, ignorance or laziness – still refer to as the 'East' and the 'West'. But this binary perspective is also a remnant of colonialism, which we should carefully examine and attempt to avoid reproducing in our scholarship.

Since the beginning of the Hong Kong protests in the summer of 2019, Bruce Lee has become a symbol of the struggle for autonomy for Hong Kongers, as he had previously been for African Americans. A wide variety of imagery and slogans were inspired by Lee, who was seen by the protesters as an embodiment of their history, identity and longing for freedom. Under the heading 'Be Water!', one widespread protest sign bore the text 'We are Formless. We are shapeless. We can flow. We can crash. We are like water. We are HONGKONGERS!' In 2020, Lee's daughter Shannon Lee (b. 1969) referred to the use of references to Lee in the Hong

Kong protests as an example of protesters 'channelling Bruce Lee's spirit' (Sherwell 2020). Shannon Lee seems to have referred not to literal channelling but to the notion that Lee's main focus in life, inspired by Krishnamurti, was emancipation, personal freedom and its creative expression. Lee inspired the cultural (and cultic) trend of combining esotericism and martial arts in the construction of identity and the pursuit of personal expression – and although the practices and teachings of Rasmus, Mizner and Mitchell are framed as traditional and, implicitly, as authentically 'Chinese', they are also examples of a cultural trend started (or at least fuelled) by Lee, the eclectic *citoyen du monde*. Whether it is ideas about the free flow of *qi*, freedom of expression and creativity, or, in the case of Hong Kong, that of political and legal autonomy, freedom is the common theme. As scholars of religion and reception, we must recognize that the freedom and creativity of the people we study cannot be contained by oversimplified terminology or old, binary juxtapositions from past imperial eras. Instead, we should understand and accept this complexity and accommodate our terminology accordingly. The cultural process of reception is continual and multidirectional, intricate and intangible. Like water or steam, it is ever slipping through our fingers if we try to hold it.

Notes

1 The ESSWE (European Society for the Study of Western Esotericism) was established in 2005. It is an affiliated society of the International Association for the History of Religions (IAHR). Its purpose is the advancement of the academic study of Western esotericism from late antiquity to the present.
2 The interview sparked some debate, including a blog post response from Hanegraaff (2021). The specifics of this debate are beyond the scope, focus and limits of the present chapter.
3 It could be argued that Lee is considered a martyr by some based on the many conspiracy theories that surround the public perception of his death. Some of these theories argue that he was killed because he criticized traditional Chinese martial arts, whereas others claim that he was killed by the Triads due to his involvement in a movie that was critical of this organization. All these martyrial narratives agree that Lee was killed because he was critical of the culture and activities of secret societies.
4 Interestingly, in his 1963 publication *Chinese Gung Fu: The Philosophical Art of Self-Defense*, he wears a traditional kung fu uniform while demonstrating traditional techniques, and included in the book is a lengthy exposition on the philosophy of *yin* 陰 and *yang* 陽, as well as seemingly traditional claims that 'gung fu' is thousands of years old and based on Daoism, Chan Buddhism and the *Yijing* 易經.

5 The Human Potential Movement refers to a loosely defined milieu or counter cultural trend from the 1960s onwards. It is used to describe a range of philosophical, literary, psychological and therapeutic practices and ideas that share the common idea that humans have an unrealized potential which can be accessed and developed to increase their agency or happiness.
6 It should be noted that at this time martial arts were already being practiced in the Chinese diaspora in the United States, just as there were examples of immigrant teachers who had arrived earlier than the 1960. Whereas the former group in general did not teach openly, some representatives of the latter did – perhaps the most notable was Gia-Fu Feng (Feng Giafu 馮家福, 1919–85), who had been in the United States since the late 1940s. He later became involved with the spiritual milieu in northern California and with the American Academy of Asian Studies – and, later, with its recalibration as the California Institute of Integral Studies. Feng was a close friend of Alan Watts and a translator of classical Chinese texts including the *Daodejing* 道德經 and the *Zhuangzi* 莊子.
7 See the episode 'The Way of the Intercepting Fist' of the TV series *Longstreet*, aired on 16 September 1971.
8 Common elements include varieties of references to Kabbalah, Gnosticism and Hermeticism. An example of such teachers is Moe Bedard who runs the website gnosticwarrior.com. A Freemason as well as a martial arts black belt, Bedard describes himself as an expert in 'Gnosticism, the Occult, and Esotericism'.
9 To avoid any confusion, it should be noted that some researchers have used the term 'hermetic' in ways that differ from its use in the study of Western esotericism. For example, Adam D. Frank (2010: 33) uses it to refer to the practices of Daoist hermits. A somewhat more obscure use of the word is found in Serge Dreyer (2017: 8), who comments on a quote by the sinologist and Taijiquan-practitioner Catherine Despeux about *yin* and *yang* and the inherent complementarity of fighting as 'seemingly hermetic remarks'.
10 For his use of kabbalah, see the video 'About Quabbalah', available online: https://www.youtube.com/watch?v=pOxEbUVWppg (accessed 15 November 2022).
11 Explained in the video 'Releasing Methods: Hermetic View of Buddhism', available online: https://www.youtube.com/watch?v=34wfrashnYw&list=PLKg7niTM6D-sc2WI4JWu549cu4gtYJWSC (accessed 15 November 2022).
12 This is explained by Mizner in a comment in a Facebook thread: https://www.facebook.com/HeavenManEarthInternalArts/photos/a.2025923977625717/2546146565603453/?type=3 (accessed 15 November 2022).
13 Available online: https://taiji-forum.com/tai-chi-taiji/tai-chi-interviews/tai-chi-interview-adam-mizner/ (accessed 15 November 2022).
14 According to the *Heaven Man Earth Taiji International* Facebook page, the organization now has branches in Australia, the United Kingdom, the United States,

Belgium, France, Italy, the Netherlands, Germany, Switzerland and Qatar, as well as affiliate teachers in several more countries.

15 https://heavenmanearth.com/en/hme-meditation (accessed 15 November 2022).
16 https://heavenmanearth.com/en/adam-mizner (accessed 15 November 2022).
17 https://heavenmanearth.com/en/testimonial/sifu-mark-rasmus (accessed 15 November 2022).
18 https://discovertaiji.com/en/testimonial/sifu-damo-mitchell (accessed 15 November 2022).
19 https://www.lotusdao.com/damo-mitchell (accessed 15 November 2022).
20 https://themartialcamp.com/ (accessed 15 November 2022).
21 The concept of an interconnected relationship between the domains of heaven, earth, and humans – at times referred to as *sancai* 三才 – is encountered in a wide variety of philosophical and cosmological theories in Chinese history. It is a somewhat fluid concept which has a variety of uses. It is also found in many martial arts contexts as a way of understanding the human body almost as a conduit between what is above and what is below. In Taijiquan the notions of 'separating empty and full' (*fen xu shi* 分虛實), letting the 'head be suspended from above' (*xu ling ding jin* 虛領頂勁), and 'sinking the shoulders and elbows' (*chen jian zhui zhou* 沉肩墜肘) express the same perception of the human body as a conduit between or an expression of the complementary forces of up and down.
22 A common English paraphrase of the Latin *Quod est superius est sicut quod inferius, et quod inferius est sicut quod est superius* from the second verse of the *Emerald Tablet*. The *Emerald Tablet* or *Tabula Smaragdina* is an important text of Hermeticism. The earliest sources of the text are early medieval Arabic versions from the late eighth or early ninth century. Latin translations are found from the twelfth century onwards. The text is often popularly attributed to the mythical character Hermes Trismegistus from the Hellenistic period.
23 The idea of a *philosophia perennis* originates in the work of Agostino Steuco (*c.* 1497–1548). As Asprem and Granholm (2013: 34) have pointed out, it is the idea that there exists a kind of wisdom which is 'eternal, always present underneath the surface of any historical period'.

References

Asprem, E. and K. Granholm (2013), 'Constructing Esotericisms: Sociological, Historical and Critical Approaches to the Invention of Tradition', in E. Asprem and K. Granholm (eds), *Contemporary Esotericism*, 25–48, London: Routledge.

Bowman, P. (2010), *Theorizing Bruce Lee: Film-Fantasy-Fighting-Philosophy*, Amsterdam: Rodopi.

Bowman, P. (2021), *The Invention of Martial Arts: Popular Culture Between Asia and America*, New York: Oxford University Press.

Chen, K. (2010), *Asia as Method: Toward Deimperialization*, Durham: Duke University Press.

Colet, R. (1986), 'Krishnamurti: The Spiritual Force Behind Bruce Lee', *Inside Kung Fu*, February: 73–5.

Crowley, B. and E. Crowley (1994), *Moving With the Wind: Magick and Healing in the Martial Arts*, Minnesota: Llewellyn Publications.

Dreyer, S. (2017), 'Pushing Hands and She spiritual Dimensions of Taijiquan' (trans. G. M. Lane and L. McEwen), *Staps*, 117–118 (3/4): 141–54.

Faxneld, P. (2016), 'Förnuftet är en dålig guide: Sekularitet och andlighetsdiskurs inom östasiatiska kampkonster i Väst', *Aura: Tidskrift för Akademiska Studier av Nyreligiositet*, 8: 57–89.

Faxneld, P. (2021), 'Martial Arts Spirituality in Sweden: The Occult Connection', in L. Pokorny and F. Winter (eds), *The Occult Nineteenth Century: Roots, Developments, and Impact on the Modern World*, 221–43, Cham: Palgrave Macmillan.

Feng, G. and J. Kirk (1970), *Tai Chi, A Way of Centering and I Ching: A Book of Oracle Imagery*, New York: Macmillan.

Frank, A. D. (2006), *Taijiquan and The Search for The Little Old Chinese Man: Understanding Identity Through Martial Arts*, New York: Palgrave Macmillan.

Frank, A. D. (2010), 'Taijiquan: Teaching Daoism through Experiential Arts Learning', *Education About Asia*, 15 (2): 31–4.

Granholm, K. (2013), 'Locating the West: Problematizing the Western in Western Esotericism and Occultism', in H. Bogdan and G. Djurdjevic (eds), *Occultism in Global Perspective*, 17–36, Durham: Acumen.

Hanegraaff, W. J. (2021), 'Nobody Wins Unless Everybody Wins', 29 March. Available online: https://wouterjhanegraaff.blogspot.com/2021/03/nobody-wins-unless-everybody-wins.html?fbclid=IwAR30_c_Gd2w_8plcQXafENfWS3Vynnk2e1AYLLU2nVbhva9hWJEWOyg8LVA (accessed 14 August 2022).

Huang, A. C. (1973), *Embrace Tiger, Return to Mountain: The Essence of T'ai Chi*, Moab: Real People Press.

Huang, A. C. (1975), *Tao: The Watercourse Way*, New York: Pantheon Books.

Kozma, A. (1999), *Esoteric Warriors*, London: Paul H. Crompton.

Lee, B. (1975), *Tao of Jeet Kune Do*, Burbank: Ohara Publications.

Lee, B. ([1963] 1987), *Chinese Gung Fu: The Philosophical Art of Self-Defense*, Santa Clarita: Ohara Publications.

Lei, S. H. (2012), 'Qi-Transformation and the Steam Engine: The Incorporation of Western Anatomy and Re-Conceptualisation of the Body in Nineteenth-Century Chinese Medicine', *Asian Medicine*, 7 (2): 319–57.

McCloud, S. (2020), 'Religions are Belief Systems', in B. Stoddard and C. Martin (eds), *Stereotyping Religion: Critiquing Clichés*, 11–22, London: Bloomsbury Academic.

Palmer, D. A. (2007), *Qigong Fever: Body, Science, and Utopia in China*, New York: Columbia University Press.

Rasmus, M. and J. Senn (2020), *Back Door Into Hermetics: A Guide to Becoming Initiated into the Mysteries*, Thailand: self-published.

Seigfried, K. E. H. (2021), 'Column: Bruce Lee and the Tao of Ásatrú', *The Wild Hunt*, 28 August. Available online: https://wildhunt.org/2021/08/column-bruce-lee-and-the-tao-of-asatru.html?fbclid=IwAR1HKGc-C7MRtKXVx1eA7gp2r57cfLohrVJilWPuLezSlqO2wYugn6MgQag (accessed 14 August 2022).

Sherwell, P. (2020), 'You're Channelling Bruce Lee's Spirit, Daughter Tells Hong Kong Protesters', *The Sunday Times*, 11 October. Available online: https://www.thetimes.co.uk/article/youre-channelling-bruce-lees-spirit-daughter-tells-hong-kong-protesters-ql3rcn3sz (accessed 17 November 2020).

Siegler, E. (2012), 'Daoism beyond Modernity: The "Healing Tao" as Postmodern Movement', in D. Palmer and X. Liu (eds), *Daoism in the Twentieth Century: Between Eternity and Modernity*, 274–92, Berkeley: University of California Press.

Sugden, C. (2021), 'Editor Interview, Asprem, Egil, and Julian Strube', *ESSWE Newsletter*, 12 (1): 4–8.

Three Initiates (1908), *The Kybalion: A Study of the Hermetic Philosophy of Ancient Egypt and Greece*, Chicago: Yogi Publishing Society.

von Stuckrad, K. (2016), 'Esotericism Disputed: Major Debates in the Field', in A. DeConick (ed.), *Religion: Secret Religion*, 171–81, Farmington Hills: MacMillan.

Index

Abel-Rémusat, Jean-Pierre (1788-1832) 3, 16, 112
Academy of Sciences, St. Petersburg 20
accomodatio, Jesuit technique of 31
Aikidō 205, 211
Akashic Records 131
alchemy 16, 19, 32, 117, 153, 169, 181-2, 187, 190, 196 n.26, 211
Alexander, George Gardiner (1821-97) 63
alternative historiography 151
Amiot, Joseph-Marie (1718-93) 7, 16-32
   prisca scientia 27
   Universal Cipher, notion of 30
   workings of universal principle 26
animal magnetism, Mesmer's theory of 17, 22-4, 27, 150
Ásatrú 206
Asia as Method: Toward Deimperialization (Kuan-Hsing Chen) 204
Astrological Judgment upon the Great Solar Eclipse of 1887 (Old) 66
atheism 153
Atkinson, William Walker (1862-1932) 212

Back Door Into Hermetics: A Guide to Becoming Initiated into the Mysteries (Cook-Edwards) 212
Bailly, Jean Sylvain (1736-93) 17, 26-31
Balfour, Frederic Henry (1846-1909) 63-5, 68-72
Bayle, Pierre (1647-1706) 3
Baynes, Cary F. (1883-1977) 135, 179
Bertin, Henri-Léonard (1720-92) 18-19, 21, 23, 28-9
Besant, Annie (1847-1933) 65-7, 70, 110
Bhagavadgītā 67, 71, 114
Bible 2, 37, 48, 150

Bjerregaard, Carl Henrik Andreas (1845-1922) 7, 69, 110, 156
   Confucius, influence of 116
   esoteric enthusiasm 109-20
   Hermetic Brotherhood of Luxor 110, 121 n.3
   Norse mythology 111
   polytheism 119-20
   sinology, influence of 116-17
   view of history 114-15
   writings on China 111-15
   wuwei, concept of 120
Blavatsky, Helena Petrovna (1831-91) 4, 37, 61, 64-67, 70-71, 88, 100, 102, 109-110, 131
Bleuler, Eugen (1857-1939) 166
Böhme, Jakob (1575-1624) 71
The Book of God: The Apocalypse of Adam-Oannes (Kenealy) 66
The Book of the Law (Crowley) 126, 132-3, 137, 160 n.12
The Book of the Path of Virtue (Old) 66-8, 75 n.26
The Book of the Simple Way of Laotze (Old) 69
Bouvet, Joachim (1656-1730) 49-50
Boxer rebellion 156
Brahmanism 114, 172
British Anthropological Society 188
Britten, Emma Hardinge (1823-99) 149
Brooks, Richard W. (1931-2013) 61
Bruce Almighty (2003) 214
Bruce Lee (1940-73) 8, 205
   creative and personal combinations 214-15
   Enter the Dragon (1973) 210
   as Li Tsung' in *Longstreet* 209
   role as Chinese cultural translator 209
   role of Cato in *The Green Hornet* 209, 210

Buber, Martin (1878–1965)   176
Buddhism   18, 43, 50, 109, 136, 147, 172, 212

Capra, Fritjof (b. 1939)   9, 170
Carus, Carl Gustav (1789–1869)   166
Castello, Julio Martinez (1882–1973)   209
Catholicism   16, 37, 48, 148
Catholic missionaries   2, 91, 146
Chacornac, Paul (1884–1964)   93
Chaldean wisdom   112
Chalmers, John (1825–1899)   62, 68–72
China(ese)   40–7
  Atlantean origins   25–30
  Christianity in   150–1
  Cosmos   125–6, 135, 138
  as descendants of Noah   25
  European understanding of   150
  inheritor of ancient truths   152
  lore   40, 50–1
  magic   149–50, 152
  Orientalist binary perspectives   152–4
  portrayal of culture   150–1
  sphinx   41
  Tarot, interpretation of   45–7
China illustrata (Kircher)   4
Christianity   18, 48–9, 109, 115–16, 146–8, 150, 156, 165, 169, 172, 186, 206
Christian Kabbala   5, 39, 50–1
Chungliang 'Al' Huang (b. 1937)   208, 210, 216
Clavelle, Marcelle (1905–88)   93, 97
Clavicula Salomonis   39, 43
Cleather, Alice Leighton (1846–1938)   65
Confessions (Crowley)   127
Confucianism   16, 18, 25, 50, 116, 120, 147–8, 151, 154, 158
Confucius   41, 43, 48, 50, 54 n.29, 64, 76 n.26, 112, 114–16, 120, 146–9
Constant, Alphonse-Louis (1810–75), *see* Lévi, Éliphas
Cook-Edwards, William (1938–2001)   212
Correspondance d'Extrême-Orient (Văn Cang)   85, 88–90, 93
Counter Culture, 1960s   8, 164
Court de Gébelin, Antoine (1725–84)   7, 16, 28, 31, 47

Crookes, William (1832–1919)   165
Crosnier, Roger   209
Crowley, Aleister (1875–1947)   8, 120, 125–37, 139 n.6, 150, 154, 156, 159 n.9, 159 n.10, 159 n.12, 211
  admiration for Laozi   134
  aspects of ten *sephiroth*   128
  Chinese and Thelemic esotericism   129
  Daodejing   132, 136–7 (*see also Daodejing*)
  Kabbalistic writings   129, 135–6
  Tree of Life, Chinese cosmos   126, 128
  trigrams, interpretation of   132–4

Dalai Lama   89–90, 93
d'Alveydre, Joseph Alexandre Saint-Yves (1842–1909)   100, 112–13, 152, 155–6
d'Ambly, Paul Boiteau (1830–86)   47
Daodejing   2, 7, 8, 61–72, 73 n.1, 74 n.11, 75 n.20, 76 n.26, 76 n.31, 84, 95, 99, 111, 115, 117, 120, 130–3, 136–8, 154, 156, 159 n.12, 171, 176, 210, 214–15
  1880s   63
  Adyar Library   67
  Besant, Annie   70
  Bjerregaard's translation of *dao*   69
  Chinese esotericism   64
  Crowley's version (*see* Crowley, Aleister)
  development of Daoism   68
  in European languages   63
  Hartmann, Franz   70
  Latin translations   62
  Old's translation, impact   67–8
  Pauthier rendition   64
  seminal translation   63
  Studies in Theosophy   67
  Tao-te-King   62
  Tao-Te-King de Yan-Tsu (Masot)   63
  theosophical   63–72, 73 n.1
  in translation   62–3
  universal Divine Wisdom   61
Daoism   18, 172, 201, 206
  as Cabala by Amiot   31
  idolatry of   151

as occult sciences   15
Taoism   64–5, 115–8
and *Yijing*, integration of   8
Daoist cosmogony   150
Daoist hierarchy   85, 99
Daoyuan   41
David-Néel, Alexandra (1868–1969)   93
De Antro Nympharum (Porphyry)   84
de Bréquigny, Louis-George (1715–95)   28
de Deulin, Charles Joseph de Harlez (1832–99)   63
de Guignes, Joseph (1721–1800)   25, 42
Deism   148, 149
de Molinos, Miguel (1628–96)   71
de Moyriac de Mailla, Joseph-Anne-Marie (1669–1748)   42
Dempsey, Jack (1895–1983)   209
De Occulta Philosophia (Agrippa)   84
de Pauw, Cornelius (1739–99)   26
de Pouvourville, Albert Puyou (1861–1938)   7, 63, 71, 83, 110, 154
  interest in Asian culture and occultism   83
  with Văn Cang   86–7 (*see also* Văn Cang, Nguyen)
de Prémare, Joseph (1660–1736)   42, 50
de Puységur, Marquis (1751–1825)   27
de Rosny, Léon (1837–1914)   65
de Saint-Martin, Louis Claude (1743–1803)   29
Deussen, Paul (1845–1919)   171, 174–5
Dhammapada   67
Diederichs, Eugen (1867–1930)   178
Die Seherin von Prevorst (Kerner)   166
divine revelation by non-Christian figures   5, 51
Doctrines religieuses et sociales   48
Dogme et rituel de la haute magie (Lévi)   36, 40, 44–7
dualism   114
du Halde, Jean-Baptiste (1674–1743)   41
du Prel, Carl (1839–99)   165
Dupuis, Charles François (1742–1809)   17

East-West binary   7–8, 145, 152, 201
Eckhart, Meister   183
Edge, Sydney V.   66

Embrace Tiger, Return to Mountain: The Essence of T'ai Chi (Huang Zhongliang)   208
Empire of Ram   112, 155, 159 n.6
Enter the Dragon (1973)   205–10
Eschenmayer, Carl August (1768–1852)   165
esoteric historiography   111–13, 151
esotericism   7–8, 10 n.4, 15, 31, 74 n.11, 112–13, 126, 133, 135, 137, 151, 154, 157, 194 n.9
  Chinese religio-physical techniques   207–8
  cultural influence of   6
  Euro-American   4
  histories   202–5
  and martial arts   211–16
  Western   6, 84, 102, 134, 137
esoteric teachings   69, 109, 158
Esoteric Warriors (Kozma)   211
Eurasian civilization   29, 31

Far-Eastern metaphysics   7, 83
Feng, Gia-Fu (1919–85)   208, 210, 218 n.6
Ferguson, Marilyn (1938–2008)   170
Figurism   2, 5
Figurist interpretative school   49
Figurist tradition   36, 42, 49–50
Flournoy, Théodore (1854–1920)   166–8
Freud, Sigmund (1856–1939)   166, 173, 175
Fullerton, Alexander (1841–1913)   67, 71
Fuxi   41–4, 112, 130

Gaubil, Antoine   42
Gems from the East (Blavatsky)   66
Germer, Karl (1885–1962)   126
Giles, Herbert Allen (1845–1935)   63, 66, 116
Gnosticism   156, 181, 218 n.8
Great Magical Retirement   130
Guénon, René (1886–1951)   89, 93, 102, 116
Gyatso, Thubten (1876–1933)   89

Haislet, Edwin   209
Hanlin Academy   25
Hartmann, Franz (1838–1912)   7, 61–3, 68, 70–2

Hauer, Jakob Wilhelm (1881–1962)   169
Hauffe, Friederike (1801–29)   166
Hegel, Georg Wilhelm Friedrich (1770–1831)   16
Hermeticism   2, 4, 169, 212–13, 215, 219 n.22
Hermetic Order of the Golden Dawn   126, 128 n.3, 138 n.3
Hermetic Taijiquan   8, 210–14
Hindu Tantra   137
Hippie movement   210
Histoire de la Magie (Lévi)   36, 40
Hoëné-Wronski, Joseph Maria (1776–1853)   38
Hongwu (1743–1811)   7, 16–21, 23, 28, 31
  and Amiot, friendship   18–19
Huang, Sheng Shyan   213
Huang, Yueting   216
Huc, Évariste Régis (1813–60)   91–2
humanity   27–8, 38, 40, 65, 87–9, 112, 114, 127, 151, 154
humankind, history of   38–40
Human Potential Movement   207, 210, 218 n.5

idolatry   20, 151
illuminism   16, 29, 31–2
Indochinese masters
  encounter with   84–7
  in *fin de siècle* occultism   30, 44, 46, 83–7, 92–3, 95, 98–9, 101–2
  teachings   87–92
The Inner Life and the Tao-Teh-King (Bjerregaard)   69–70, 111, 114, 115, 120, 122 n.9
Introduction to the Science of Religion (Müller)   66
Islam   110, 137, 206
Islamic mysticism   137

Jennings, Hargrave (1817–90)   155
Jesuit Collegium Romanum   4
Jesuit missionaries   48–51, 146–7
  in Beijing   16–18
  in China   146
  Christianity   49
  and Figurist penchant for the Yijing   48–51
  in India   90

sources about   95–6
Jones, Charles Stansfeld (1886–1950)   136
Judaism   172
Judge, William Quan (1851–96)   67
Judge affair   67–8
Julien, Stanislas Aignan (1797–1873)   62
Jumnien, Ajahn (b. 1936)   213
Jung, Carl Gustav (1875–1961)
  active imagination   168–9
  collective unconscious   170
  concept of the Self   169–70, 193
  culture and religion   165
  on Daoism   171–5
    Chinese sources   171–2
    God and morality   172–3
    reconciliation of opposites   172
  interest in Asian religious literature   193
  lectures on Kundalini Yoga   163
  meditative self-experimentation   167
  orientalism   185–7
  psychological types   174, 190, 196 n.25
  psychotherapy   164, 166–7
  religion   164–71
  spiritualism   166–7
  synchronicity, concept of   167
  and Wilhelm   171–84 (*see also* Wilhelm, Richard)
Jung and Eastern Thought (Coward)   163–4

Kabbalah   28, 39, 43, 50, 65, 126, 128, 135–7, 211–12
Kempis, Thomas a (1380–1471)   71
Kerner, Justinus (1786–1862)   166
Keyserling, Hermann Count (1880–1946)   174, 176–8
Keyserling's School of Wisdom   177–8
Kierkegaard, Søren (1813–55)   111
Kircher, Athanasius (1601–80)   4–5, 25, 50
Konishi Masutarō (1862–1940)   63
Konx Om Pax (Crowley)   127
Koo, Wellington (1889–1992)   126
Krishnamurti, Jiddu (1895–1986)   207, 209, 214–15, 217
Krygier, Kieren   213
Kung Fu
  postures   22

true theory of 20
The Kybalion: A Study of the Hermetic Philosophy of Ancient Egypt and Greece (Atkinson) 212, 215

La Bible de la liberté (Lévi) 37, 48
La clef des grands mystères (Lévi) 36, 48
La Haute Science (de Pouvourville) 84–5, 95, 97
Lao, Naixuan (1843–1921) 179
Lao-Tse Táo-Tĕ-King. Der Weg zur Tugend (von Plänckner) 62
Laozi 61, 63, 65, 67, 71, 73 n.8, 74 n.11, 114–18, 120, 134, 141 n.31, 149–50, 171
La science des esprits (Lévi) 36, 47
La vie inconnue de Jésus-Christ (Notovitch) 90
La Voix de la famine (Lévi) 36–7
Lectures on Mysticism and Nature Worship (Bjerregaard) 113
Lee, Jun-fan 205
Lee, Shannon (b. 1969) 216–17
Legge, James (1815–97) 63, 65, 68, 70, 71, 72, 117, 131–3, 151
Le Grand Arcane: ou l'occultisme dévoilé (Lévi) 36, 48
Leibniz, Gottfried Wilhelm (1646–1716) 3, 43, 49, 149
Le maître des sentences (de Pouvourville) 86
Les Cartes a jouer et la cartomancie (Boiteau d'Ambly) 47
Lettre de Chine 85–90
Lévi, Éliphas (1810–75) 7, 28, 35–41, 43–51, 151–2
    on Confucius 112
    existence of Tarot 47
    magic 35–40, 43, 152
    occult publications 38
    socialism and Catholicism 37–8
Liang, T. T. (1900–2002) 208
Liber Trigrammaton (Crowley) 129
Liu, Yongfu (1837–1917) 156
Liu Shu (1032–78) 41–2
Lotus Nei Gong International 213

magic 7, 16, 19, 25, 35–45, 51, 141, 152, 171, 175, 192

magnetism 17–18, 20, 22–4, 27, 150
Marie, Countess of Caithness (1830–95) 63
martial arts 201, 202, 204–16, 217 n.3, 218 n.6, 219 n.21
    cultural entanglement 205
    and Hermatism 212–213
Martini, Martino (1614–61) 7, 16, 29, 62–3
Martinism (illuminism) 16, 29
Masot, Salvador (1845–1911) 63
materialism 145, 153–4, 157–8, 177
Matgioi, un aventurier taoïste (de Pouvourville) 84–5, 94–5, 102, 103 n.4
Mead, George Robert Stow (1863–1933) 65
Medhurst, Charles Spurgeon (1860–1927) 61, 110, 116, 150, 152
Mémoires concernant les Chinois (Amiot) 18, 24
Memories, Dreams, Reflections (Jung) 165, 178
Mesmer, Franz Anton (1734–1815) 22–3, 27, 44
mesmerism 15–17, 20–1, 23, 27, 30–2, 44, 165–6
    and Chinese occult sciences 16, 20–5
metaphysics 7, 83, 102, 136–7
microcosm 174, 191
Mitchell, Damo 212–13, 215–17
Mizner, Adam 212–17
Mohl, Julius (1800–76) 49
Monde primitif analysé et comparé avec le monde moderne (de Gébelin) 16–17, 28, 47
Montesquieu, Charles-Louis de (1689–1755) 149
Moving with the Wind: Magick and Healing in the Martial Arts (Crowley and Crowley) 211
Müller, Friedrich Max (1823–1900) 63, 66, 68, 71, 72, 74 n.11
Mysterium Coniunctionis (Nietzsche) 191
The Mystery of the Ages, Contained in the Secret Doctrine of All Religions (Marie, Countess of Caithness) 63

mysticism   72, 112, 116, 128, 135, 137, 138 n.2, 155–6, 158

neidan   201, 212–13
Newton, Isaac (1643–1727)   23, 29
Nguyễn, Văn Cang   83
   contributions   85, 87–8, 97
   French occultism   87, 90, 96
   and Huc   92
   identity details   86
   in Paris   94, 98
   representation as a Vietnamese soldier   85–6
   sources   86–7, 94–5
   spiritual performances   91
   on Tibetan religion   88–9, 91–2
Nguyễn, Văn Luật (1850–1930)   83–4, 86, 94, 96, 99–100, 102
Nicoll, Maurice (1884–1953)   175
Nietzsche, Friedrich (1844–1900)   191
Noak, Friedrich Wilhelm   63, 73 n.6
Noëlas, Jean-François (1669–1740)   62
non-action, concept of   118–20, 132, 139 n.6, 150, 183, 210
Notovitch, Nicholas (1858–1916)   90, 102

occultism   8, 31, 36–8, 48, 83–5, 87, 102, 126, 166
Olcott, Henry Steel (1832–1907)   67–8, 70
Old, Walter Gorn, see Old, Walter Richard
Old, Walter Richard (1864–1929)   7, 61, 65, 69, 71–2
Old Testament   5, 50–1
Ōmoto, religious movement   205
On the Nature of the Psyche (Main)   189
Opium Wars   150
Orientalism   145–6, 152–5, 157
   culture   185–6
   Jung's   185–7
   orientalist East/West polarity   185–6
Orientalist binary   152–4, 156–7
orientalist East/West polarity   185–6

paganism   109, 147, 151
Passavant, Johann Karl (1790–1857)   165
Pauthier, Guillaume (1810–73)   62, 64, 71, 72

philosophia perennis   215, 219 n.23
Physique et psychique de l'opium (de Pouvourville)   101
polytheism   3, 117, 119, 151, 186
The Power of Chi (2022)   214
Preiswerk, Helene (1881–1911)   165
prisca scientia   27
prisca theologia   5, 50–1
Prjevalsky, Nikolay Mikhaylovich (1839–88)   88
Psychologische Typen (Jung)   171
Pythagoras   5, 23, 30, 48, 51
Pythagoreanism   30

"qi"   215–16
Qianlong   18
Qigong   212
Qing authorities   16, 18
Qingjing jing   70, 130–1, 133
Quesnay, François (1694–1774)   149

Rasmus, Mark   212–13, 215–17
Red Book (Jung)   169, 172, 181–2, 196 n.25
Régis, Jean-Baptiste (1663/1664–1738)   49, 91
The Relationship between the Ego and the Unconscious (Jung)   169
religious comparativism   15, 31
Renaissance   2, 215
Rhine, Joseph B. (1895–1980)   167
Ricci, Matteo (1552–1610) 50, 146, 148
Robinson, Ronnie (1953–2016)   213
Rosicrucians   109

Sacred Books of the East (Muller)   63
Said, Edward (1935–2003)   145, 152
Scholem, Gershom (1897–1982)   135
scientific occultism   166
The Secret Doctrine (Blavatsky)   71, 74 n.11, 88–9
The Secret of the Golden Flower (Wilhelm)   181–2, 185, 187, 190, 196 n.25
Seigfried, Karl E. H.   206–7
Sepharial, see Old, Walter Richard
Shiji (Sima Qian)   42
Silesius, Angelus (1624–77)   71
Sinnett, Alfred Percy (1840–1921)   152

Sinology 3, 116, 151, 175
Sinophilia 3, 5
Sinophobia 3, 5
Skirving, Alan 213
Smith, Hélène (1861–1929) 167
The Soul of the Desert (Crowley) 127, 130, 133
The Speculations on Metaphysics, Polity and Morality of 'The Old Philosopher' Lau-tsze (Chalmers) 62
spiritual wisdom 149, 153
The Story of God (2005 documentary) 214
Sufism 31, 110–12
Suzuki, D. T. (1870–1966) 209
Swedenborg, Emmanuel (1688–1772) 44, 65, 205
Swedenborgianism 65
Symbols of Transformation 182–3
synarchy 155–6, 159 n.6
synchronicity 164, 167, 180, 183, 187–92
Synchronicity: An Acausal Connecting Principle (Jung) 190

Tai Chi, a Way of Centering and I ching: A Book of Oracle Imagery (Feng and Kirk) 208
taiji 29
Taiji Forum 213
Taijiquan 8, 207–8, 210–13, 215–16, 219 n.21
taijitu 46, 53 n.20
Tang, Zonghai 216
Tang Dynasty 70
Tantra 130, 137
Tao: The Watercourse Way (Huang Zhongliang) 208
Taoist Texts: Ethical, Political and Speculative (Balfour) 63
Tao of Jeet Kune Do (Lee) 206, 209
The Tao of Physics (Capra) 9
Tao-sée 20, 24–5
Tarot 16, 28, 35, 39, 45–7, 53 n.19, 53 n.23, 159 n.9, 170, 212
Thai Buddhism 212–13
Thelema 121, 126, 129, 132, 134, 136–8, 154, 156, 160 n.12

Thelemic spirituality 126
The Theosophical Glossary (Blavatsky) 64
Theosophical 7, 61–4, 68–9, 71–2, 110–13, 152–4
Theosophical Society 4, 62, 65–7, 70, 109, 111, 131
Theosophist/Theosophists 7, 61, 63–72, 152, 156
Theosophy 37, 63, 70, 72, 109, 113, 120, 145–6, 153, 157
Thien Tao (Crowley) 127
Tingley, Katherine (1847–1929) 71
tongjian waiji 42–3
Traditionalism 94–5, 97, 104 n.20
Transcendentalism 110, 121 n.3
treaties of Nanjing 150
treaty of Tianjin 150
Tree of Life 8, 126, 128–9, 133, 135
typological exegesis 5, 50

Ueshiba, Morihei (1883–1969) 204
Ular, Alexander (1876–1919) 171
Upanishads 84

van Manen, Johan (1877–1943) 61
Volney, Constantin François (1757–1820) 17
Voltaire (1694–1778) 3, 110, 148–9, 154
von Plänckner, Reinhold (1820–84) 62, 72
von Strauß, Viktor (1809–99) 61–2, 69, 72, 171

Wang, Chang (1724–1806) 28
Wang Lun, uprising of 1774 18
Watts, Alan (1915–73) 207–10, 214
The Way of the Dao (Crowley) 128–9, 132
Western esotericism 6, 84, 102, 134, 137, 202–3, 217
Western materialism 153–4, 158
What Is Theosophy? (Old) 66
Wicca movement 171
Wilhelm, Richard (1873–1920) 8, 164, 171–5
  commentaries on *Yijing* 179–80
  Golden Flower, impact of 180–2
  Jung's relationship with 176–84

Reisetagebuch, impact of 176
translation of Chinese alchemical treatise 180
Wing Chun 212
wisdom 38–9, 50, 61, 65, 67, 109–10, 112–15, 128, 145, 159 n.5
   Chinese 8, 23, 29–30, 157–8, 209
   Daoist 176
   Eastern 145–6, 149–58, 185
   eternal oriental 97
Wolff, Toni (1888–1953) 174–5
wuwei 118, 150–8, 183, 193, 210

Xifre, Josef 65

yang 17, 20, 22–3, 25, 45–6, 125, 128–9, 133–4, 174, 213
Yang-style Taijiquan 213
Yijing 7, 8, 132–4, 140 n.23, 150, 154, 158 n.2
   Crowley's interpretation of the eight trigrams 132–4
   Figurist penchant for 48–51
   Jung's reflections on synchronicity 188
   oracle practice of 192
   as synchronicity-based science 187–93
   synchronistic principle 188–9
yin 6, 17, 20, 22–3, 25, 45, 126, 128–9, 133–4, 174
Yoga 31, 117, 137, 163, 186–7
Younghusband, Francis Edward (1863–1942) 89

Zarathustra 40, 191
Zen Buddhism 8, 201, 211
Zend-Avesta 48
Zheng, Manqing (1902–75) 208, 213
Zhuangzi 66, 69, 116–17, 120, 156, 190–1
Zhu Xi (1130–1200) 42
Zimmer, Heinrich (1980–1943) 169
Zohar 84
Zöllner, Friedrich (1834–82) 165
Zoroastrianism 114

www.ingramcontent.com/pod-product-compliance
Lightning Source LLC
Chambersburg PA
CBHW071831300426
44116CB00009B/1512